*/2. 50*

# A MAN'S GUIDE TO LIFE AND LOVE IN THE PHILIPPINES

## By Larry Elterman

# TABLE OF CONTENTS

# Part 1: *Introduction and Overview*

## Topic i: *Purpose of this Book*

**THIS BOOK IS A PRACTICAL GUIDE DESCRIBING WHAT YOU NEED TO KNOW TO FIND LOVE and/or LIVE IN THE PHILIPPINES.**

**This is not your family oriented travel book. This is a hard-core, no holds barred, no subjects avoided, non sugar coated look at all aspects of Expat life, love and sex in the Philippines.**

There are many travel books about the Philippines. They will tell you about beautiful sights to visit, the nicest beaches, the best hotels and the good restaurants. These are good books if you are on vacation and your purpose is to travel and explore. But what if you are looking for more than a vacation? What if you are considering living in the Philippines? What if you are looking for a Filipina woman to be your wife or girl friend? How do you go about it? Where do you live? How do you handle your money? How do you meet women? What are the dangers? How do you own property? How do you become a permanent resident? What is it really like to live in the Philippines?

If these are the kinds of questions you have the normal travel books do not help you very much. So how does one obtain such information?

You can attempt to gather this information from the Web. Sure, there are millions of web pages about the Philippines. The problem is in the integration. Piecing it all together in your mind is a difficult and time consuming task. Another problem with the Web is that often the sites, especially those Philippine sponsored, are sugar coated, making everything sound great and never discussing the negative aspects.

The purpose of this book then, is to remedy this situation. To provide a single easy to read source about living and loving in the Philippines. This book will also help you if you don't necessarily want to live permanently in the Philippines, but wish to find a Filipina wife to bring back to your own country.

## Topic ii: *Why the Philippines?*

People often ask me: "Why the Philippines?". There are many places in this world to live or retire. Is there something special about the Philippines? Actually the answer is "Yes!". The Philippines is unique in it's set of characteristics. They fulfill a set of requirements that few, if any, other countries can fulfill. Any one of these requirements taken alone rule out many countries. Taken as a set they rule out perhaps all countries except the Philippines. Well? What are the these characteristics? I will list them as follows then talk about each one.

- Inexpensive living

- English language widely spoken

- Open to western visitors and Expats

- Westernized Christian somewhat liberal culture

- Easy to find a woman

- Younger women do not mind older men

- Society does not judge younger women with older men as bad.

### ♦ Inexpensive Living

This isn't a requirement for all people. If you are wealthy there is no need to choose an inexpensive country to live in. However, if you are like most of us, you don't have unlimited resources and you want to make the most of your money. People are always trying to invest their money wisely. Normally if you can make 10 percent a year this is considered very good. How would you like to triple your money instantly? Well, if you choose the Philippines as your retirement location instead of a western country such as the USA, you effectively triple your money. I estimate that to maintain a given life style in the Philippines costs you about one-third as much as in a western country such as the USA. This 3 to 1 ratio is not based on any scientific study, or any hard numbers. It's more my intuitive conclusion based on experience. The comparative cost of things in the Philippines is not a straight forward formula such as everything costs three times less. For example, the cost of labor is probably a factor of 20 to 30 times cheaper than in the USA. However if you want to buy a tennis racket or a set of golf clubs it will cost you more in the Philippines than in the USA. Everything has it's relative costs. I will describe this further in subsequent chapters.

The requirement for inexpensive living rules out most developed countries such as the USA, Australia, Canada, New Zealand, most of Europe, and first world Asian countries such as Japan, Singapore and Hong Kong.

### ♦ English Language Widely Spoken

For some people this is not so important. Some people have the skill and inclination to learn the local language. Some people don't really care because they plan to live in an Expat enclave and communicate mostly with other Expats. For me personally, this is very important. It's very tiring to never be understood. It's very tiring to be never able to communicate with the locals. It's also very nice to have local friends. For me, wide spread English comprehension was a mandatory requirement. This eliminates a country such as Thailand where very few people speak English. The level of English varies widely in the Philippines between educated and non educated people. However, in general, sufficient English is spoken so that you will never feel you need to learn the local language.

### ◆ Open to Western Visitors and Expats

This is important. You don't want to feel that everywhere you go you are hated. You don't want to be embarrassed or afraid to say you are American. Of course the Philippines is a big diverse country, and it has its occasional "foreigner hater", but in general most people are open to, and friendly towards western foreigners.

### ◆ Westernized Christian Somewhat Liberal Culture

I mention that it is a Christian culture not to indicate that this is so important to me in particular, or for you to feel you must be Christian to live here. I mention it because Christianity is a religion/culture most Westerners can relate to even if you are say Jewish or non religious. You sort of know what you are getting. You are not in for any big surprises. Most people here in the Philippines are not fanatics about their religion. In contrast consider the poor school teacher from England teaching in Sudan who in November of 2007 innocently named the class teddy bear Mohammad and was thrown in jail and sentenced to 40 whip lashes. There were protests in the street that the sentence was too lenient and that she should be executed. You don't want any surprises like that! (For those not familiar with the story, thankfully she was finally pardoned by the president and sent back to England).

The people of the Philippines are more westernized in their thinking than probably any other Asian country. This is because the Philippines has a history of western occupation and Christian missionaries. The Philippines was occupied first by the Spanish from 1565 to 1898 and then by the USA from 1898 until 1946, so it is only relatively recently that it has been an independent nation. The Spanish and American occupations have had a lasting and continuing effect on the culture in the Philippines. If you are just on vacation it is not so important to be in a country with western culture. In fact it can be very interesting to see other cultures. However, when you are living someplace, it's nice to feel you can relate to people, and not feel like these people are from another planet.

My statement that the Philippines is "somewhat liberal" applies more to life style than political or religious views. What I mean is, that free speech is allowed, women are valued members of society (consider that they have a woman president) and sexuality is a definite part of their culture. Women enjoy being sexy and dressing sexy. Sexiness is ok. Contrast this with say, Dubai, where they just passed a law making it a crime to dress sexy. Also in the Philippines gay culture is out in the open and well tolerated - far more so than in the USA.

### ♦ Easy to Find a Woman

It's easy to find "a" woman in the Philippines. Of course, like anywhere, it's harder to find a "good" woman. If you are a relatively normal person with a kind nature and you make it known you are available, you will have many opportunities to date women. In fact there is a large percentage of women whose dream is to meet a nice, "rich" foreigner. Of course "rich" to them means able to live a comfortable life style, not rich in the sense of Bill Gates or Donald Trump.

### ♦ Younger Women Do Not Mind Older Men

Let's face it, the protests of the women's movement not withstanding, most of us men are attracted to younger women. It's in our genes. It's nature. We have no control over it. No matter how old we get, we are still attracted to the same age of women. Depending on your personality for most men that means women anywhere from 18 to 35. Well in the Philippines younger women do not have the same stigma against older men as they do in western cultures. For a western man hoping to meet a younger woman in the Philippines your most important assets are a decent and kind personality, some money, and a willingness not to be too cheap, at least in the courting stage! Looks and age are secondary. Of course if you have good looks and are not too old, so much the better and easier for you. But even if you are 70 years old, and your goal is to meet an 18 year old girl, you can probably succeed at your goal. Incidentally the legal age for consensual sex in the Philippines is 18 years old. If not for moral reasons then for your own legal safety I strongly recommend you not to get involved with anyone less than 18.

### ♦ Society Doesn't Judge Younger Women with Older Men as Bad

If you are in a western country and you are a 55 year old man dating a 20 year old woman the natural reaction of most people is: "**PERVERT!!!**". If you are 55 year old man living in a western country, and you see another 55 year old man dating a 20 year old woman, your natural reaction is "**PERVERT!!!**", followed by , "Lucky bastard, I wish that was me!"

Well in the Philippines you don't have to be ashamed. It is quite accepted and tolerated. Besides foreigners, many older wealthy Filipino men have young mistresses. It's sort of like this: If you are rich and living in a western country, and you buy an expensive car, does anyone object and say that's wrong? No, you have money and you are entitled to the finer things in life. Well in the Philippines, if you have money, one of the finer things in life is a young sexy woman. It seems that the honest feelings about this are much more in the open, and they are not hampered down by the oppressive weight of political correctness.

## Topic iii: *What is an Expat?*

For Westerners living in other countries the word Expat is so ubiquitous that they may be shocked to learn that many non traveling people do not understand the term. If you read books about living and traveling in other countries you will come upon the word constantly. Yet, when I first started hearing the word, I was quite confused by it, and had a hard time figuring out exactly what it meant. Pretty soon I figured out that it had something to do with living away from your own country, but I assumed that the word "Expat" had something to do with the word "patriot". I thought an Expat was an ex Patriot. A dictionary definition of the word "patriot" is as follows:

*"A person who loves, supports, and defends his or her country and it's interests with devotion"*

Thus I assumed that an Expat was somebody who no longer loved their country, and as a result, was living somewhere else. I was also amused to find out that some people think the word "Expat" has something to do with the word "expert". Thus, "Expat" is a person who has become an "expert" at living in another country. While in a sense both the above misconceptions might have some truth to them, nevertheless the word Expat has nothing to do with either the words expert or patriot.

The word Expat is short for Expatriate, which has a Latin route, namely "expatriare", which means "to leave your native land". Until relatively recently the word was used in a more negative sense, to mean someone who was exiled from their native land.

The modern usage of the word, as it is used among Expats, implies a lot more than you will ever find in the dictionary. Expat refers to a person that for one reason or another has chosen to live in another country. More specifically it usually implies someone of a western culture living in a country of non western culture. A Filipino living in America would not usually refer to himself as an Expat, and neither would an American living in

England. The word also implies that it was the persons own choice to live in a different country. An American in the armed forces being stationed in another country would not consider himself an Expat. The word "Expat" also implies long term living and an adaptation to the new culture. An American traveling in the Philippines for a few weeks is not an Expat. A retired and divorced American choosing to live in the Philippines because it is less expensive, and who has a Filipina girl friend or wife is a perfect example of an Expat.

## Topic iv: *About Currency - What is a Peso?*

Well of course the "peso" is the Filipino unit of money. Since this book is about the Philippines it is best if you develop a feel for the value of currency stated in pesos. In this book, when talking about small amounts of money the values will be stated in pesos only. For example:

The cost of a beer at a restaurant is about p40.

When discussing larger amounts of money the costs may be stated in pesos and U.S. Dollars. For example:

In the Philippines you can buy a very nice house in a good location for as little as P2.000,000 ($40,000).

When converting the value of pesos to U.S. Dollars I will use the exchange rate of one dollar is equal to 50 peso. One peso is equal to two cents. Of course I can't know what the exchange rate will be at the time you read this. As of the moment I am writing this the exchange rate is 47 pesos to the US dollar. Thus using the value of 50 peso to the dollar is a simplification. Please keep in mind that the exchange rate is always changing. Also, I am assuming you have a feel for US dollars, but you may come from another country other than the USA. The UK, Canada, Australia, New Zealand and Europe all have their own form of currency. It is up to you, the reader, to know the exchange rate for your own country and to develop a feel for the value of a peso. Do a Google search on exchange rates to find several sites that will convert any currency to any other currency.

## Topic v: *Who Am I?*

Well this book is not about my life, so I'm not going to go into a lot of detail about it, but a little background may give you some insight as to where I am coming from, and may help you to relate to this book and your own circumstance.

First of all I am of course an Expat. I have been living in the Philippines since 2001. I was born in 1953, so I started living in the Philippines when I was 48 years old. Although everybody has their own story and circumstances, I think my path to Expatriatism is a fairly typical one.

By the way, "Expatriatism" is not a real word. I made it up, but I like it, so I think I'll use it!

I am a college graduate and was a software engineer while I was working. I was considered pretty good at my job and in my heyday I made a pretty decent salary. I was married, and my relationship was great at first – at least I thought so. My wife was a lawyer, and we lived in a nice house in the suburbs, we were typical yuppies and everything was cool and the story could have ended – and they lived happily ever after. Except as is so often the case, it didn't end that way. The relationship between my wife and I slowly changed and deteriorated. It's still amazing to me and still bothers me to this day that something that started off so well ended up so badly.

At the same time as my marriage was falling apart I was also becoming disillusioned with my work. The company where I had worked for many years was bought and the culture of the company started to change. Then I was passed over for a project that I wanted to be involved in, and it was very upsetting for me, and I started to lose my incentive to work hard and diligently. I was quite depressed and started to hate my life.

Finally I got an offer to consult for a large drug company so I quit my job and moved from Massachusetts to Connecticut. There, although I was making great money as a consultant, I was miserable. I didn't know anyone, had no friends, and was very lonely. Working in a large drug company was also a miserable experience. I was used to small companies with small company cultures. Working for a large drug company was like being a robot. You were asked to do your job without having any feelings, causing any waves, or offering any opinion. If anybody stepped outside the lines they were squashed like a bug.

One evening after work, feeling lonely and bored, I decided to go to a bar. After a few beers I started talking to the guy next to me at the bar. He was an Ex-Expat. He started telling me what it was like to live and travel in Thailand and the Philippines, what the women were like, what the culture was like, etc, etc. I became intrigued. After I left the bar I couldn't stop thinking about it. It's funny, I'm sure that man has no recollection of me or that day, yet he changed my life completely. Maybe if you read this book it will change your life. So here is a real example of the butterfly effect!

Shortly thereafter I booked a four week trip to Thailand and the Philippines. I had the time of my life. A few months after I returned back to the USA I booked another longer trip. A few months after that I moved to the Philippines for good.

## Topic vi: *Who are You and What Do You Want (In General)?*

As you read on, most likely I will be describing you. You are from a western country. I come from the USA, but this book will apply equally well to People from Canada, UK, Australia, New Zealand and Europe. In fact, this book should help anyone from a western culture who speaks English (either as a first language, or speaks it well as a second language).

Most people interested in the Philippines as a vehicle for life changes fall into several categories. They have gone through a certain process. If you are reading this, chances are unlikely you are under 40 years of age. Most likely you are between 45 and 65. Most likely you are divorced. Almost for sure you are disillusioned with something. The attitude of the western woman, the attitude of western society, the day to day grind of a working job, or some combination of the above. You realize you are not getting any younger. You want to enjoy your life before it's too late. You want to find a younger sexy woman to enjoy life with. You want to make changes in your life but you are not exactly sure how. Well that's the purpose of this book. To help you use the Philippines as a vehicle for such life changes.

## Topic vii: *Marriage .vs. Girl Friend for Expats Living in the Philippines*

I decided to put this topic in the introduction because it is important for you to have some idea of your goals and desires relative to marriage and children. Your attitudes about these choices will greatly influence the type of woman you are looking for and how you go about looking for them. Some women really want marriage and that is their top priority and absolutely mandatory. Others may be willing to live with you as a girl friend without being married. You should have an idea of your goal or anti goal. That is, perhaps you don't merely not want to get married, but you most sincerely don't want to get married!

So this section will give you a little practical information to help you formulate this in your mind, assuming your mind has not already been made up. Basically you will probably fall into one of three categories: you want to get married, you don't want to get married, or either way is ok. Keep your views on marriage in your mind as you read about the different kinds of women available to you.

If you plan on living in your own country with your Filipina partner you really don't have much of a choice. You will have to get married so that you can legally settle down with your wife in your own country.

If you plan on living exclusively in the Philippines the question of marriage becomes less obvious. I will discuss some of the pro's and con's of marriage vs. non marriage in this section.

If you don't need to get married I would strongly suggest you don't rush into it. You will have many opportunities to meet women in the Philippines, and if you rush to get married you may very well regret it when you later discover how many young, sexy and beautiful women are available to you! As a single you will be very desirable. As a married man not many good women will be interested in you. So better to keep your options open.

Of course if you develop a serious relationship with a woman she will probably pressure you to get married, one reason being that she knows how desirable you are as a single, and she wants to take you off the market! Most Filipina want a feeling of security.

Some Filipina women may not be willing to live with you if you are not married. This is especially likely if the woman is young and living with her parents or her parents or relatives live near by. If the woman is living in a separate location from her family then she will be much more likely to be willing to live with you.

There are some women who will not be willing to have sex unless they are married but in these days they are a small percentage. Most Filipina realize that if they want to attract a foreigner they can't insist on celibacy. In any case if a woman is so conservative that she insists on remaining a virgin until married, this is probably not the kind of woman you want, unless you yourself are a very conservative type.

So, that being said, is there any reason to be married other than to please your woman? The answer is yes, as discussed below.

### ♦ Visa Convenience

Being married to a Filipina citizen allows you to apply for permanent residence. If you don't have permanent residence you will have to renew your travel visa every couple of months and leave the country every 16 months. You can also get permanent residence without being married by obtaining a Special Resident Retirement Visa (SRRV). See the section about Philippine Visas for more information.

### ♦ Status and Protection

Getting married to a Filipina also offers you some additional status and protection, not in a formal way, but in a subtle way. Filipinos will be more accepting of you and treat you more like you belong if they know you are married to a Filipina woman. Filipinos will be less likely to take advantage of you knowing you are married to a Filipina. If you get in any kind of trouble or are accused of something, there will be somebody on your side to be your advocate and stand up for you. These are not overt issues, they are subtle issues, but they definitely exist.

### ♦ Operating a Business

A business can't be opened in your name. You need to operate a business in the  name of a Filipino citizen. Most foreigners of course operate the business in their wife's name.

### ♦ Owning a House or Land

A foreigner can't own property in the Philippines. Most foreigners who want to buy or build a house do so in their wife's name. I will discuss the pro's and cons of owning property in a later chapter of this book.

## Topic viii: *Marriage and Visas for Those Living in Their Own Country*

If you plan on living in your own country, you will need to get married.

Since you plan to live in your own country then it is important that you have some idea of the Visa laws that apply to help you in making your decisions and in deciding how to go about things.

If you don't live in the USA you should learn the Visa laws for your own country. As I understand it many western countries have similar visa laws to the USA, so this section still might be helpful, but please don't rely on it.

If you are from the USA and plan on getting married, read on.

### ♦ Fiancée Visa

If you are planning on being married and living in the USA the Fiancée visa is by far the easiest method. With this visa you can bring over a woman to the USA for up to six months while you decide whether or not to get married. At the end of six months you must either be married, or she must be out of the country. The Fiancée visa is a reasonably quick and easy visa to obtain if you go about it properly. It usually takes 4 to 8 months to process. However, you can't just meet somebody over the internet and apply for this type of visa. The rules state that you must meet the woman in person, and you must have proof of your meeting and courtship. This means that you must visit your prospective fiancée in the Philippines. There is no rule about the length of your visit, but obviously the longer it is, the better it looks.

**VERY IMPORTANT**: Keep all documentation supporting your meeting and courtship including Airplane tickets and phone records. Take many pictures of the two of you together looking like a happy couple. Anything that supports your visit and courtship, even before your trip, will be helpful. Yahoo Messenger supports a feature called "archiving" which will record all your conversations. Turning this feature on might be a useful way to prove that you have had many conversations together. Of course it may need to be edited for general consumption, depending upon the kinds of things you and your Fiancée talk about.

### ◆ I30 Visa (Spousal Visa)

This kind of visa is a request for permanent residence for your wife in the USA due to the fact that you are married. In other words, you got married in the Philippines, and now you want to bring your wife over to the USA to live with you. The problem with this type of Visa is that the Visa request takes much longer to process than a Fiancée visa. Why? I don't know. It's just the way it is. An I30 request takes anywhere from eight months to two years to process. It can be tempting to get married in the Philippines, as you can get married right away and don't have to wait for the approval of a Fiancée Visa. However, unless you are willing to live in the Philippines, or at least go back and forth to visit your wife while the application is in progress, I don't recommend this. If you are planning on living in the USA the fiancée visa is a better option.

### ◆ Having Your Cake and Eating It Too

Maybe after reading about the first two Visas you feel a little discouraged. You want to live with your wife right away in the USA, you don't want to have to wait six months for a Fiancée Visa, and you don't want to live in the Philippines. Isn't there any other way?

Well actually there is one other possibility, but it is expensive, risky and you have to make sure you understand all the legal subtleties. This is how it works.

Your internet girl friend comes to the USA on some other kind of visa. Perhaps she is a nurse and can get a visa to work, or perhaps she has relatives and can get to the USA to visit them on a travel visa.

Once she is in the USA you get married and then have her apply for a change of status. While the change of status is pending she can usually remain in the USA. If the change of status is eventually approved she can remain permanently in the USA.

However this option is risky because if the change of status is rejected she will then have to leave the country.

There are many legal subtleties associated with this method so it is absolutely essential that you  obtain the services of a good lawyer specializing in immigration law before initiating any part of the process.

If you do wind up hiring such a lawyer to process the change of status it will cost you plenty and the application could take several years to approve.

You might be wondering, "Can I get married in the USA even if she is not a permanent resident?" The answer is yes, the ability to get married has nothing to do with immigration law.

I don't really recommend this method but I described it anyway, because this method has been used.

## Topic ix: *What About Kids?*

So in addition to your views on marriage you should also keep in mind your attitude towards children, specifically whether  you want to have more. For many of the younger Filipina this can be a big issue because they definitely want to have kids! If you marry a woman who has a dream of having a family and then you refuse to have kids,  or you don't tell her you had a vasectomy or some such thing, this could be a very big cause of friction! You will have more options if you are open to having children, but if you don't, that's ok. But you should be honest about this so you don't run into big problems down the road. So if you are sure you don't want children this will also effect the type of woman you are looking for. So be aware of your views on both marriage and children as you read the sections that follow.

# Topic x: *Bailing Out: Philippines .vs. Your Home Country*

This book is mainly about finding a Filipina partner and living a new life in the Philippines. However I also want this book to help people who only want to find a Filipina wife to bring back to their home country. For some people there is no choice. Living in the Philippines is out of the question. Other people may definitely want to live in the Philippines, and still others may be undecided.

For those who want to bring a woman back to their home country and especially for those undecided about where to live, I want to point one important difference about a new life with a new woman (girl friend or wife) in the Philippines .vs. a new life with your Filipina wife in your home country.

Unfortunately, in discussing this topic, I have to dwell on the negative. Everybody wants to believe things will work out great. Nobody goes into a new relationship thinking it will fail. Yet, sometimes that is what happens. So even though it's not pleasant, sometimes we should address the negative possibilities.

Suppose you go to the Philippines, find a woman that you think is the girl of your dreams and marry her. Now suppose things turn out bad. Your relationship falls apart, you hate your wife, you hate the Philippines and you hate your new life. Well good that you are in the Philippines because you can just bail out. You can simply leave it all behind, go back to the home country and there is pretty much nothing your Filipina wife can do about it. Sure you may be still legally married but all in all your life won't be much effected. Even if you want to get divorced you can probably do it for a small settlement since your wife, at this point, has no leverage. She either agrees to the divorce with a small settlement or else she gets nothing at all. Keep in mind a small settlement for you, like a few thousand dollars, is a very significant amount of money for her.

If while in the Philippines you never got married, you only had a girl friend, well in that case it's even easier for you to leave it all behind. Simply go back to your own country and you have no remaining ties whatsoever to the Philippines.

Now lets contrast this with bringing your new Filipina wife back to the USA (other western countries probably have similar laws).

In order to bring your new wife or fiancée home you will have to be the one to sponsor her Visa. You will be responsible for her. Once you are married and she has attained permanent residence status she basically has all the rights of any wife living in the USA. This means that if things fall apart and there is a divorce she will be entitled to a significant portion of your assets. In addition you may have to pay her alimony. Your life could become a mess and maybe you look back on your decision to bring home a Filipina wife as one of the worst decisions of your life.

Imagine how you would feel if after a two week courtship you brought home a Filipina to be your wife, and then a short time after you are married it falls apart, and you have to give her a large part of your assets and you have a life long responsibility to this woman. If wouldn't feel too good.

So again, I don't like to dwell on the negative. Many men bring home Filipina wives and it works out great. However, I just want you to be aware of the danger. It's a lot safer to try your new life in the Philippines. You are not forced to get married right away and you can bail out back to your home country if things don't work out.

# Part 2: About Filipina Women and You

## Filipina Beauty!

# Chapter 1: Who Are You and What Do You Want (More Specifically)?

So let's get down to details. Let's describe several categories of men that may be interested in reading this book. These categories are based on actual experience, from people I have met, and their goals. Later, after describing the basic categories, subsequent chapters will detail how you can reach your goals. When describing the categories, I will use the following abbreviations, which I basically made up.

**YEX**: Means YES to EXPATRIATism. Somebody who definitely wants to leave their own country and make a new life for themselves in the Philippines. They are ready, and they are not afraid.

**NEX**: Means NO to EXPATRIATism. Somebody who definitely does NOT want to leave his own country. A NEX only wants to find a Filipina wife to bring home to his own country.

**MEX**: Means MAYBE to EXPATRIATism. Somebody who is not sure what they want. They are open to the idea of a new life in the Philippines, but they are afraid to jump right into it. They want to proceed slowly and keep their options open.

## Topic i: *The Typical NEX (No to Expatriatism)*

You are in your late 40's, 50s or early 60s, sometimes even older. You are probably divorced or widowed. You still have a job. Your kids are basically grown. You don't have the money or inclination to retire yet. You want to stay at your job. You want to live in the United States, but you are lonely. It's very hard for you to find a woman to be with. You are not attracted to 50 year old women, and younger women are not interested in you. Basically your goal is to find a wife, and you have heard that you can find one in the Philippines. Can You? Most definitely, and your challenge is not so much to find "a" woman willing to marry you and come to the United States, as it is to find the "right" woman.

## Topic ii: *The Typical MEX (Maybe to Expatriatism)*

You are in your late 40's, 50s or early 60s, sometimes even older. You are probably divorced or widowed. You probably still have a job but you are seriously thinking of retiring. The idea of living in the Philippines intrigues you. The much lower cost of living will make retiring more feasible. You want to find love again. You are open to the idea of living in the Philippines, but you are reluctant. What's it like? Will you really be happy living there? Will you really be able to find a woman there? You want to test the waters. You want to see what it's like there. You want to make the transition slowly if at all.

## Topic iii: *The Typical YEX (Yes to Expatriatism)*

You are in your late 40's, 50s or early 60s, sometimes even older. You are divorced or widowed. You may or may not still have a job but you are ready to retire. You like the idea of a younger woman, but they are not interested in you. You are disillusioned with western women and their attitudes, you are disillusioned with the work place and your job, and quite frankly you are disillusioned with the general attitudes and life style in your own country. You are ready and eager for a change and an adventure. You are not afraid. Let's do it!

## Topic iv: *The Swinger*

You are in your late 40's, 50s or early 60s. You have had more than a few women in your life. You are charming with women, and still have a strong sex drive. You feel old age closing in on you and you want to enjoy yourself and experience a full sex life before it's too late. You have a craving for a young sexy woman that you can't have in your own country. You have no desire to be married or be involved in a serious relationship. Neither, however, are you interested in prostitutes. Part of the fun for you is in the chase and the challenge. Also you want a woman that enjoys sex, not a woman that has sex for money, even if she is young and sexy. Fortunately, (or unfortunately - depending on your point of view), this type of person can get what they want in the Philippines. If you are charming, reasonable looking, have some money to spend, and are willing to lie, you can have a very successful sex life. By lying, I mean two things:

- Claiming your are single even if you are not,

- Pretending to be looking for a wife or at least a serious relationship, even if you are not.

## Topic v: *The Drinker*

The drinker is interested in two things: drinking and having sex with prostitutes. I have good news for you. You can find what you want in the Philippines. There are many cities that can cater to your needs, and it will be far cheaper to drink and obtain prostitutes in the Philippines than in your home country.

## Topic vi: *The Bad Person - A Word of Warning*

Here I want to describe a type of person who should not come to the Philippines. If you are an alcoholic who can't control yourself when drunk, if you are a drug addict, if you are a mean or violent person who likes to get into fights, if you are the type of person who likes to control women or even beat them, if you think the Philippines is a place where you can find a woman to be your slave, if you are loud or obnoxious, if you have a short temper, if any of the above even remotely describes you, I urge you to stay away from the Philippines.

Filipinos, for the most part, are very open and friendly to foreigners. By and large they are a tolerant and kind people. But they expect foreigners to behave appropriately. If you are reasonably kind and friendly and have a sense of humor, you will have no problems. Most Filipinos will accept you with open arms.

However, Filipinos are not tolerant to foreigners that cause problems. If you are loud and obnoxious and easy to argue and offend, you will have problems. In mild cases you will simply be ostracized. In extreme cases you may get deported, beat up or even killed. In particular, if you are a violent type that likes to beat up on women, you will be heading for big trouble, as Filipino society is very protective of their women.

## Topic vii: *In Conclusion*

Well, did I describe you? Most likely I did. Or perhaps you are a bit of a combination of some of the categories I described. Well anyway, all these categories (except the "bad person") can all be successful in the Philippines, so read on!

# Chapter 2: Who are They (Filipina Women Looking for Foreigners) and What Do They Want?

## Topic i: *General Discussion*

First let me describe who they are not. They are not usually educated upper class young Filipina women. Such women have no need for older foreign men. Such women will be looking for true idealistic perfect soul mate love with other young educated upper class Filipino men. So don't expect everything in one package, it's not in the cards.

Now in general terms, without getting into specifics, there is one common thread in all Filipina women looking for foreigners. They are poor. They are hoping for a better and more secure life either for themselves, or themselves and their family. Let's face it, you don't get something for nothing.

Does this mean that they are only gold diggers, who will secretly scorn you, and never fall in love with you? No, not at all. Filipina women are easy to fall in love. If you find the right woman, and treat her well, she will love and care for you. Really the situation is not as different as you might at first think from relationships in a western country. Even in western countries women are not looking for unemployed lazy uneducated partners. They want a provider, someone with a good job and education.

Well it's the same in the Philippines except that the situation is much more exaggerated. The women are poorer, and from their point of view, even if you are only of middle class in a western country, to them you are rich. In a western country an older man can find a young attractive woman if he is very rich. The women that he finds may be attractive, may be friendly and fun, but she is unlikely to an educated woman from an upper class family, such a young women willing to be with an older rich man will be looking for a shortcut to an easier and more secure life.

So, same in the Philippines, except that, lucky for you, there are many more very poor women looking for a means to a better life, and lucky for you, even your modest financial resources will make you seem rich to many Filipinas. Of course, if you really are wealthy or rich, so much the better. Without sacrifice on your part you can make your potential partner and her family that much more happy and content.

However, if you really are poor and have no money to spend, then you will not find what you want. In order to find the Filipina woman that you are looking for you have to be able and willing to provide them with a better life. This means, particularly in the courtship phase, you can't appear to be cheap. In the Philippines they have an expression for this concept , as follows:

**NO MONEY NO HONEY!**

Now in the above discussion, I said the situation is not as different as it might at first appear from relationships in a western country. Well that is partly true, as I discussed, but there is one very big difference between your western country and the Philippines.

In a western country if you are an older man with a very young woman you are looked down on as a PERVERT! Of course underneath this façade is extreme hypocrisy. The older men are secretly jealous, and the older women are secretly angry. Why is it these older men want younger women? What's wrong with them? Why don't they grow up? In the Philippines age is much more respected. Children are taught to respect and appreciate older people as having experience and wisdom. In the West children are often taught by example that it is fun to make fun of older people! It's a very big difference! The Philippines is much more family orientated than a typical western country, and it is common for three or even four generations of relatives to be living together in the same house.

In the Philippines the concept of an older man with a younger woman is much more accepted. In fact, nobody thinks twice when they see an older man with a younger woman. It is completely accepted, and in fact expected.

The attitude is if you are an older man of means, well of course you are going to enjoy the pleasures of a younger woman, just like, if you are a man of means in a western country, you are going to enjoy the pleasures of owning a nice car.

It is common in the Philippines to see older foreigners with their young girl friends or wives, and common to see older wealthy Filipino men with their young mistresses. People don't really give it much of a second thought, and to be honest, it's a very refreshing difference from the hypocrisy of the West. It's kind of funny, in the USA, there is much less age discrimination in the work place, but much more age discrimination in relationships. In the Philippines it is the opposite.

If the idea of a much younger woman is appealing to you, and you are thinking whether you want to live in your own country or live in the Philippines, well this alone is a good reason to live in the Philippines. Your relationship with your much younger wife will be accepted here in the Philippines, unlike in your own country, where you are likely to get dirty looks everywhere you go.

Another thing to keep in mind when choosing a Filipina woman is the family baggage that comes with her. In most cases these women have strong family ties and their family may be constantly pressuring you for money, feeling that you, as a foreigner, have an endless supply. Sometimes it can be a very difficult thing. I will discuss this problem in the topics below as well as in other sections of this book.

Oh, and, by the way, do you want kids? This is an important question to ask. Many of the younger women will want to become a mother. If you don't want kids with your Filipina wife then choose a woman who already has kids.

So now that we have discussed some background information, we can actually get into the different categories of Filipina women looking for foreign men. The categories are as follows:

## Topic ii: *Young, Smart, Ambitious (YSA)*

**Young, Smart and Ambitious**

This is a very young woman, usually 17, 18 or 19. She is smart, ambitious, usually attractive and she speaks English well. She wants to make something of herself. She wants an education, but of course the problem is, she is poor. Perhaps she is hoping to go to college or perhaps she is in college but is struggling mightily to make the payments. Either way she figures her best way to get an education is to find a foreign man. This type of woman is a big gamble. If you are lucky you can hit the jackpot and find a young woman who is smart and beautiful with a great personality, who falls in love with you and is grateful to you for giving her the life she wanted, and who will remain loyal to you. However, there is also a very good chance (a much better chance) that once she gets her education she will have no need for you. That while being with you, she secretly craves young men of her own age and can't wait for the time she will be independent. Whether or not you want to take a chance on such a woman depends on you and your attitudes. Perhaps you feel good about giving a young woman a chance in life and don't mind if she leaves after a few years. In that case, this type of woman can be a good choice. However, if you are looking for stability, a woman likely to remain loyal to you, and content to stay and take care of you in your old age, I don't recommend this category. If it does work out, she will probably want kids.

## Topic iii: *Young Without a Clue (YWC)*

This type of woman, often attractive, is poorly educated and not that smart. She is typically 18, 19 or early 20s. She is reaching adulthood and realizes she has no idea what she wants to do. She has no skills to find a good job. Her only real choice is to get married. Maybe she has Filipino suitors from poor families, but if she is going to get married and have babies why not marry a foreigner who can provide her with a good life? Depending on what you want, this type of woman can make a perfectly fine wife. She does not have any ambition, so she will be content to stay with you. If you are good to her, she will fall in love with you. She will desire to have babies and a family. There are two downsides to this type of woman. First, you may feel intellectually lonely. This type of woman provides companionship, but not intellectual stimulation, she usually lacks pizzazz or charisma. Second, she might have strong family ties that are always pressuring you for money.

## Topic iv: *Young, Pressured by her Family (YPF)*

This category is very similar to YWC above, but there are subtle differences. Although typically uneducated, this type is more likely to be attractive and charismatic. This is because the family realizes they have a girl who foreigners will find attractive and they want to take advantage of that and gain some money out of the situation. I guess this does not sound too good, but you have to call it like it is. This does not mean the family will "sell" their daughter to anyone. Of course they want a kind man to give a good life to their daughter and at the same time help out the family. This type of woman can actually make a perfectly good wife, but the situation is not right for all men. You have to be comfortable getting involved with the family. The family will want to meet you, and get to know you. You will have to do things like take the family out to dinners and things like that. The courtship phase will be watched over by the family. It may be more difficult to have sex before the marriage. After the marriage there may be pressures over money. The family will always want something, how much will be a constant negotiation! For many this type of situation is just too stressful. However, for some people it might be just fine. If you have a bit of money to spare, and you are generous by nature, it can work out for you. You have to strike a balance. You have to help the family out sometimes, but you have to also know when to say no. They will take as much as you are willing to give. In particular, if someone gets sick or dies, they will expect you to help out. This type of woman is not for me personally, nor for many of you, but if you are willing to accept the baggage, she will usually make you a fine loyal wife. Most certainly she will also want to become a mother.

## Topic v: *Nice Working Girl (NWG)*

If you live in the Philippines, or choose to take a reasonably long vacation of a month or more in the Philippines, you will come across, in your normal day to day activities, many young women at their jobs. This may include sales women, women at the grocery store, laundromat, at the post office, or waitresses at restaurants and bars, secretaries at doctor or dental offices, etc, etc. You will find some of these women to be attractive, intelligent, funny, and so very helpful. You may see such a woman and think to yourself, wow, that's the kind of woman I want, and in fact, such women are often high quality women. Such women are often college educated, speak English well, have a good personality and a high moral character. They are this way because they would not have been hired if they were not that way. Jobs are hard to come by in the Philippines, even simple low paying jobs, so the people that are hired usually have something to offer.

**Four Typical Nice Working Girls (NWGs)**

NWGs fall into two general categories, those with the lowest level jobs, such as sales assistant, waitress, worker at McDonalds or some such similar job and those with slightly better more secure jobs, such as secretary, office worker or dental or doctor's assistant.

The girls in the former category typically make very little money and are often on a six month contract. Why is this? Well under Philippine law permanent workers working for more than six months are entitled to certain benefits, such as minimum wage and health insurance. The employers get around this by hiring the girls to six month contracts. After six months the girls are let go, and they typically wind up landing another six month contract at a similar establishment doing a similar job. Girls in this category are usually very open to meeting a foreigner.

The girls in the latter category are usually not as desperate for a man, or foreigner in particular. They have a good job, and they are happy and grateful to have that job. They are likely to be content at what they are doing. Still, if you go about it the right way, there is a good chance they will be interested in you.

However even if a NWG is interested in you, there is still a problem. The problem is finding time to date them. They will not be willing to give up their jobs unless they feel the relationship is very serious. Most jobs in the Philippines are long hours and six days a week. During their day off they may have other obligations, like visiting family, washing their clothes or going to church. So you will have a hard time finding quality time to spend with them. It will be a hard process. If you do convince them to give up their job, you are expected to follow through. If they give up their job and you dump them a week later, that is very bad. Perhaps you had better leave town. Still for some men with patience and time, a good woman can be found this way. If it does work out, she will probably want kids.

### Topic vi: *Career Woman Looking at the Ticking Clock (CW)*

This category probably isn't as common as some of the others, still I have seen it a few times now, so I decided to include this category in my discussion. In the previous section I already discussed Nice Working Girl. The difference between NWG and career woman is the level of job. The career woman almost always has a college education and has a higher level of job, like a manager, mid level position in a bank, position in a government office, or some such thing. The career woman looking at the clock is typically in her late 20's to early or mid 30s. The Career woman has always put her education and job before her social life, and now maybe she is beginning to have second thoughts. She feels her biological clock ticking and feels maybe she wants a family.

The problem is, she feels stuck. Her job is too good to give up unless there is a very good alternative. She does not want to give up her job to marry a typical low paid Filipino man. In any case she is already too old for most Filipino men looking for a wife. Thus she begins to think that maybe a foreigner is her best hope.

Of course one problem with this category of woman is the same problem as with the NWG, even more so. It is finding time to date and be together. Like the NWG, the career woman won't give up her job unless she feels secure that the relationship is very serious.

If you are the kind of man that likes the company of an intelligent educated woman with a  strong opinionated personality this could be a good choice for you.  Sometimes it's nice to have real intellectual conversation about serious topics with your GF or wife. On the other hand, honestly speaking, this kind of woman is more likely to be a pain-in-the-butt.  More opinionated, more sensitive, more prone to arguing than a less high powered Filipina.  When evaluating the tradeoff between intelligence and how much of a pain-in-the-butt they are likely to be, use the following scientifically proven correlation, which applies to women of all races, not just Filipinas.

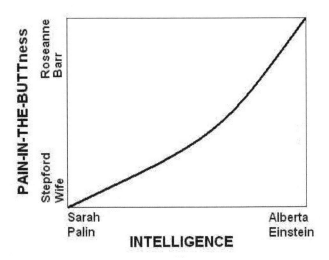

Scientifically proven correlation between a woman's intelligence and her PAIN-IN-THE-BUTTness

## Topic vii: *Single Mom (SM)*

There are a surprising number of single moms in the Philippines. Why is this? Well it's due to a number of circumstances that interact with each other. Filipina women are often very ambivalent about the subject of sex. They live in a Catholic society where the church condemns pre-marital sex. Most women profess to be religious and believe in the teachings of the church and thus would say that sex before marriage is bad. On the other hand the teachings of the church are not really consistent with other aspects of society. Philippine society is a pretty liberal society in many ways. People are not shy to talk about sex. They love Hollywood movies and TV that is full of sexual content . Even if you watch Filipino TV, produced in the

Philippines and spoken in Tagalog, it is full of sexy women and sexual content. Honestly, Filipina women enjoy being sexy.

Well, because of the Catholic Church there is no real sex education in the Philippines. As a matter of fact, as I am writing this in November 2008, there are a number of politicians trying to change this with a new bill promoting sex education in schools. It is running into fierce opposition from the Catholic Church who condemn condoms and most methods of birth control. It is yet to be seen who will prevail. At any rate because there is no sex education there is no real knowledge about birth control. Many girls have ridiculous notions that they have heard from friends, things like, if the girl is on top they can't get pregnant  I personally knew a young woman who enjoyed sex and was sexually active but insisted she would never get pregnant as long as she stood on her head after sex. No, I did not make this up! Guess what. She is now a single mom with two kids. Big surprise!

Ok, so you have a situation where young single women don't like to admit they want sex because of their religious upbringing, but who deep inside are much more sexually liberated than they like to admit. They would never do something like take birth control pills or carry condoms with them, because to do so would be to admit they expect to have sex.  Filipino men don't do much to help the situation because most Filipino men would readily admit they hate condoms.

So what happens is this. The first time they are in a serious relationship and are turned on, they wind up having sex without birth control. If they are lucky enough to get away with it the first time, you would think they would then get birth control. But no, most of them don't. They just keep on having sex and hoping. Then, when they get pregnant abortion is not an option. Besides being illegal in the Philippines (it is available illegally and dangerously) it is also strongly against their religious beliefs and family oriented culture. Thus they wind up continuing the pregnancy. Meanwhile, the boy, who is not really ready to be a father takes off. In the Philippines the laws governing child support are not very strong. As long as the boy takes off to another location it's almost impossible for the girl to get child support. In any case the boy is usually poor anyway, and in most cases the women does not even attempt to get child support.

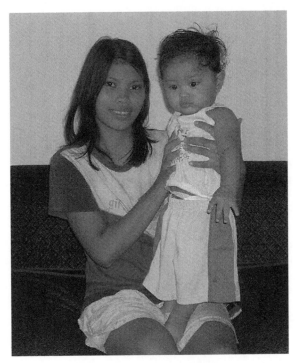

**Young Filipina Mother**

The good news for these women is that they are accepted in Filipino society. There is not a big stigma against being a single mom. Furthermore because Filipinos usually have very close knit families, the parents of these singles moms, after an initial period of shock, almost always accept the circumstances and welcome the baby into the extended family.

The bad news is that most Filipino men do not want a woman who already has a baby so it is very hard for these women to get married to a Filipino man. This is why many of them hope to find a foreigner who is more open to their circumstances.

If you don't mind the baggage of becoming a step dad, SMs can be a very good choice for many reasons. First SMs are more liberal, attractive and charismatic on average. They had to be not that conservative to have had sex before marriage, and they were desirable enough so that someone wanted them. They won't have any qualms about having sex before marriage, obviously, since it's something they have already done. Also, you often don't have all of the problems of family associated with single mothers. Even though there is not a big stigma against SMs, still they have a very difficult time in the Philippines. Either they stay at home, which means they are a burden on their family, or they work, in which case their family has to take care of their child while they work. Either way it is difficult on the family. Since you are doing the family a huge favor by solving this problem, they often don't expect as much from you. Also, since it is difficult for a single mom to get married to a Filipino man, they are likely to be loyal and grateful. Of course the most important thing to a single mother is to provide a good life for her child, and you will of course be expected to treat the child as your own, providing a good life and education for the child. If all that is ok with you, then it can be a good situation. If you don't want any additional kids, this can also be a good choice as often a single mom will be content not to have more kids.

## Topic viii: *Older Widowed Woman (OWW)*

Maybe this woman is in her late 30s, 40s or early 50s. She has lost her husband a few years ago, and now she is ready to move on. Well the problem is, will you be disappointed in yourself when you see all the other foreigners with pretty girls in their teens and 20s. In the Philippines it's not easy for an older woman to date and find love again, the men definitely like the younger women. If you don't mind the woman's age, and you will not be jealous of men with younger women and if you are sure you will not regret it, well, it's probably a perfectly good way to go. Many of the problems associated with younger women will not be an issue. Family will usually not be an issue. There might be kids in the equation. Is that ok with you? Well, bottom line is, you can probably find a good woman in this category if you don't mind that she is not young and beautiful. This is also a good choice if you don't want any more kids in your life.

### Topic ix: *Older Separated Woman (OSW)*

Since divorces are not granted in the Philippines this means there are many unhappy couples, and some of them simply choose to live separate lives. They are separated from their husbands but still legally married.

This category is similar to OWW, described above. The same positives and negatives in general, but of course there is one big difference. This woman is still married. Well, this can be good or bad, depending on your point of view and philosophy. Since she is married, she can't pressure you to get married. Since she is already married it's easier psychologically to break it off, you don't feel the same sense of obligation. The problem is, there are sometimes benefits to getting married. One good reason for getting married is that you can then obtain permanent residence, and you don't have to worry about the hassle of renewing visas. Another important reason is that without marriage it will be very difficult to bring the woman back to your own country. It will force you to live in the Philippines. If you are a NEX you will not want to consider this type of woman.

Suppose you are together a number of years and decide you want to get married. Is there anything you can do? Well, yes, but it is difficult, expensive and iffy. You can try to get an annulment to the woman's marriage. Whether you succeed depends little on whether an annulment is justified. It depends on the people trying to help you, the officials and clergy involved and most of all, how much money you are willing to fork out. It's easy to be ripped off. People will promise you anything, and then keep on demanding money to continue the process. If you are lucky, eventually you will succeed after spending lots of money. If you are unlucky, you will throw your money away. You really need somebody you trust completely to help you in the process.  I discuss annulment in more detail in a later section.

You can also try and get a divorce while in another country, but this is also a difficult task, and there is some question as to whether the divorce will be recognized in the Philippines. Unless you are sure you don't want to get married, better to avoid this category.

## Topic x: *Very Conservative Older Virgin (VCOV)*

When describing this category, this is a good opportunity to discuss Filipina attitudes towards sex. I would say they fall into roughly three categories.

The first category is "the sexually liberated". Typically these women live in cities, in many cases they have gone, or are going to college. They have grown up with western views towards sex. They see nothing wrong with sex, and desire to enjoy sex with a man they care about. Typically these woman lose their virginity between the  ages of 16 and 20.

The second category is the conservative type who absolutely, and without exception, insist on getting married before sex. More typically from the province, typically very religious, they believe it's a sin to have sex before marriage.

The third category starts out exactly like the second category, thinking they are going to wait to be married before having sex. However, as time goes by they slowly find their attitudes relaxing, and at some point they lose their will to say "NO" all the time. Typically this type of woman loses their virginity between the ages of 20 to 35.

Now let's go back to the second category. Girls in this category have a "window of opportunity" to find what they want. If they are attractive and have a good personality and are young, let's say 17 to 22, there is a good chance that there is some guy willing to date them without having sex, and willing to marry them. However, if they pass this age, they start to find things turning against them. Filipino men are no different than western men in this regard. As they get older, they have less and less patience for women insisting on staying virgins. So as these women get older, they find men start to lose interest in them, and they become VCOVs. Most VCOVS start out thinking that they are going to marry a Filipino man, but many at some point become disillusioned at the lack of interest in them, and mistakenly think that perhaps they can find a foreigner to marry them. At age 30 or maybe 35 they get on the internet and start looking.

Well I'm not sure what to say about VCOVs. I suppose for the right man maybe they could be a good match, but certainly I am not that type of man, and I doubt most Expats or potential Expats would find them a good match either. Who wants to wait until marriage to have sex? Also, they are likely to be overly conservative, overly religious, and just plain un-fun loving. Most likely they will desperately want to have a child, before it is too late. I don't recommend VCOVs unless you are also very conservative.

## Topic xi: *Dancer or Entertainer (DOE)*

Ok, this category needs a lot of explanation and discussion. Before I start, let's get to the bottom line:

The dancer or entertainer is the quickest, easiest and most painless path to finding a young sexy attractive partner. It is also (in my opinion) the path least likely to result in long term happiness.

Still interested? Read on.

First of all, what is a dancer or entertainer? A dancer is a woman who dances scantily dressed (or sometimes naked) at a girly bar.

An entertainer (Sometimes called GRO – for guest relations officer) is a girl who will sit down with a man and keep them company, as long as the man keeps buying them drinks. These drinks are called   ladies drinks, and they are special drinks, small, low in alcohol, and more expensive than normal drinks. The girls get a commission from these drinks, usually about 40 or 50 percent of the price of the drink.  A good entertainer will of course make the man feel good, by being very friendly, by touching him, and acting in a seductive and sexy manner, so that the man is inclined to keep on buying drinks. Some might say that the terms dancer and entertainer are really euphemisms for prostitute. Well, sort of – but not exactly,  there is a lot of grey area, which I will get into.

Almost all dancers are also entertainers, since when watching the girls dance, you can request that a girl you find attractive sit with you and keep you company. The girl will join you and stay with you so long as you buy them drinks.

All dancers are entertainers, but not all entertainers are dancers. Some entertainers work at a different kind of bar, such as karaoke bar, or just normal looking bar, where there is no dancing.

If you have the money and inclination, what can you eventually do with (or to) your dancer or entertainer?

Well this depends on a number of factors, such as the city you are in, the policy of the bar, and the attitude of the girl herself. In hard core areas such as Angeles, Makati, Parts of Cebu, Puerto Galera and others, you can pay what they call a bar fine. This might be in the neighborhood of a two or three thousand pesos. The woman gets a percentage of the bar fine. You pay it, and you can take the woman back to your hotel and have sex with her, just like a normal old fashioned prostitute. She will usually beg you for additional money (better to negotiate ahead of time) and she will often try to finish and get away as quick as she can, so she can make more money. If you choose to do this, make sure she knows what is expected of her, and how long she is to keep you company.

**Dancers performing at a Girlie Bar**

In other cities or bars you may not be allowed to take the girls out, but they may have what they call "VIP" rooms. These are private rooms where you can have "fun" with the girl. This "fun" may include sex, but not usually. More commonly it involves masturbation or oral sex. Of course these VIP rooms cost plenty of money and again, the girl gets a percentage of this money.

Still in other cities or bars, you may not be able to do anything with the girl, only talk, touch and kiss in a public area. In these bars and cities anything more you may want to do has to be arranged unofficially.

In addition to the different levels of HARD-CORE-NESS in different cities and bars, there is the attitude of the girl herself. Dancers and entertainers are usually not overtly pressured to do anything more with the customers than have drinks. If they want to do more, it is their choice. They are free to refuse a customer's request to take them out, or take them into a VIP room. In fact this freedom has a lot do with how they attract girls into the profession. I will discuss this in further detail below.

Let's now change direction, and look at how and why girls are attracted into the profession in the first place. Let's start by comparing entertainers and dancers to street prostitutes and self employed bar prostitutes as they exist in the Philippines.

Street prostitutes are the lowest of the low. They are extremely desperate lowlifes or drug addicts. They usually have pimps, (called bugaw in the Philippines) and they don't have much of a choice to refuse a customer. Their job is to have sex as much as they can, as often as they can, with as many customers as they can. It is truly a horrible life, and most women with even the smallest amount of self respect don't want to go down that road. Needless to say, you would not want to choose a street prostitute to be your girl friend or wife!

The next level up is the self employed bar prostitute. These girls are usually quite pretty and sexy and also much more intelligent and have much better personalities than the street prostitutes. These girls usually hang out in bars where Expats or western vacationers hang out. They will approach a man and pretend to be just a normal girl interested in meeting a guy. If you are inexperienced you may get fooled into thinking they are just a normal girl who for some reason really likes you. The tip off is typically is the way they are dressed and that they are overly affectionate and touchy feely. They will often spend an hour or two accepting drinks from and cultivating a potential customer. At some point, if the man does not initiate it, the women will get down to business and suggest they go somewhere for sex. If the man accepts she will talk business. Some naive men might be shocked when they all of the sudden realize this pretty sexy woman they thought they were hitting it off with is just a prostitute. Unlike the street prostitute, sometimes these girls invest considerable time with a potential customer, and then get nothing to show for it. It goes with the territory. From the girl's point of view, the huge difference between being a street prostitute and a self employed bar prostitute is that with the latter, it's the girl who usually initiates the contact, and she has complete control over who she chooses or accepts. She will not in general choose someone she finds disgusting. The more desperate for money she is, the lower her standards will be.

In contrast, the profession of dancer or entertainer seems much more palatable. Let's see how it all starts out.

It starts with a young attractive woman who is desperate for money. She may be desperate because she wants to help her family, or her sick dad, or her baby, or any of a number of reasons. Perhaps she has looked for a job and failed to find a regular job. Or perhaps she is in a regular job, or looked at regular jobs and thought the money is just not enough. Typically a low level job earns between 150 and 300 pesos a day depending on the job and city. This is like $3 to $6 dollars a day. This is not enough money for her needs.

She has a friend who works in a bar and makes 1000 pesos a day or more. The friend will say to her, "Come on, try working at the bar". The reluctant girl may say something like, "But I don't want to have any sex with the customers". The friend will tell her, "No problem, you don't have to, you can make all your money just by having customers buy you drinks. Try it, if you don't like it you can quit". So the girl goes and talks to the manager (or Madame) of the bar and asks questions. She might say, "But I don't want to have sex with the customers". The Madame will assure her (and is honest in this respect) that she is never forced to do anything with a customer. The bar is happy to hire her because they have nothing to lose. The girls are paid a very low base salary, if any salary at all. All the money is to be made on commission.

So, the girl decides to give it a try. Once there, she quickly finds out it is not that easy. There are typically many more girls than customers, so it is like survival of the fittest. The girls that survive are the ones that are most attractive with the best personalities and most seductive natures.

She might fail right away and give up. Or, if she is attractive and has a nice personality, she may get by making a few hundred peso a day from commissions on drinks. The girl might be a little discouraged but figures she is still making more money than a normal job. In a typical day she may meet a customer or two and get some money from drinks, but the customer quickly gets bored when he realizes that the girl will not do anything "extra" with him. She does not get any repeat customers as repeat customers learn to stay away from her. She may continue on in this way for a few weeks or even months just getting by. Meanwhile she sees some of the other girls making much more money. Some of the most successful ones can make thousands of pesos a day, by first milking a customer for drinks, then going out for sex, and repeating the process two or three times a night. She sees this, and she is jealous of how much money the other girl is making, but still, she does not want to have sex with the customers.

Then one day she has a customer that she genuinely likes. He is funny and attractive and seems like a nice guy. So she figures what the hell, she really needs the money, and so she lets herself get bar fined or brought to a VIP room, and the journey down the slippery slope has begun.

Well, as a man looking for a wife, should you consider this type of girl? I would personally say no, avoid this scene and look elsewhere. However I suppose there are some positives to be said for this method. For one thing it's just so easy. Many of these girls are desperate to leave the bar life and hoping for a foreigner to come along and save them. You can "date" many girls, if you want to call it dating. You can try them, have sex with them, and then decide. Unlike girls in a normal job, it is easy for these girls to quit, and then go back to their bar or another bar if things don't work out. So if you find one you like, you can ask her to leave the bar and live with you. Many will be happy to live with you. You don't have to worry about their parents because they are already far away from them. Of course she will want to be supported in a comfortable manner and have an allowance.

I suppose you could make the case that some of these women have good reasons for doing what they do. If a woman is doing this to pay for medical care for her dad who has cancer, can you say she is bad or morally corrupt? Perhaps you could say she is a saint, for making such a sacrifice. Perhaps, but not usually. I lived in Angeles (which has a very hard core bar scene) for two months. I had a friend who was heavily into trying to find a girl friend in this manner and I did not like what I saw. Most of these girls live day to day and will say or do anything to get what they want. There may be exceptions but most of these girls are not the type of girl you would want for your wife.

As an aside, of course having unprotected sex with any kind of prostitute, dancer or entertainer is extremely dangerous. However, supposedly the employed bar girls are supposed to be tested for STDs every month. How well this is enforced probably varies from bar to bar and city to city. An Expat bar owner from Cebu related the following information:

"Girls are tested once a month for basic sexually transmitted diseases. They are not tested for AIDS or HIV because the test is too expensive. Health inspectors typically visit a bar every few months to check each girls medical certificate. If one has not been tested for over one month she is stopped from working and the bar owner is fined". Of course it is not hard to imagine a bar owner getting around this problem in the "standard" Filipino manner.

# Chapter 3: Who is Good for Whom? Interactions Between Categories

Let's review the categories:

**FOREIGN MEN**

| | |
|---|---|
| NEX | No to Expatriatism |
| MEX | Maybe to Expatriatism |
| YEX | Yes to Expatriatism |
| Swinger | The Swinger |
| Drinker | The Drinker. |

**FILIPINA WOMEN**

| | |
|---|---|
| YSA | Very Young Woman, Smart And Ambitious. |
| YWC | Very Young Woman Without A Clue. |
| YPF | Very Young Woman From Province Being Pressured By Her Family. |
| NWG | Nice Working Girl. |
| CW | Career Woman looking at the ticking clock |
| SM | Single Mom. |
| OWW | Older Widowed Woman |
| OSW | Older Separate Woman |
| VCOV | Very Conservative Older Virgin |

DOE            The Dancer Or Entertainer

Well what kind of women should you look for? Well that depends partly on your personality and partly on your situation. Here is a quick summary of some considerations, by type.

## Topic i: *If You are a NEX*

**YSA**. You do not want to live in the Philippines, and bringing a very young woman back home could be a source of ridicule. Another problem with the YSA is that they want an education. Education is cheap in the Philippines, but you don't want to stay in the Philippines. Do you want to spend the money to give her an education in the USA? Very expensive, very risky. She could get her education and then divorce you. Well as with this category in general, you can hit the jackpot, but it's a big risk.

**YWC**. Again, bringing a very young woman back home could be a source of ridicule. Also, will you be happy with her lack of experience in life, and lack of intellectual stimulation. It could work, but there are probably better options. Also, this type of woman may not be happy away from the Philippines, she may feel lost and homesick.

**YPF**. Again the ridicule problem but still this could work. This woman is motivated to help her family. You could get her a job and let her send some or all of her money back home. She might miss the Philippines.

**NWG**. Could work out, but the problem is in the dating process. As a NEX you have limited time to be in the Philippines and a NWG will have limited time to get to know you.

**SM**. Could work, but you have to get two or more people into your country. More difficult. Of course there is the question of whether you want to be a step dad. Could be rewarding but you have to be the right type of person.

**OWW**. If the age of the woman is ok for you, why not.

**OSW**   Not a good choice. She is already married, so how are you going to get her back to your home country?

**VCOV**   Well if you are very conservative, I suppose this could work, but most Westerners want to have sex with a woman before marriage.

**DOE**   Not recommended. Among other reasons already discussed, here is the problem. You will be going back to the USA to work on the Fiancée visa. You will have to support her and trust her. Most DOEs can't be trusted, especially with money. She is likely to tell you she needs money because she is no longer working, then she is likely to take your money and keep on working. In the mean time she might find another man.

## Topic ii: *If You are a YEX or MEX*

If you are a YEX all categories are open to you. What you want depends on your personality. If you are a MEX all categories are initially open to you, however if you decide you don't want to live in the Philippines, then you will be guided by the choices available to a NEX

## Topic iii: *If You are a Swinger*

Since you are interested in sex and having a good time, your best categories are as follows:

**YSA**. Actually this may be your best match since it can be mutually beneficial. This type of woman is likely to be liberal, sexy, and fun loving. Since her main goal is to have an education, she won't be as devastated when you move on. You will have to pay for her education while you date her. This is not nearly as expensive as in a western country.

**SM**. Sex should be no problem. A single mom can be sexy, smart, fun. As long as you help support her kid while you date her, she will be happy. She may be sad when you move on, but she should be ok since she still has her kid.

**NWG** Finding time to date is the main problem. In good conscience you should not fool her into leaving her job, that would be very bad. If you have the patience and don't mind the limited time, it could be a good match. She will be ok when you move on, because she still has her job.

**OWW**: Could work, if you don't mind the age.

**OSW**: Could work, if you don't mind the age. You don't have to feel guilty since she is married anyway.

The following categories are **not** for you:

**YWC**: You will probably be bored, and she may be devastated when you move on.

**YPF**: You don't want to get involved with her family, that's not for you. If you have sex and pretend you are serious and then move on, her family may be angry. Avoid this.

**VCOV**: Not your type.

**DOE**: May not be what you are looking for, many swingers want the challenge of the chase.

### Topic iv: *If You are a Drinker*

Your main goal is to drink and have sex with Prostitutes and DOEs. Well, if you have money, and if you are a nice drunk that doesn't get angry or violent when drinking, then there are some good places for you in the Philippines, such as Puerto Galera, Angeles, Makati, parts of Cebu and many others.

If you do want to establish a relationship, a DOE is your best bet, since they will not mind that you are a drunk so long as you keep giving them money.

# Chapter 4: General Strategies for Specific Types

In the section titled "WHO ARE YOU" I described a number of different categories or situations you might be in. In this chapter I will say a few words about your general strategy for finding women depending on which category you fall into.

## Topic i: *About Courtship*

In a normal relationship in your own country you would usually date or "go out" together a long time before you made any decision to get married. This, of course, is the way it should be. The longer you know someone, the least likely you will be surprised or shocked about something in their personality.

However, if your goal is to find a Filipina wife and bring her back to the USA, and if you don't have time to live in or take a long vacation in the Philippines, then you can't afford this luxury. You must make this decision quickly. Hopefully, if you are a good judge of character, then you have a good chance of success, but there is no doubt, mistakes can be made. This is a chance you just have to take. It goes with the territory. However, you can increase your odds by not ignoring warning signs. Maybe you want a woman or wife so bad, there is a tendency to ignore the warning signs, then later, you will say, I should have known. If you find a woman always lying to you, or trying to cheat you out of money, or being overly obsessed about money, don't ignore it.

Of course, the best way to avoid this problem is to give yourself plenty of time to visit in the Philippines, or even better, to just live here. If you are here for a long time you will not feel the pressure to make a decision quickly. If you are living here permanently you really should feel no pressure to get married at all. This is the best way, but I realize not everyone can do it this way.

## Topic ii: *NEX with Limited Time*

A NEX (No to Expatriatism) is not planning on living in the Philippines.

In the United States as well as some other countries there is the concept of a Fiancée visa which I described earlier. With this visa you can bring over a woman to the USA for up to six months while you decide whether or not to get married. However, you can't just meet somebody over the internet and apply for this type of visa. The rules state that you must meet the woman in person, and you must have proof of your meeting and courtship. This means that you must visit your prospective fiancée in the Philippines. So it's a given that you must visit the Philippines for at least a short vacation, perhaps only a week or two. Since your time is limited it is unrealistic for you to think that you can find a girl to marry in the short amount of time you are in the Philippines. You must have the woman or women you want to meet picked out ahead of time. You do this by establishing Internet relationships ahead of time as will be described in a subsequent chapter. It will be easier if you pick out women from one or at most two different areas in the Philippines, as this will reduce your travel time.

## Topic iii: *MEX with More Time*

A MEX (Maybe to Expatriatism) will have more time available to visit the Philippines. It has to be that way, otherwise how could he consider and evaluate whether he wants to live permanently in the Philippines? Suppose you are planning a six week trip to the Philippines. I would say six weeks is the minimum time you would need to acclimate yourself and have a good chance of meeting a woman in the Philippines. If you are planning such a trip, what should your strategy be for meeting women?

Well it is still a very good idea to have some women picked out ahead of time. It's a nice thing to look forward to, and it can only increase your chances. Plus, it's a fun hobby. However, if you will be spending six or more weeks in the Philippines the internet need not be your only method. If you are not totally ugly, if you have a half decent personality, and if you are not shy you will have no problem finding women to date, even if you are old and you want to date young women. The key thing is to have no fear of rejection. If you have some skill in picking out the girls who might be interested, and in presenting yourself, you will find that the odds of a woman accepting your request for a date are very high. There are a lot of Filipina women interested in dating western men. Don't be afraid to try, even if your initial thought is, "This woman is too young, too sexy and too pretty to be interested in me". Put that thought out of your head. When you date, many women will want to bring along friends or relatives the first time. You will have to accept this.

## Topic iv: *YEX with Unlimited Time*

As a YEX (Yes to Expatriatism) you have all the time in the world. I strongly suggest you don't make any quick decisions. There is nothing wrong with finding some possibilities ahead of time using the internet, but unless one of these women is the girl of your dreams, it's better just to come to the Philippines, get acclimated, look around and just have some fun. As a single Westerner living in the Philippines you will have plenty of opportunities.

# Part 3: *Using the Internet to Find Love in the Philippines*

**Computer screen with yahoo messenger**

# Chapter 5: The Internet in general

Ok, so you want to find a Filipina woman to be your wife or girl friend and lover. How do you go about it before you  actually travel to the Philippines?  In the sections that follow I will explain how to use the internet to achieve this goal.

When you finally do visit the Philippines, if your time is limited, having women picked out ahead of time is really your only option. You will not have time to find a quality woman in the short amount of time you will be visiting. If you plan a long vacation, or you plan on living in the Philippines, then this is not mandatory. Still, most men will want to have woman picked out ahead of time if for no other reason than that it's fun. It's nice to look forward to meeting a woman you have picked out ahead of time, and the process of getting to know someone on the internet can be enjoyable in it's own right.

In the old days trying to find someone and getting to know them ahead of time was a daunting task. You would have to sign up for some expensive mail order bride service just to get a list of names, pictures and contact addresses. Then you had to write letters and send pictures by regular postal service with a turn around time of weeks. Perhaps you could afford one or two very expensive phone calls, but that was it. The chance of being fooled or mislead (by a false picture, or other false information) was very high.

Well lucky for you times have changed. In the modern era of the internet you can send instant email, chat on line, send pictures back and forth, see each other with live video and talk cheaply using internet phone services such as provided by Yahoo or Skype. You have a much better chance of getting to know someone accurately and less chance of getting fooled than in the old days.

What if you are not computer literate? Well too bad for you! Learn how to use a computer or give' up. The old methods will not work anymore. If you want to meet women ahead of time before visiting the Philippines, the internet is your only reasonable choice.

Ok, are you ready to meet Filipina women on line? Well be patient!   Before I get into detailed specifics I want to go over a number of general points. I will get to specifics later

## Topic i: *Honesty, Safety and Scams*

*"Mr. Knox now, come now, come now, you don't have to be so dumb now!"*
> - From "Fox in Socks" by Dr. Seuss

- Are you new to the internet?

- Are you by nature a trusting person?

- Are you by nature a gullible person?

If you answered yes to all three questions you could be in deep trouble! You are prime meat! You are just what the scammers are looking for!

You had better have some idea of internet safety and scams or you **WILL** get burned. It's easy to catch a virus if you don't know what you are doing. If you trust people right away you are likely to get scammed.

Hopefully this will not happen to you, because in this section I'm going to educate you. If you are an experienced internet user and chatter you can skip this section. You already know all this stuff. If not, you had better read this section carefully!

There are three basic ways you can get hurt, as follows:

- You can catch a virus

- You can get scammed

- You can get emotionally involved with a fake

Let's take a look at each of these items

### ♦ What is a virus?

I realize learning about viruses does not have anything directly to do with finding love on the internet! However, when looking for love on the internet the possibility of catching a virus is very real, so it is important that you educate yourself on this topic.

What is a virus? It's a hard concept to get a handle on if you are not a computer expert. A computer virus is not really like a real life virus. They call it a virus only because of it's ability to replicate itself.

Basically a virus is a computer program that is written by someone. This is an important thing to understand. Unlike the nature version, a virus is not a randomly occurring thing. Behind every virus there is a person or persons. There is somebody with great computer knowledge who spent a lot of time, thought and energy into developing and deploying the virus.

So, a virus is a clever piece of software (computer program) designed to somehow install itself on your computer and once there, perform a task, and also replicate itself to other computers.

This brings up two questions, namely:

- Who writes these viruses?

- What do they do once on your computer?

If we examine the latter question first then the former will become more obvious.

Some virus do nothing bad. They are seemingly on your computer just for fun. They might do something like display a certain message or picture, but not in general cause any real damage.

Some viruses don't appear to do anything bad, but their purpose is to steal information. This information can be used for marketing purposes or worse. In the worst case the virus can steal personal or financial information used to scam you or raid your identity or bank account.

Some viruses go about destroying your data and software so that your computer becomes unusable. A virus can not usually destroy hardware, but it can make your software and data so unusable that you must re-install your computer from scratch.

So who writes these viruses?

Well nobody knows for sure exactly who writes the viruses and where they come from. If they did, they would arrest all the people, put them in jail and there would be no more viruses. However, we can make some pretty good guesses about what kind of people write these viruses.

The viruses that do nothing really bad and seemingly have no purpose are most likely written by students and hackers who just want the challenge of seeing if they can write a successful virus. Basically it's an endeavor undertaken for fun.

The viruses that steal information are written by people looking for financial gain. Either for marketing purposes or to otherwise use the information in devious ways.

The viruses that destroy your computer? Who knows. Maybe they are written by someone with an axe to grind, or by terrorist groups trying to cause havoc to the capitalist world.

### ◆ How to Not Catch a Virus

Knowing what a virus is fine, but what you really want to know is how not to catch one! First of all you should have a reasonably modern and up to date operating system. The newer operating systems have more safety checks in place to prevent you from catching a virus. For PC users this means having at least Windows XP with service pack 2, or a more modern operating system such as Vista or Windows 7. Whatever operating system you have, all the latest security patches should be applied.

You should have the firewall activated and in internet options you should have the safety setting set to medium or higher. You should purchase and install a well known Anti Virus program. You should set your operating system to AUTOMATIC UPDATE so that all the latest security patches are automatically downloaded.

If you don't know how to perform the above tasks you will have to get someone to help you, it is beyond the scope of this book to help you in this area.

Even if you follow all the procedures listed above it is still possible to catch a virus if you don't know what you are doing. Here are some additional precautions:

**NEVER** click on an imbedded hyperlink from an unknown source, especially while having a chat conversation or receiving mail from an unknown or untrusted source. Sometimes viruses steal mailing lists so that it appears you get a mail from a trusted friend, but it is really the virus sending the mail. Always be careful when clicking on imbedded hyperlinks. If there is any doubt in your mind, don't click on it.

For example, while chatting in YAHOO MESSENGER it is common to get a message something like the following:

- Me and my friends are getting naked! Want to watch? <u>Click on this link to see!</u>

If you click on such a link you are likely to catch a virus.

Be very careful when you download files being sent to you. For example, if they say you are receiving a picture, make sure the extension is either JPG, BMP or GIF. If you see a file with an unknown extension never download it. In particular files with EXE extensions are extremely dangerous. If you go to execute something or do some task and you get a warning from the operating system, a dialog box something like:

"you are about to initiate an EXE program, do you trust the source?"

Better to always be conservative. Unless you really trust the source and unless you really need what they are trying to send to you, better to reject the attempted task.

Even with all this it is always possible to catch a virus, so keep your virus protection software up to date and run the scan at least once every few days. And finally, Good luck!

### ♦ Scams and Scammers!

A "Scam" is a technique or story to fool you into giving your money away. A scammer is a person employing a scam.

- Unfortunately there are many scammers on the internet.

- Unfortunately, if you are trusting and gullible it is easy to fall prey to a scammer.

- Fortunately, if you are skeptical and not gullible, you should always be able to avoid getting scammed.

Scammers attempt to take advantage of your generosity, emotions, greed, stupidity or some combination of the above. There are many types of scams and many types of scammers.

**Example Scam**: You have been communicating with Jane, a seemingly beautiful and friendly Filipina. One day she suddenly tells you: Joe, I have a big problem! My mother stepped on a rusty nail and now she has a serious blood infection. The doctor says she needs a very expensive antibiotic or she may die! Please Joe, I can't afford the medicine. Please help me! I need just p15000. Please can you send right away? I will be forever grateful, and I will pay you back next week when I get my salary.

**Example Scam**: You have been communicating with Jane, a seemingly beautiful and friendly Filipina. One day she tells you: Joe, I have great news! For three years I have been trying to get a travel visa to the USA. Yesterday it finally came through! Joe, I want to visit you! I am ready to come right away! Joe, just send me the money for the ticket and I can come next week!

**Example Scam**: You have been communicating with Jane, a seemingly beautiful and friendly Filipina. One day she suddenly tells you: Joe, I have a great opportunity for you! My rich uncle wants to send money to his son in the USA, but he has no bank account. Let me have the Full name and number of your account and he will transfer $100,000 to your account. You will then transfer the money to my cousin. You can keep $5000 just for your trouble and assistance in this matter.

The moral of these stories? **NEVER** communicate with a Filipina named **Jane**! No – just kidding! The moral is: Don't be gullible!

There are so many scams and scammers. Most scammers are looking for reasonably big bucks. However, there is even a class of scammers looking for very small money. There are Filipina women whose only source of income is small donations from foreigners. They will maintain many on line relationships, occasionally asking for a few hundred pesos here and there from each of their "clients" for such items as rice, load or internet costs. These girls know that if they only ask for small sums of money every once in a while you will assume they are not scamming you. They assume your thinking will be: "who wants to bother scamming someone out of just a few hundred peso".

It's very easy to avoid getting scammed if you remember two very simple rules.

- Never give out personal information such as your full name, your address or your bank account or credit card numbers.

- Never send money

It seems so simple, but yet people still get scammed all the time. They get fooled into trusting someone, then they get burned.

Does this mean you should never ever send money under any circumstances? I won't go that far. I will discuss this subject in more detail in later sections.

### ◆ Emotional Involvement with a Fake.

There is also the possibility of getting involved with someone who has something to hide. Somebody trying to fool you in some way, not to scam you out of money, but because they know if they don't fool you, you will not be interested.

Examples include:

- An ugly or old woman trying to fool you by sending you fake pictures of a beautiful woman.

- An underage woman pretending to be at least 18 years old

- A woman who is perhaps separated (but still married) claiming to be single.

- A woman who has children but does not tell you.

- A woman that has a physical, mental or medical problem, but does not tell you.

- A gay person or transvestite trying to get his (her?) jollies by fooling you into on line sexual activity.

One way to avoid some of these problems is to insist that your partner have a web cam. A web cam is a very valuable tool in this process. I would strongly recommend that you not get involved with anybody who refuses to show themselves on web cam, no matter what their excuse is.

Other than that, look for and be alert to inconsistencies and don't ignore them when you see them. A person lying about an important issue usually slips up sooner or later.

### ♦ Other Safety Tips

- Be Skeptical! It's so very easy to lie on the internet. If you are not an experienced chatter, don't fall into the trap of believing everything someone tells you. Always be skeptical, always look for inconsistencies. Look for women of good character who genuinely seem to be honest. If you are skeptical and alert, you will almost always catch the liars in the act of lying.

- Don't believe just because you see a picture. Anyone can send you a picture of a beautiful woman. Pictures must be backed up with live web cam for verification.

- Use a separate email address for your on line searching. When you start this process create a new free email address for the sole purpose of use during your on line search. Don't use your normal email address or you are likely to be sorry as your level of spam is likely to shoot up dramatically. It's easy to sign up for a free email account on Google, Yahoo or HotMail as well as many other sites.

## Topic ii: *Don't Put All Your Eggs in One Basket.*

Don't make the mistake of "falling in love" with a single woman on line. No matter how much you think you like a certain girl, or how great the conversation is, or how pretty or sexy she is, or whatever. Remember, you can never really know until you meet in person. Even when you meet in person it's not always easy to make a correct judgment of a person's character and personality in a short amount of time, and it's almost impossible to be sure about a person from the internet only. People that have played this game know there is nothing more discouraging than thinking you have met somebody great on the internet and then being so disappointed when you meet for real. I'm not saying don't be optimistic or excited about the person you meet on line, I'm just saying, always keep in the back of your mind that it's easy to fake a persona on line.

Now if you meet a local person on line and then meet for real, and it does not work out, it's no big deal, but the stakes are magnified when you are going to travel thousands of miles to meet this woman. For this reason I most strongly recommend that you don't put all your hopes into a single on line contact. You should strive to meet a number of potential girl friends on line, so that when you finally visit, if one does not work out, you have alternatives.

As an aside, it's better not to tell any of the on line girl friends that you have other girl friends on line. They will likely be jealous. Filipinas are very jealous by nature.

## Topic iii: *Patience is a Virtue*

If you think you are going to go on line and quickly obtain a list of quality women, then you are in for a big disappointment. Finding quality women on line is a very time consuming process. You will have to make a hobby of this and put many hours of effort into finding women you can relate to. The good news is that many people enjoy this process and some even get addicted to it. But if you are impatient and expect immediate results you are sure be discouraged.

For one thing, the internet in general, and chat rooms in particular are a bit crazy. The chat rooms contain many entities that appear to be either crazy or fake. The fake people are called bots, which is short for robot. These are automated programs that at first appear to be real people. If you say hello to a bot you might get a reply like "hi there sexy, I'm feeling so horny now, how about you?", or any other of a million stupid replies. If you are experienced it usually does not take you long to figure out you are talking to a bot. I often wonder who exactly is infesting the room with bots, and what is their purpose? It's hard to get a handle on this, as nobody really seems to know. There are probably a variety of reasons bots infest the chat rooms. Well it's beyond the scope of this book to figure that out, but from your point of view you must realize that many, if not a majority of the people in the rooms, are fake, or stupid, or mentally retarded or weird. Thus it will be your job to patiently seek out the real people that exist, and find the quality women to talk to. I estimate that for every 50 people you attempt to chat with, perhaps one will turn out to be a possibility, meaning someone you don't immediately reject. Someone that you can have a nice conversation with. Maybe one in ten of those will be somebody with whom you establish a lasting internet friendship. Anyway, I don't really know the exact numbers but the point is, you must make many attempts, and you must be patient.

## Topic iv: *Learn How Not to Waste Time – Rely on Webcam*

Since, as I just described, on the average, you have to make many attempts for every quality contact you find, it's good if you learn how not to waste time. You will get better at this as you gain experience. As you gain experience you will quickly learn how to separate fake bots, idiots, gays and liars from legitimate women. One tool that is invaluable and which you should rely on heavily is the web cam. You MUST have a web cam if you want to play this game, and my suggestion to you is that you MUST insist that your contacts also have a web cam. Most internet cafes offer web cam, often for free, sometimes for a small additional fee. After a short amount of conversation the topic of web cam should be brought up. Do you have a web cam? If they answer "NO" I suggest you just move on. You might say something like, "I'm sorry but I like C2C" (cam to cam). If they say they will have a cam some other time, then just say, "ok, we add each other as friends and talk when you have cam". Don't waste your time talking when there is no cam. The odds are too great you will waste your time and be disappointed later. You have to learn to be efficient. When broaching the subject of web cam there are many tricks that people play. Here is an example

**You**: Do you have web cam?

**Them**: You first

Notice they did not answer the question. They may be tricking you so that you think they have a web cam, but what they really mean is, "you first, me never" They rationalize to themselves that they did not really lie. This tendency towards dishonesty about web cam can actually be used to your benefit.

Many women will want you to show your web cam first before they show theirs. That's ok, but you should always get direct straight forward responses to the following questions.

- Do you have a web cam? Make sure they specifically answer YES, not something like "you first". If they give some non descript answer, say "but you didn't answer the question, do you have a web cam?"

- If you establish they have a web cam ask this. "If I start my web cam, do you also promise to start yours?"

Again make sure you get a direct straight forward answer, not something like "you first". If you can't get straight forward answers, time to move on. Don't waste your time. If you get YES answers to both questions, then by all means, start your web cam first, make them happy.

Now, sometimes you will start your web cam, only to find that even after their promises, they don't start their web cam. Although this is kind of annoying, really, for your purposes, it's ok. It means one of two things:

- They are liars and never had a web cam.

- They have a web cam, but they looked at you and didn't like what they saw. In addition, they are liars because even though they are not attracted to you, they didn't keep their promise.

Either way, it's ok, you have eliminated them. You have to see it this way and not take it personally.

## Topic v: *Decide on Your Geographical Area*

Continuing on the subject of not wasting your time, you might want to consider limiting your geographical area.

When you live in the USA and you look at the Philippines on the map, it looks like a small place, and in fact, if you were to take the total land area of all the islands and add them up, they add up to about the same total area as the state of New Mexico. However, this is very deceiving. When you are actually here, it feels immense. There are hundreds of inhabited islands spread widely apart in the ocean, and even what looks like a small Island on the map feels pretty big when you are here. Part of this is because, with a few exceptions, there are no real highways so it takes a long time to drive from place to place. When going from island to island, many islands have no air service at all, and others have air service only going through Manila as a hub. For many islands a boat trip is the only way to get there and again, often you might have to go through a hub to get to your final destination. So traveling around the Philippines is not always as quick and easy as you might think. So unless you have both lots of money and lots of time it's better not to be traveling all over the Philippines to meet the women you picked out on the internet. For this reason I suggest you concentrate on one or two geographical areas.

Fortunately with both Yahoo Messenger and FilipinaHeart (two services I will be discussing later) it is easy to meet Filipina women from a given area since with Yahoo Messenger the chat rooms are organized by location and with FilipinaHeart you can search by location. Again, I will describe the details of this later.

## Topic vi: *Think About What You Are Looking For*

And still continuing with the thought of not wasting time, have an idea of what you are looking for. Earlier I discussed the different kinds of Filipina women available. Have some idea of what's acceptable to you, what you want and try to stay on track. It's easy to get side tracked. Remember you have a goal.

## Topic vii: *About Internet Cafes and Home Computers*

In the USA there is not really the concept of cyber cafes. Most people have their own computers. In third world countries such as the Philippines people often can't afford their own computers, so they rely on internet cafes. Internet cafes are basically business establishments where a person can rent a computer that is connected to the internet. Typically there are many computers packed into a small room, and the cost usually ranges from p15 to p40 per hour, depending on a number of factors. The more comfortable they are, the faster the connection and the more privacy they have, the higher the cost. Cities typically have higher costs than rural areas. Some Cafés offer private booths that typically rent for about p100 an hour. I mention internet cafes for a couple of reasons. First because you have to be aware that when a person is at a café they typically don't have much privacy. Second, that they usually have a time limit. They pay for a certain amount of time, and when that time is over they must stop. Most café users don't have a lot of money, so they don't like to extend their time. Thus it is very common for your chat mate to say things like, "Sorry, my time is up, I have to go now". This can be a bit frustrating, but what can you do? Some women will use this as an excuse to have you send them money. I will discuss the topic of sending money in more detail in the next section.

## Topic viii: *About Sending Money*

If you read the HELP section about security on FilipinaHeart they will suggest that you never send money under any circumstances. Earlier in this section I discussed scams and scammers and how so many of them will attempt to fool you into giving them money. The natural conclusion is simply: Never send money.

Still, I would not go so far as to say NEVER. Never say NEVER as they say.

Under some circumstances it may be appropriate to send small amounts of money. I will however say this: Only send money if you have a well established online relationship, only send small amounts of money and if you do send money be prepared for the fact that the money may not be used as intended.

Think of it like buying a lottery ticket. You should not buy one unless you can afford to buy one. If you do buy one, hope to win but don't expect to win.

If you develop an on line relationship with a Filipina woman there is a good chance that at some point she will ask you to send her money. I guess this is never really a good thing, but how bad it is, how you perceive the request, and whether you want to honor the request depends on several factors.

If you are just starting your on line relationship and a girl asks for a lot of money, this should be an immediate red flag. Most likely it's time to move on. Don't be suckered or scammed. Often the request will sound something like this: "My mom is sick and in the hospital, if she does not get her medicine she may die. Please can you help me?". Or like this: I'm in school, but my tuition is due next week, please can you help me to stay in school?". These statements may or may not be true, but it is irrelevant. A quality woman will not make these kinds of requests at the beginning of the relationship. If she promises to pay you back, you can be especially sure she is a born liar and scam artist, because once you send money you will NEVER get it back.

On the other hand, if your relationship continues on for a period of one month or more then the dynamics change. Under some circumstances it may be reasonable to send some money. In some cases it may be a means to build trust, or for her to know you are serious about her, or for you to know if she can be trusted. Also, if you offer money, but she refuses, that's usually a sign of good character.

Let's consider a couple of examples. Suppose her web cam is poor quality and when you suggested she buy a better one she tells you, as they always do, "I have no money to buy one". Maybe you want to offer to buy her a good one. So you tell her that you will send her the money so that she can buy a good quality web cam.

Now when you make the offer, if she says something like: "No, I really don't want you to send me any money", well that's a sign of good character. However, if she says "ok", that's not bad either. The test will come later. Send her the money but make her promise, that no matter what, that money is only to be used to buy a web cam. Sometimes when you insist that they promise that the money only be used for it's intended purpose they get offended. They might say something like "What do you think of me?". Well a response like this does not mean much one way or the other. If they are an honest person this may be their honest reaction, if they are dishonest, this is the reaction they give to fool you. At any rate, whether they are offended or not, make sure they promise to use the money as intended.

Then send the money and see what happens. If she keeps good on her promise and buys the web cam, well that's a very good sign. However, if she says something like, "I'm sorry, but an emergency came up, and I had to use the money, I hope you understand". Well don't understand. It's a very bad sign. Or a very good sign that she can't be trusted. Suppose she says that she never received the money, but the Western Union office says it was signed for. That's an even worse sign. Now you know she is liar and can't be trusted. Move on. When you send money for a specific purpose, and this purpose can be verified, this is a good method to see if she can be trusted.

Here is another example. Perhaps she is a student, and after a few weeks she begs you for a few thousand peso so she can pay her tuition. Well this is not easy to verify and you are under no obligation to support someone who is nothing more than an internet contact. However, if you feel the girl is special and you really like her, and your intuition tells you she is telling the truth, maybe you want to send her some money to prove that you are serious about her.   That's your call, there is no right or wrong answer. But don't send a lot, and be aware of, and ready to accept that,  you might be getting scammed.

If you do decide to send money Western Union is the simplest way. There are Western Union offices in most cities in the Philippines. If you have never done it, it's easy. You go to a Western Union office and just give the exact name of the person and the city you are sending the money to. They will give you a numbered receipt. To the person getting the money, give your exact name, the exact amount sent, and the transaction number. With that information and proper identification the receiver can pick up the money from a local Western Union office.

### Topic ix: *What Hardware Will You Need to Use the Internet Effectively?*

Of course you will need a reasonably modern (although not necessarily top of the line) computer. The computer must have a reasonably modern operating system capable of running modern software. You should have at least  256 (better at least 512) megabytes of internal RAM memory to run this software effectively.

You must have a broadband (fast) internet connection such as DSL or cable. Don't even think about dial up, it will be too frustrating. You must have the broadband capability to send and receive pictures quickly, have voice chat and send and receive live video.

You must have a microphone and speakers (or headphone) connected to your computer. Almost all modern computers have this.

You must have a web cam so you can send live video. A web cam is a very important item in this process. It provides reality and proof that you are who you say you are, and it allows you to have much more fun with your prospective girl friend/wife. Web cams are not that expensive and I strongly recommend a top of the line web cam capable of operating in low light conditions. A cheap web cam will be a constant source of frustration. The one I use is excellent, although I am sure there are many good choices on the market. My web cam is the A4 tech flexi cam, low light version.

Finally you need a digital camera or a scanner or both. A digital camera will allow you to send high quality pictures of yourself to your friend over the internet. A web cam, although extremely useful and fun does not send high quality pictures. A scanner will allow you to scan and send old style photographs as well as other information from books or maps etc. You will also need to create digital pictures to upload to your Profiles, so prospective Filipina women can see what you look like.

# Chapter 6: Overview of Internet Dating Strategies and Software

In this section I will first give an overview of the suggested Software. Then I will go over some general strategies to use the software. Details follow in subsequent chapters.

## Topic i: *Overview of Suggested Software*

### ♦ Internet Browser

Of course you will need a modern internet browser such as Internet Explorer or FireFox. All modern computers come with this software standard.

### ♦ www.FilipinaHeart.com

FilipinaHeart (FH) is a very good site specializing in Filipina match making. The only down side of this site is that it is a pay service.

### ♦ Friendster

Friendster is a social networking internet site located at (www.friendster.com). There are, of course, other social networking sites such as FaceBook and MySpace, but for some reason Friendster is by far the most popular here in the Philippines.

### ♦ Yahoo Messenger

YAHOO MESSENGER is free downloadable software available from WWW.YAHOO.COM. Yahoo messenger is a full featured messenger service allowing texting, voice, video as well as file and photo sharing. Of course there are other messenger services such as AOL, Paltalk and MSN messenger, but again,

YAHOO MESSENGER is the one used almost exclusively here in the Philippines.

### ◆ Skype

The Skype application from www.skype.com allows free voice chat (i.e. telephone like conversation) between computers, and very low cost conversation from computer to regular land line phone. Skype also supports live web cam video. Although Yahoo Messenger also supports voice chat Skype is a much better application for this purpose. Skype specializes in voice chat and the quality and service is far superior to Yahoo messenger for this purpose. Skype is not used to meet people. It is used to communicate with people you already know. Your friend will also have to have Skype installed on her computer. Skype can also be used for texting with a user you already know.

### ◆ Clipboard Magic

Clipboard Magic is a simple and free program that makes it easy to cut and paste from a library of existing messages. This will save you typing and hand cramps.

## Topic ii: *Overview of internet strategies*

- Is your attitude: "Why spend money when I can accomplish my goal without spending money"?

- Or is your attitude: "What's the big deal about spending 30 dollars a month when the goal of finding a partner is so important"?

- Is your attitude: "I don't really feel comfortable with technology. I want to keep things simple"?

- Or is your attitude: "I love technology. Give me all the options so that I can maximize the probability of finding my partner"?

The answers to these questions will determine what strategies you will use on the internet.

If you don't want to spend money for a pay service then you will not want to use FilipinaHeart (FH). FH costs about $30 for a one month subscription. Discounts are available for multi month subscriptions.

However, if you don't mind spending the money, and you want to keep things simple, then you might want to ONLY use FH.

If you don't mind spending money, and you don't mind technology, then you will want to use a combination of FH, Yahoo Messenger, Friendster and Skype.

# Chapter 7: FilipinaHeart (FH) and other Pay Dating Services

## Topic i: *History and Overview*

In the old days, when dinosaurs ruled the earth and the internet was not yet born, when a Westerner wanted to hookup with a Filipina or other third world women, they would buy a magazine, often known as a mail order bride catalog, listing "mail order" brides.

These magazines would have a lists of women, each with a short description and picture and listing ID or number. If you were interested in corresponding with one you would send a check to the magazines office stating the number of the girl you were interested in, and they would send you back the address of the girl. Typically it cost a few bucks per address.

The process was excruciatingly slow and highly susceptible to scamming. First you would send a check to the office and wait for the reply, a week or more. Then you would send off an international letter to the woman by normal postal mail, and wait for the reply. Assuming you got a reply each round of letters could take two weeks or more. Sometimes the pictures supplied to the magazines were fake, and after all this, if you finally did visit the woman you were highly likely to be mightily disappointed.

Well "mail order bride services", you've come a long way baby! This ain't your fathers Oldsmobile!

When the internet came along these "mail order bride services" knew they had to adapt, but the first generation of improvements was basically just a transfer of the service to the internet.

That is, you scanned the list on their internet site instead of in a magazine. You paid on line instead of sending a check, and for your money you got an Email address rather than a regular postal address.

When free messenger and social networking services came along such as Friendster and Yahoo messenger complete with texting, voice, video, profiles and pictures the "Mail order bride services" had to adapt big time or risk going out of business. To stay in business they had to offer something more than what you could simply get for free. Well I am happy to tell you they succeeded!

To be honest, when I wrote my first pass at this book I did not even include pay services such as FilipinaHeart (FH) in this book's internet section. I was still remembering the first generation of internet "mail order" services which were only one technological step up from the magazines. My feeling was, why burden the reader with this option when you could do everything you need to do for free.

When one of my Expat friends reviewed the book he was amazed that I was advocating the free method when the Dating Services made things so much easier. Given this feedback I decided to test drive some of the Internet Pay Dating Services. Originally I had picked out four services which specialized in Filipina Dating, namely:

- www.FilipinaHeart.com

- www.Blossoms.com     (Cherry Blossoms)

- www.Cebuanas.com

- www.FilipinoFriendFinder.com

I decided to try FH First since that was the one most recommended and had the most Filipina Listings. So I purchased the Platinum membership (most expensive membership) of FH and gave it an extensive test drive. I was so impressed that I decided not to even try the other services. I am not saying they are not as good. Maybe they are even better. Please feel free to investigate these and others. But I can say without equivocation that FH is an EXCELLENT service!

## Topic ii: *FilipinaHeart (FH) Overview*

### ♦ High Praise for the User Interface

In my previous life before retiring to the Philippines I was a software engineer designing end user products and interfaces. I know good software when I see it and I know bad software when I see it. FH is an exceptionally well designed site and I am extremely impressed with it. It does everything you want it to do, and the interface is very simple and intuitive. Experienced internet users should feel comfortable with this site almost instantly. Even inexperienced users should be able to use this site comfortably in a short period of time.

There are many features about the interface that make FH easy to use, but I will list in this section a few of the traits that make it particularly user friendly.

Every member has their own home page. From the home page you can easily navigate to any of the other features or pages. Furthermore, no matter where you are or what you are looking at, they always provide a link back to the home page. Thus you never "get lost". One click will always bring you back to the home page and from there one or two clicks will get you wherever you want to go.

The other feature I really like is that whenever you are looking at a member in any way, whether it is their profile, a listing from a search query, a "show interest" entry or whatever, they always have the same five buttons directly under the name or picture, namely:

**On line Status button**: Blinking if the member is on line. If the member is on line, click on this button to initiate an instant message chat.

**Send mail Button**: Click on this button to send email to the member you are interested in. This is not real email, but rather special FH email sent from within FH, and received from within FH.

**Show Interest Button**: This button is really designed for non paying members as will be described subsequently. Paying members will instead choose to send email.

**Add to Favorites:** A single click will add this member to your Favorites list so you can easily find the member again in the future.

**See Profile**: A single click will bring you to the detailed profile of the member you are interested in.

These features as well as other features of the user interface make it a joy to navigate around the FH web site.

### ♦ About Membership Options

First let me dispel one idea you might have. Perhaps you think you can start off with  the free membership, and if you decide you like FH, then you will upgrade to a paid membership. Useless idea! You can't even begin to really use the features of FH unless you buy a paid membership, thus you will have no idea if you like it or not. So if you want to try it, just bite the bullet and pay for at least one month.

FH offers three levels of membership, namely

- FREE (or standard)

- GOLD

- PLATINUM

The Costs of these memberships (rounded off to the nearest dollar) are shown below (as of January 2009). The first figure is the total cost, the second figure is the cost per month.

| | 1 month membership | 3 months | 6 months | 12 months |
|---|---|---|---|---|
| Free | $0 | $0 | $0 | $0 |
| Gold | $25/ $25 | $50/ $17 | $75$/ $13 | $100$/ $8 |
| Platinum | $30/ $30 | $60/ $20 | $100/ $17 | $120/ $10 |

The details about the membership options follow:

**Free membership**: The free (or standard) membership is basically for the Filipina girls who can't afford to pay for (what is to them) an expensive monthly service. The free membership allows you to list your profile, do basic searches, read member profiles and to "Show interest". The free membership does not allow you to initiate email exchanges or video or voice chats. It does allow you to respond to email, video or voice invitations from paying members.

If a free member is searching through the member lists and profiles and sees a non free member they are interested in, the only thing she can do is click on the "Show interest" button. This action will list the name, picture and summary of the interested free member on the home page of the paying member they are interested in. If a paying member receives a "Show Interest" entry from a Free Member, they can choose to either throw away the entry, or respond with an email, or, if the initiating member is on line, the paid member can initiate a live instant message text chat.

It is useless for a free member to show interest to another free member because, although the free member will receive the "show interest" entry, there is no way for the free member to respond, other than also clicking on the "show interest" button.

The memberships are very cleverly designed to allow free members to only communicate with paying members. Thus, as a Westerner you definitely do NOT want the free membership.

Basically it comes down to this: Almost all the Filipinas have free memberships and almost all the Westerners searching for Filipinas have paid memberships.

**Gold Membership**: My recommendation about this membership is simple: Don't get it! One of my few complaints about FH is that the web site does a poor job of explaining the differences between the services, especially between Gold and Platinum. There are important differences that are not explained. For example a Platinum membership allows you to activate video from an instant message window. The gold membership does not. The Platinum membership costs just a little more and you won't run into any road blocks.

**Platinum membership**: Does everything, no road blocks, costs just a few bucks more. Do yourself a favor and purchase this membership.

## Topic iii: *Features of FilipinaHeart (FH)*

When discussing the features of FH I will assume that you have purchased the Platinum membership. Some of these features are not available in the Gold membership.

### ♦ Profiles and Pictures

Like Yahoo Messenger, Friendster and other Social networking sights FH allows you to create a profile and upload pictures that other members can see. The profiles and pictures must be approved before they are available for other members to see. You may also attach a voice/video message to your profile.

Unlike some social networking sites the profile feature is very limited, consisting of answers to standard questions and two "essay" sections, one asking you to describe yourself, and one asking you to describe what you are looking for.

### ♦ Searching, Displaying and Sorting

FH has a very nice searching, displaying and sorting capability. The following table summarizes all the different items and options available to you when searching on FH.

| SEARCH or SORT ITEM | EXAMPLES |
|---|---|
| Sex | Male, Female, Male or Female |
| Ethnicity | Any, Asian, White, Black |
| Nationality | Any , Philippines, United States |
| Minimum Height | Any,  160cm (5 ft 3 in) |
| Maximum Height | Any,  168cm (5 ft 6 in) |
| Minimum Weight | Any,  40 Kg (88 lb) |
| Maximum Weight | Any,   60Kg, (132 lb) |
| Religion | Any, Catholic, Protestant |
| Country | Any , Philippines, United States |
| State or Province | Any, Negros Occidental |
| City | Any,  Bacolod |
| Astrological Sign | Any, Leo, Virgo |
| Marital Status | Any, Single, Divorced,  Married |
| Appearance | Any, Very attractive, Below Average |
| Education | Any, High School, Bachelors degree |
| Eye Color | Any, Blue, Brown |
| Hair Color | Any, Brown, Black, Blonde |
| Drinking Habits | Any, Yes, No, Occasionally |
| Smoking Habits | Any, Yes, No, Occasionally |
| Children | Any, Yes, No |
| Type of Relationship | Penpal,Friendship, Dating, Marriage |
| Profiles must have Photos | No, Yes |
| Last Active | Any, Last month, Last 3 months |
| Sort By | Newest Members, Last Active |

**Table of FilipinaHeart Searching/Sorting Capabilities**

The searching options shown in the table above far exceed anything available in Yahoo Messenger (which basically has no search capabilities) or in social networking sites such as Friendster.

A few of the capabilities shown in the above table are really impressive and useful. As far as geographical area goes, you can search the Philippines in general, a particular Province (similar to a State in the USA) or even get down to the city level.

Membership sites always like to boast how many members they have, but often these figures are wildly exaggerated because the majority of members are not active. Many may have joined just to try it, and then never used it again. This is why the "Last Active" filter is so important and useful. By choosing (for example) the "active in last month" option you can assure that you are seeing only real and active members, those that have signed on within the last month.

You can also sort by Last Active date. Besides being useful for seeing the most active members first, this option also allows you to see at the top of the list members that are currently on line, and you can click to chat with these members.

### ♦ Chat Rooms with Video

FH has both standard and member created chat rooms. If you are not familiar with chat rooms they are basically a window (virtual room) having many listed occupants. Each listed occupant of the virtual room (these occupants in real life spread out all over the world) sees the exact same window on their computer. When any occupant of a room types a message on their computer the message shows up in the window of all the listed occupants. For a more complete description chat rooms see the Yahoo Messenger section under the topic heading "**Here Are Some Of The Ways You Can Use Messenger**" and the sub heading "**Live Internet Chat With Many People In a Room**"

Chat rooms in FH are similar to Yahoo messenger but have a few key difference. In FH there is always a profile associated with each room member. In messenger there may or may not be an associated profile. FH heart also allows you to post or see a video (web cam) of other members of the room.

As with most chat rooms, you can also initiate an instant message (private chat) with any listed member of the room. When you attempt a private chat the member may or may not accept your invitation to chat.

One good thing about FH chat rooms is that in general FH is a much more tightly controlled environment and thus there seems to be less fake room members (sometimes called Bots).

### ♦ Instant Messaging with Video and Voice

An instant message chat is a live chat between to members. The members can exchange messages with each other by typing into an instant message window.

You can initiate an instant message conversation in a number of ways. You can do it from a chat room, you can do it from your list of on line friends, or you can do it when looking at a list of members if the "on line" button beneath the member entry is blinking. Click on the blinking "on line" button to start a private instant message chat.

When engaged in an instant message chat, voice and video can be activated so that you and your instant message partner can see and hear each other (assuming you both have microphones and web cams).

### ♦ FilipinaHeart Email

First of all FH email is not real email. Real email can be sent to or arrive from any email address in any domain. FH email can only be sent and received from other FH members. FH email is initiated by clicking on the SEND MAIL icon under a listed member and is received by a member when your message shows up in their message list.

FH email does not allow attaching documents or files nor does it have any other fancy features such as different fonts or text sizes or spell checker. It is basically a simple email feature allowing you to send and receive simple text messages to and from other FH members.

One fancy feature FH mail does have is the ability to attach a voice and/or video message to your email. Simply click on the ADD VOICE OR VIDEO button and you have 30 seconds to record a video and voice message which the recipient can see and/or hear.

FH email is simple, but it is sufficient for the needs of this environment and because it is a tightly controlled environment you are unlikely to get lots of junk mail or spam in your "in" box.

I do wish, however, that it had a spell checker.

One other very nice feature of FH email is the ability to "filter" your email. Suppose you are getting a lot of messages from older women. Well you can create a filter such that if the woman is more than 40 years old her mail will be filtered out. Unfortunately you can only filter on a few attributes, like age, sex and country. You can't (for example) filter out tall or short women.

### ◆ Blocking

If there is a member who is always bothering you with email messages or instant message invitations you can block that member so that they can't see or communicate with you.

### ◆ Approval Services

Profile content (Text, Pictures and Video) have to be approved by the staff of FH before they can be viewed by other members so that objectionable material is unlikely to get posted.

### ♦ Abuse Reporting Services

Yahoo messenger and most Social Networking sites have the ability to report abuse, but the feature is largely a joke because they don't have the resources to follow through. Particularly on Yahoo where it is so easy to throw away an account and start a new one, it is almost impossible for Yahoo to prevent objectionable people from using their chat rooms and instant message service.

FH seems to take their abuse reporting seriously.

### ♦ Currently On Line List

FH allows you to see a list off all members that are on line so that you can easily start an instant message conversation with any on line member.

### ♦ Favorites List

Add any person you might be interested in to your FAVORITES list so that you can easily find them at a later time.

### ♦ On Line Friends List

Add someone to your Friends list so that you can instantly see if they are on line and initiate a chat if you so desire.

## Topic iv: *What does FilipinaHeart (FH) Give You that Free Services Do Not?*

Actually a lot. First of all it offers you a simple easy to use Integrated environment where you can do everything you need to do (relative to finding Filipina women) from this environment. This is especially important for inexperienced computer and internet users who don't feel comfortable learning many complicated software applications.

FH also offers you searching and filtering capabilities well beyond what most free sites offer. Finally FH offers a membership base with a single common purpose, connecting! I highly recommend FH and honestly, if you are serious about finding a Filipina woman, I don't think the money to join should be a major issue.

# Chapter 8: Free Internet Methods for Finding Filipina Women

The free methods for searching for Filipina woman involve using the social networking site called **Friendster** and Yahoo's instant messenger software, called **Yahoo Messenger**. The details follow:

## Topic i: *Setting Up Computer Accounts and Friendster Profile*

First go to www.yahoo.com and create an account for yourself. Even if you already have an account I strongly suggest you create an account for the sole purpose of using it for your search for Filipina women. This will prevent pollution of your already existing account and make all your names and accounts you present to women consistent. Pick out a name for yourself that might attract a Filipina women. Picking a name is very personal, but it should be obvious you are a man, and catchy if possible and easy to remember. You will use this account for both email and Yahoo Messenger. Suppose the name you pick out is Bill_USA_51, meaning your name is bill, you are from USA and 51 years old. This means your Messenger chat name will be Bill_USA_51, and your email address will be Bill_USA_51@Yahoo.com. Of course not all names are available and there is a good chance the simple name you pick will already be in use, so you may have to keep trying till you get an available name. Yahoo also allows you to set up a profile, but I don't necessarily suggest spending a lot of time on this, since you will be doing this in Friendster anyway. However if you have the time and inclination, it can't hurt. Read the next section to learn about profiles.

For the second step forget about Yahoo for the time being and go to the Friendster site (www.Friendster.com) and create an account for yourself. When you create a Friendster account you need to have an already existing email address to use as your account name. You will of course use the email address you just created on Yahoo, in the example above, Bill_USA_51@Yahoo.com. A password will also be asked for to make your account secure. In Friendster, when you create an account you use an email address as your ID, but that email address is not published, instead you pick a nick name that people will see in your profile. You may or may not want to use your real first name and or real last name. I suggest at least using your real first name, and up to you as to whether you use your real last name.

Now learn how to use Friendster without any thought of yet finding someone. Learn how to look at profiles and do profile searches. A profile is a user written description of themselves, containing any information the person wants to share with you. Look at both Filipina women's profiles to get an idea of what they are looking for, and also look at men's profiles that are looking for Filipina women. Pretend you are a Filipina woman looking for a man. How would you go about it? What would you search for? This will give you an idea of how to create your own profile.

Once you are thoroughly familiar with how to search and examine profiles, and once you have examined many profiles, it is time to create your own profile. Hopefully you will have an idea of what you want to do from having looked at other profiles. There are many variations and ways to create a profile, but of course you want to make sure you include the key facts and that you come across as a nice guy. Here are two important things to include:

1. PICTURES!!! Most women (or men for that matter) will ignore profiles that don't include pictures. You need digital pictures available to upload to the Friendster site. You can create these with a digital camera, or by scanning regular pictures to make them digital.

2. Include your Email/Messenger/Friendster ID. As mentioned above the Friendster ID is not automatically published. However,

you can display it in the text of your profile. Since the ID is the same for Friendster, your email and for your Messenger, this makes it very easy for prospective women to remember and contact you using any of these three methods. By publishing your Friendster ID somebody can locate you directly without having to do a search. Here is where my suggested method of creating a YAHOO account expressly for meeting women comes into play. If you were using a regular email account you would not want to publish it in this way because doing so might subject you to lots of SPAM (electronic junk mail). So for the example above, you might want to include something like the following in the body of your profile:

My Friendster ID and email address is Bill_USA_51@Yahoo.com, my yahoo messenger id is also Bill_USA_51. Please feel free to send me an email or contact me on yahoo messenger.

Friendster also provides a method called Messages for you to contact other Friendster users but by publishing the above information it gives the prospective women more options for contacting you.

Ok, now that you have Friendster set up, you could now try to find women on Friendster and send them Friendster messages, or wait for women to send you messages. However there is a problem. Once you have made contact, how do you communicate effectively and easily with this person? Friendster messages are not an effective way to communicate, they are only good for making first contact. This is where Yahoo messenger comes in. With Yahoo messenger you can do live text chat, live voice chat, and live video. So your next step is to learn how to use Yahoo messenger. So my suggestion is, once you have made contact with a person via Friendster messages, try to set up a date to talk or chat with each other on Yahoo messenger. If you are not familiar with what I'm talking about, your Friendster message might go something like this:

I would love to chat with you on Yahoo messenger service. I will be on at Sunday (May 23) at 6pm, if you want to meet me on line. My id is Bill_USA_51, or if you can't make it, send me an offline message when you can. What is your messenger ID?

I will describe Yahoo messenger offline messages in the following sections. As an aside, here is a good time to bring up another point. Of course your time and her time are not the same. You are in different time zones. All of the Philippines is in a single time zone and there is no daylight savings time in the Philippines. Learn how to convert your time and date to Philippine time and date, and don't confuse some poor girl by talking about your time and her time. Probably half the women are not even aware there are other time zones. Just speak in Philippine time. There are many internet sites, such as www.thetimenow.com, to find the current time in any time zone.

## Topic ii: *About Yahoo Messenger*

Yahoo Messenger will be your main tool for meeting and communicating with Filipina women. In fact, you could argue that you don't really need Friendster, you could just use Yahoo messenger and not use Friendster at all. However, you can't do it the other way around and use Friendster but not Messenger. You need Yahoo Messenger as it is the overwhelming favorite and most commonly used communication software among Filipinos. To give yourself the most options use Friendster and Messenger to complement each other. For example, if you meet somebody on Messenger, tell them to look at your profile on Friendster. If you meet somebody on Friendster, set up a time to communicate on Messenger.

Yahoo Messenger (here after referred to simply as Messenger) does many different things for you, and is a pretty good tool when it's working properly. Unfortunately it also has a lot of problems. It is constantly crashing. By crashing I mean it just dies and goes away, and you have to restart it. Or it freezes up. Or the voice quality is poor. Or the video freezes up or crashes.

Sometimes the Messenger grabs all the computer CPU and the whole computer freezes up, or any of a number of other problems. In terms of it's functionality Messenger is an excellent tool. In terms of it's quality control, it's pretty poor and does not, in my opinion, reflect very well on Yahoo. As a former software engineer I can say with pretty good confidence that they have a major quality control problem. This is an aside and is neither here nor there, since you don't really have a choice. I just give you some up front warning. You have to learn to accept it's flaws and not get frustrated. Hopefully Yahoo will eventually fix these problems, but I'm not holding my breath.

## Topic iii: *Here are Some of the Ways You Can Use Messenger*

### ♦ Live Internet Chat with Many People in a "Room"

The live chat room and Friendster messages are the two primary means of making contact with a Filipino women.

For those not familiar with Chat rooms, I will offer an analogy. Pretend the internet was never invented, and instead somebody created a city, called Yahoo city, and the purpose of this city was to provide a way for people with similar interests to meet and talk. The city is divided into city blocks with names like MUSIC, RELIGION and REGIONAL. If you want to talk about music, go to the music block. If you want to meet people from a particular region, go to the Region block. Since you want to meet Filipina women, your best bet is to go to the Regional block of the city. Once there you see a number of buildings with names such as USA, Canada, Japan and Philippines. You walk into the Philippines building and go to the Elevator. On the elevator is a list of the different floors. Each floor has a name such as Manila, Cebu, Visayas, etc. You have heard that women from Cebu are nice, so you take the elevator to the Cebu floor. Once on this floor you see a hallway with many rooms, each numbered, there is room CEBU1, CEBU2, CEBU3, etc. You notice some of the doors are closed indicating the room is full. You walk into an open room. Once inside the room you see typically 20 to 30 people, all wearing name tags. The room is in chaos. Everybody is talking at once, and you can hear all the conversations. There are men in the room who you are not interested in, and there appear to be a number of retarded people as well (sorry, mentally challenged). Maybe if you are lucky you will also see one or two Filipina women that catch your interest. If you want to get their attention, you have to shout to them, and everyone can hear you. If you have no luck in this room you can leave and try another room. Maybe you decide you don't even like the floor, so you take the elevator to the Manila floor and go in one of those rooms. If you do catch a woman's attention you will find it hard to communicate in the noisy room, so you will probably make arrangements to meet privately.

To convert this pretend example from the physical world to the cyber world of Yahoo messenger, this is what you would do and see. From the Messenger main window you would choose the menu item MESSENGER, then sub menu, YAHOO CHAT, then sub menu JOIN ROOM. You will be presented with a list of categories (city blocks in the example). Choose Regional. You will then get a list of regional entries (buildings in the example) Choose Philippines. You will then get a list of Philippine sub categories (Elevator floors in the example), Choose CEBU to see a list of numbered CEBU rooms. Click on a room to enter. A "Room" is a window on your screen. The window will have on the right side a list of everybody in the room. The content of the window will be conversation from the people in the room. At the bottom of the window is a place to enter your text. If you enter text and press RETURN, your message will be broadcast to all the people in the room, and everybody will see your message. They will know you sent the message because your name will be attached to the message.

### ◆ Live Instant Message Chat with an Individual Friend

The problem with chat rooms is that there is no privacy. Everybody in the room can see any message you send. To get around this problem you can send what's called an instant message, which is a message to an individual person. First you get the persons name from the chat room, then instant message them with a personal message. If they want to communicate with you, they will message you back.

### ◆ Live Voice Chat

While instant messaging with a friend, you can request live voice chat, which is similar to a normal phone chat, but much lower quality.

### ◆ Live Video

While instant messaging with a friend you can request video, so that your friend sees you live, and you see your friend live, providing you both have Web cams.

### ◆ Offline Message

Offline messages are similar to a simple form of Email. If you have a friend's ID, and you go on line, but your friend is not on line, you can send them a message anyway. Your friend will get the message the next time they logon to Messenger.

### ◆ Create an Official Friend

Create an official friend so you can see when they are on line. Yahoo messenger has the concept of official "friends". Suppose you are chatting with someone and decide you like each other. You might say to them: "Can I add you as a friend?". If they say yes, then you click on the ADD FRIEND button, and Yahoo goes thru a procedure verifying that both people want to be friends with each other. After you are friends, each of you can see when the other person is on line. When you sign into Messenger you will see a list of all your friends, and Messenger will indicate which ones are currently on line. You can also add somebody as a friend even if they are not on line. The next time the friend logs onto messenger, messenger will verify with them that they want to be your friend.

### ◆ Share Pictures and Files.

Messenger also allows you to easily share digital pictures and/or files with each other. You can use the File sharing feature to send your friend a file. This file could be a picture if you want. If you are sharing a picture you have a choice. You can send the picture as a file, or you can start a photo sharing session, which allows you to see the pictures right in a messenger window without downloading the file. Ok, I said it allows you to easily share pictures and files. Let me amend that. It's easy when it works. For reasons I don't understand much of the time it simply does not work. This is part of the frustration of using Messenger.

### ◆ About Yahoo Profiles and Member Searches

As in Friendster, Yahoo allows you to create a profile. Wouldn't it be good if Yahoo allowed you to create a nice profile, and to effectively search other member profiles? Yes, it would be good. Then, why would you need a separate social networking program like Friendster? Simply create your profile on Yahoo Messenger, do all your searches on Yahoo Messenger, and when you find someone, their ID is automatically available to you, so that you can immediately instant message them. Yes it would be so good. Unfortunately, for reasons unknown, and that are hard to fathom, the capability does not exist.

The first problem is that, unlike social networking programs like Friendster, Facebook and MySpace which have been designed from the start to allow you to easily create fancy sophisticated eye appealing profiles, the profile feature on Yahoo is more like an afterthought. It is easy to create a simple profile, but much harder to create a nice eye appealing profile. It's worth it to create a simple profile on Yahoo, but  if you want to create a fancy one, put your energy into your Friendster Profile.

However, the inability to easily create fancy profiles is not the main problem. The main problem, which is a complete killer, is that there is no way to search on the profiles. If you know someone's ID, then you can pull up their profile, but there is no way to do a search like this:

"Find me all girls between 18 and 25, single, living in Cebu".

Now interestingly enough, there is supposed to be a way, called "advanced member search", but it simply does not work. It does not work at all, not even a little bit. To make sure it was not just me doing something stupid, I went on Google to research why the advanced member search does not work, and sure enough I confirmed that it does not work for anyone, and nobody knows why! It's just plain weird.

Well, software is not static, and they are always fixing bugs and adding features, so maybe someday soon it will be easier to create nice profiles and more importantly to do member searches on Messenger,  but for now, as of the time I am writing this, use Friendster for this purpose.

This section was intended to give you a general overview of what Messenger is all about and how you can use it. There are many other features I have not described. This section is not intended as a tutorial. You will have to take the time to learn how to use Yahoo Messenger.

## Topic iv: *Specific Techniques for Using the Software*

The previous section gave you some general guidelines and tips for using the internet. This section will be more specific. This book is not a tutorial on how to use the software, so my suggestions will be basic, it is up to you to learn how to use the software, but here are some specific techniques.

### ♦ Converting a Friendster Contact to a Messenger Contact

Suppose you get a Friendster message from a woman saying she wants to get to know you? Well how do you go about it? Just sending Friendster messages back in forth is pretty slow. So what you do is this. Perhaps she has published her Yahoo Id on her Friendster account, perhaps not. You should have your Yahoo id published. If you don't see her Yahoo ID published, ask her to send it to you in a message. Then when you have her Yahoo ID, tell her you will add her as a friend, and you will look for her on line.

After you obtain her Yahoo ID sign on to Yahoo Messenger and add her as a friend. You do this as follows: From Messenger main window, choose ACTIONS, then "send an instant message", then choose "OTHER CONTACT", then type in the Yahoo Id of the person you want to communicate with. Then send her a message, which will open up a message window. From the message window, click on the ADD USER button to add her as a friend. If she gave you a name that does not exist in the Yahoo database, you will get an error. If the name exists, she will be added as a pending friend. The next time your friend logs on, she will see your "add friend" request, and after she verifies it, you will become full friends. After becoming full friends, you will see her name light up whenever she is on line, and you can send her an instant message.

### ♦ Using Yahoo Chat Room to Find Contacts

Other than Friendster, a good way to find contacts is through use of the Yahoo chat rooms. Yahoo has chat rooms specifically dedicated to the Philippines. From the Messenger main window choose menu item MESSENGER, then YAHOO CHAT, then JOIN ROOM. You will then be taken to the lists of categories and rooms. Expand the REGIONAL section, then double click on the PHILIPPINES category. Then you will have a list of different rooms to choose from, such as:

Cebu Tambayan

Luzon

Metro Manila

Mindanao

Visayas

Chose the room you want, and press the GO TO ROOM button to enter a room. Now personally I find the chat rooms useless as a way to actually talk and communicate. It's sort of the equivalent of being in a bar with a band so loud you can't even talk. There are typically many BOTS in a room with a lot of meaningless fake conversation going on. However, the good thing about a chat room is that on the right side of the window it lists the members of the room. Click on a member and then click on the IM button to send an instant message to that member. If you are lucky a conversation will ensue.

Remember, this is a patient man's game, most attempts at contacting a user will not end up in a meaningful conversation. As you become experienced you will learn how to weed out certain names and certain responses quickly.

## Topic v: *Clipboard Magic – A Nice Little Copy and Paste Program*

When you have on line conversations with new contacts you will find yourself repeating the same statements and questions over and over and over again. To save time and hand cramps use a simple "clipboard extender" program. A clipboard extender allows you to save a set of stock responses in a list. To use one, click on the list entry and then go back to your message window and PASTE. There are many clipboard extender programs available, but I can recommend CLIPBOARD MAGIC as a very simple and totally free program that does what you need it to do for this purpose. You can easily find where to download this program by typing CLIPBOARD MAGIC into your GOOGLE search page.

Here, for your benefit or amusement is a list of some of my stock responses from my own Clipboard Magic List.

*Do you have cam?*

*Hello, how are you today?*

*Hi, are you female?*

*I'm American, I only speak English*

*I'm in Dumaguete, Negros Oriental, Visayas, you know it?*

*I'm male, American living in Philippines, and you?*

*I'm male, are you female?*

*I'm sorry, but I only like cam to cam*

*Just living here, came here to Philippines to retire early*

*Ok, so if I start my cam first, you promise to also start your cam?*

*Sorry but I like cam to cam and you don't have cam*

*Sure, you start your cam and I PROMISE to follow*

*To start with, I'm male, are you female?*

*What part of the Philippines are you from?*

*Where are you now? In cafe? Or are you at home?*

# Chapter 9: Voice Conversations

I have already mentioned in passing about using some of the listed software to have voice conversations. In this section I will discuss voice conversation in more detail.

Suppose you are tired of texting and you want to talk live and hear a real voice. Nothing wrong with that. You have several options. All internet options require a broad band internet connection.

### Topic i: *Use Yahoo Messenger to Have Voice Conversation*

If you have a microphone attached to your computer, you can make calls from your computer to her computer or vice versa. Yahoo messenger itself allows you to have a voice chat. From a message window you can click on the CALL button to initiate a voice chat. The problem is, as I have mentioned several times, Yahoo does not really have their act together. Half the time it does not work at all, and when it does work the quality is usually poor with long delays and dropped words being a very common occurrence.

### Topic ii: *Use FilipinaHeart to Have Voice Conversation*

Similar to Yahoo Messenger, FilipinaHeart also allows you to have a voice conversation which you establish from an instant message window. You must be a Platinum member to establish a voice conversation with a standard member from an instant message window. If you are a Platinum member, simply click the SEND AV button at the bottom right of the window and then turn on or off the video and voice capabilities.

## Topic iii: *Use Regular Phone to Have Voice Conversation*

Well – what's wrong with a regular phone? Nothing - if you don't mind spending money. Most Filipina do not have regular land line phone, they only have a cell phone, so you will have to make a call from your phone to her cell phone which can be expensive, or you can send her money so that she can call you from her cell phone, with a rate of about 20 pesos per minute.

As an aside, this is one of those verifiable money situations you can use to see if she is trustworthy. Send her a little money and tell her to use it only for calling you from her cell phone. See if she follows through. If you get an answer something like: "I got the money and I tried to call you, but it doesn't work", well, she is probably lying.

Of course one of the downsides of using a regular phone is that you don't see each other, there is no video. You could however, sit by your computer, use messenger for the video and talk on the phone.

For your information I will describe the numbering system in the Philippines, and how you make calls from the USA to Philippines or Vice versa.

Philippine local numbers and cell phone numbers are 7 digits long, just like in the USA. Philippine land line phones have an area code, but unlike in the USA where the area code is always 3 digits, in the Philippines the area code is variable length. Philippine cell phones have something similar to an area code, but it has nothing to do with area, it has to do with the Carrier (or company) you are using. The carrier code is always 3 digits.

A typical Philippine cell number might be something like:

919 - 502 - 8936, and if given to you by a friend, she might give it to you in any of several formats, such as:

0919-502-8936, 63919-502-8936 or 063- 919-502-8936

The important part is the last ten digits.

To call from the USA to her cell phone you would dial as follows:

011-63-919-502-8936

| | |
|---|---|
| 011 | United states code to indicate international call |
| 63 | Philippines country code |
| 919 | Cell phone carrier code |
| 502-8936 | Local phone number |

To call a land line in the Philippines you have to know the area code as well as the local number. The area code will usually be stated as a number with a zero in front of it. For example, 02 for Manila, 032 for Cebu. You will not actually use the zero. For example, to call from the USA to a land line phone in Cebu you would dial as follows:

011-63-32-502-8936

| | |
|---|---|
| 011 | United states code to indicate international call |
| 63 | Philippines country code |
| 32 | Area code for Cebu |
| 502-8936 | Local phone number |

Or if the call were going to Manila, It would look as follows:

011-63-2-502-8936

| | |
|---|---|
| 011 | United states code to indicate international call |
| 63 | Philippines country code |
| 2 | Area code for Manila |
| 502-8936 | Local phone number |

To call from the Philippines to your land line phone in the USA your friend would dial something like the following:

00-1-617-502-8936

| 00 | Philippine code to indicate international call |
| --- | --- |
| 1 | USA country code |
| 617 | Area code for Boston Massachusetts USA |
| 502-8936 | Local phone number |

## Topic iv: *Use Skype to Have Voice Conversation*

### ♦ SKYPE in General

Skype is a free internet based software available for download from WWW.SKYPE.COM. The main purpose of Skype is to allow telephone like conversation between parties using the internet. Skype allows conversation from computer to computer, or from computer to telephone. Computer to computer conversation is free, and use of a web cam is also supported. Computer to Telephone conversation costs money, but is still far cheaper than regular telephone to telephone conversation. I use Skype to call from my computer in the Philippines to land lines all over the world for about 3 cents (0.03 dollars) a minute. The quality, while not quite as good as normal telephone to telephone conversation, is surprisingly good and quite acceptable. The costs of calling computer to telephone can vary greatly with Skype depending on where the Land line is located. Where the computer is located is irrelevant, since from the point of view of Skype, the computer is simply connected to the internet. However Skype has set up local relay facilities in some countries which facilitate a cheap internet to phone line interface. In other countries they don't so the cost is much higher.

For example a call from a computer to a USA phone costs about 3 cents a minute., but a call from a computer to a Philippine phone costs ten times that amount.

Unlike Yahoo Messenger and Yahoo in general, which has big issues with quality control, Skype is a quality product and works as advertised and works very well. I recommend it.

### ♦ Use SKYPE for Computer to Computer Voice Chat

Both you and your friend will need to have Skype installed on your respective computers. Both you and your friend will need Skype Accounts. If she has her own computer this of course is no problem. If she goes to an internet café, they will have to have Skype installed on the computers. Most cafes now have Skype installed. You will be able to watch each other on video at the same time as you chat.

### ♦ Use SKYPE to Go From Her Computer to Your Phone

This works well because a call to a phone in the USA is cheap. The problem is she will need an account loaded with some money. To load an account you need a credit card. She is unlikely to have a credit card. The easiest way to get around this is for you to set up the account using your credit card and let her use it.

### ♦ SKYPE From Your Computer to Her Phone (Not Recommended)

This is really not a good option because using Skype to call a phone in the Philippines does not really save you any money, since SKYPE is not really set up in the Philippines.

# Part 4: *Making a Life for Yourself in the Philippines*

This part is for YEXs (yes to Expatriatism). It's for people who are serious about making  a new life for themselves in the Philippines and contains practical information about how to go about it and the choices you will have to make.

# Chapter 10: How to Find Woman While Living in or Visiting the Philippines

## Topic i: *Get Yourself a Cell Phone*

If you plan on trying to meet women it is absolutely essential that you get yourself a cell phone. Without one you will be at an extreme disadvantage.

Later in the chapter titled: "**All about cell phones**" I will describe in detail how cell phones work in the Philippines, how to buy one, how they are used, etc. For now, I just want to mention that they are essential in the meeting and dating process, and a bit about how you can use them to your advantage.

Asking for a cell phone number is a lot easier and less stressful than asking a woman straight out for a date. Most Filipina are willing to give out their cell phone number, even if they are not interested in you. Most of the time they will give out their correct number even if they have no interest. It's an easy way for them to show you they are interested or an easy way to get rid of somebody if they are not interested, as she can subsequently ignore your text messages.

Notice that I keep on mentioning "text messages", and not "telephone calls". If you get a number don't start out calling her. That is not the normal way in Philippine culture. The normal way for initial contact is with a text message. Filipina that may be very shy face to face or in a voice conversation may be much less shy when texting. This is sort of the same phenomenon as texting on the internet. It's easier to be open when it's only the written word. If you are not used to texting, my answer is simple: learn how to do it, and become comfortable with it, no excuses!

Here is an example of how you might use your cell phone in a real life situation. Suppose you go to a store to buy some clothes, and you like the sales lady, who is very sexy and seems very nice, but she is also busy so it is hard to have a private conversation with her. Here is an opportunity to use your cell phone. You might say something like: "You are so very nice, would it be ok if I have your cell phone number?" or "You seem very nice, can we be text mates?". Something simple like that. No need to go into long explanations. Of course sometimes you might get rejected with answers such as, "I don't have a cell phone now" or "My cell phone is broken" or I don't have it with me and I don't remember the number" or sometimes (a disconcerting cultural habit) your question might just be met with a blank stare and silence. Well that's ok, move on, no big deal. However, you will find that a large percentage of the time she will give you the number.

By the way, when asking for the number, try to do it in a discreet way without other people knowing what's going on, if possible. If she is with friends, it's no problem, but if she is with co-workers and they are watching, she might say no even if she really wants to give you the number because she is embarrassed.

Ok, so now let's assume she gives you her cell phone number. Does this mean she is interested in you? No, not necessarily. So what is your next step?

Well of course your next step is to send her a text message and see if she replies. When sending a text message you can afford to be much more direct than you would in a face to face situation. Exactly what you say and how you say it is of course up to you, you will have to develop your own style that you feel comfortable with, but it would not be inappropriate to send a messages something like the following:

"Hi, this is Bill, remember me?, I met you while buying shirts. You know I'm single, and hoping to meet a nice woman. You seemed so nice, so I was hoping you could be my friend."

Now if she is not interested, she will most likely simply ignore you. That's Filipino culture, the Filipino way. If she is interested she will respond to you, unless of course, she does not have any load.

A text message costs 1 peso to send. Often Filipinos simply run out of load so they can't text you back. Sometimes they have load, but they will use that as an excuse anyway. If they ever see you again, they will say, sorry I didn't return your message, but I didn't have any load.

Even if they have load and even if they are interested in you, they may send you back a message something like the following: "Yes, Hi Bill, I remember you. Thanks for texting me! I'm almost out of load, can you send me some load?". From the point of view of the Filipina woman, if you are interested in courting her, then you should be willing to pay for the conversation.

The best way to avoid all of this is to just send her some load ahead of time, this way she will have no excuse, and if she doesn't answer you, you can be pretty sure she is not interested.

If they have the same cell phone carrier as you (for example Smart to Smart) you can use a technique called Pasa Load to transfer a small amount of credit, like 5 or 10 pesos, directly from your phone to her phone. If you don't have the same carrier you can go to a local store (like a local mini market, called a sari sari store in the Philippines) and buy load for her. Buy the minimum allowed, typically 15 or 20 pesos. You pay the store clerk, and then the clerk will use a special service on their phone to transfer the load to your friend.

If you like, you can wait around for a "RECEIPT", so you can be sure the load was transferred. A "RECEIPT" is a text message sent to the clerk's phone verifying the transfer. The message will be something like this:

"SMART load of 20 pesos was successfully transferred to 0919-555-3333"

You can request that the clerk show you the verification message. Personally, if I don't know the person I'm sending the load to that well, I will usually wait around for the verification message, which usually takes a minute or two. When you look at the verification message make sure the "sent to" telephone number is correct. Some nasty unscrupulous women play a game where they pretend they didn't get the load in the hopes that you will send them more load. If you saw the verification message and they are still claiming they did not get the load, don't get fooled by this scam, time to move on, this is not the kind of woman you want.

Now assuming this is not the case, and that you have sent your prospective date some load, you can now change your initial message to be something like the following:

"Hi, this is Bill, remember me?, I met you while buying shirts. I am the one that just sent you some load. You know I'm single, and hoping to meet a nice woman. You seemed so nice, so I was hoping you could be my friend."

Sending load ahead of time sets a nice tone, shows you to be a thoughtful person, and allows her to text back and forth with you without worrying about money.

Even if she is not interested in you personally she might very well have a friend she can recommend. It's good to network in this way. In fact, you will probably find that after you have let a number of people know you are single and available, and you have given a number of people your cell number, you will start to get unsolicited text messages from women. Typically these messages may say something like:

"Hi, is this the phone of Bill? This is Amy. Can you be my text mate?"

### Topic ii: *Your Best Assets: A Decent Personality, Perseverance and Money*

Let's talk a little about what kind of person will be successful in dating many women and the kind of women they want while in the Philippines, with the ultimate goal of finding the right woman. What assets do you need?

Well let's approach this backwards, what assets don't you need? You don't need to be handsome, you don't need a great body, you don't need to be tall, you don't need to be slim and you don't need to be young. In fact, you can be reasonably old, fat and ugly and still have great success. Now let's be honest, if you are tall, handsome, slim, muscular and relatively young of course that will make you that much more desirable, but none of these are needed.

What is needed is a decent, charming and kind personality, a sense of humor, plus some money, and a willingness not to be cheap - at least while dating!

Why is this the case? What's going on here? What are the underlying factors? Well think about it. If the main goal of these women was to find soul mate type love with somebody they were deeply attracted to, they wouldn't be looking for older foreigners, they would be looking for young Filipinos that share their culture. These woman are basically looking for a short cut to a better life. This is the hard reality of the situation. Now, will they have a better life if they live with a man that has money but is a mean spirited jerk? No, their life will be miserable. These women are realistic. I'm not sure they think about it in terms of words they could write down, but they know instinctively it's not in the cards to get everything. Thus they are satisfied with living a comfortable life with a decent man, even if that man is not the most handsome man in the world.

What if you are a nice guy with a good personality, a good sense of humor, very kind, very generous, young, rich and very handsome? Ha ha, the women will probably be swarming around you like flies around honey. However, if you had all that you probably wouldn't be here in the Philippines in the first place, would you?

So besides just being a decent kind guy, what else will serve you well? Well, the ability to be charming, start a conversation, and not be shy. The ability to have no fear of rejection! Most Filipina women are shy, at least initially. Usually you have to make the first move. However, if you force yourself to talk to many women and are not afraid of rejection, you will find that a good percentage will be interested. Thus it is in your best interest to not be shy and to persevere in your goal of finding a woman.

### ◆ How Do You Physically Go About Meeting Women?

Ok, you are here in the Philippines. You are settled down in your hotel or apartment. You are rested. You are ready to go. What do you actually do?

Well a lot of that depends on what kind of area you are in, what kind of woman you are looking for, and your own personality. Hopefully you are living here or on a long vacation, and you have plenty of time. It's not good to feel rushed.

Let's quickly recap the different kinds of Filipina women we described earlier:

| | |
|---|---|
| YSA | Very Young Woman, Smart and Ambitious. |
| YWC | Very Young Woman Without a Clue. |
| YPF | Very Young Woman From Province Being pressured by Her Family. |
| NWG | Nice Working Girl. |
| CW | Career Woman Looking at the Ticking Clock. |
| SM | Single Mom. |
| OWW | Older Widowed Woman |
| OSW | Older Separated Woman |

VCOV              Very Conservative Older Virgin

DOE              The Dancer or Entertainer

If you are interested in meeting a NWG or SM, one of the best ways is simply to go about your life. In the course of going to restaurants, going shopping, or doing any of your normal errands you are sure to come in contact with many NWGs, some of these NWGs will also be SMs. Take every opportunity to be friendly and start a conversation. Let it be known you are single and looking for a wife. Don't say looking for a girl friend, they will be more excited if you say looking for a wife. You will find that often, even if the particular person you are talking to is not interested, they will know other people that may be interested. Don't pass by any opportunities, you want to start networking. Give out your cell phone number freely, remember the simple technique of asking "would you like to be my text mate" which is non stressful for both of you and allows you to break the ice later from the ease of your cell phone.

My friend told me that he knew of two Expats who made up small slips of paper, sort of like business cards, containing their name, cell phone number, and the fact that they were available, and simply passed them out to any pretty girl they saw. Personally this is not my style, but evidently it worked for them, as a large percentage of the women texted back showing interest.

Now as you go about your business in stores, restaurants, movie theaters, or whatever, you will find yourself coming into contact mostly with NWGs or SMs that are also NWGs. These are nice girls, but as I mentioned before, the problem is, it's really hard to date these girls because they are always busy. Their job is their main priority and you can't ask them to quit their jobs unless you are really committed to them. So how do you go about meeting other types of girls?

Well if you want to meet a DOE this is also easy, so long as you are in a location that has the type of bars and karaoke establishments that hire DOEs. If you are really fixated on DOEs you should choose a location that specializes in this market, such as Angeles, Makati, Puerto Galera and some parts of Cebu.

What about going to normal bars? Bars that do not employ DOEs, bars where friends simply meet to share a few drinks and have a good time? Perhaps you are interested in meeting a young college student. Will you have success if you go to a bar where young college students hang out?

Well anything is possible, and of course it also depends on your personality and skill, and often on luck, but in my experience this is not the best way to meet people.

For example, suppose you are at a college hangout. Well most of these girls have families that have money or they would not be in college. Most of these girls are not interested in meeting an older foreigner. Perhaps somewhere in the crowd are a few YSA girls that are in the market for a foreigner. Even if this is the case, in this environment they will be hanging out with their friends and probably not give you any notice. Well I'm not saying don't try. It's possible to have success anywhere, but I wouldn't rely on bars as your best choice to find women.

Ok, so then what is the best way to find women other than NWGs and DOEs?

Let's talk about YSAs (young smart ambitious) for a little while. There are many college Filipina girls hurting financially that are desperate to stay in college and get an education. Some of these girls are open to trading sex for money and some may be open to relationships with an older Westerners, some both. The problem is how to find them.

Even if you are in the Philippines the internet is a good choice since these girls are smart and like to spend time on the internet. I have been told by a few people that they have had success just hanging out at parks that are close to colleges, especially before a semester starts when tuition is due. Take a book, find a shady place to sit, and just relax for a few hours and see if any girls smile at you or approach you.

Here is another idea. At many colleges they have tutoring services that set up expert students with people that need tutoring in a particular area. Usually the cost is something like p150 per hour. Find a subject you need a little help in, could be anything, and request a female student tutor. The odds are increased because these are both students and students that need money or else they would not be tutoring. Even if you have no attraction to the particular student you get, you can network in this manner. Ask her if she has friends that might be interested. You can go from college to college, and subject to subject requesting a variety of tutors.

Now let's talk a little about SMs (single moms) that are not NWGs. Since these women are not working, and since they don't have a husband, they spend a lot of their time with their kid or kids. Maybe on your day to day routines you come in contact with them at the department store or the grocery store. You know they are a mom because you see them with their child, but how do you know if they are a single mom? Well you don't, but if you are clever it's not so hard to find out. First off, if you see her with a guy, that's a pretty good clue she is not a single mom. If she is alone you can try to engage her in a conversation. The conversation might go something like this:

You:    You have a very beautiful child

Her:    (hopefully smiling) Thank you!

You:    How old is she?

Her:    Two years old.

You:    You and your husband must be very proud of her.

Then see how she responds. If she says nothing, or she says something like "Yes we are", then it's time to move on. If however she responds something like: "I don't have a husband,

I'm a single mom", well then you are in business. Time to engage her in further conversation and try to get her cell phone number. Can we be text mates?

Ok, continuing on,  this leaves the following:

| | |
|---|---|
| CW | Career Woman looking at the ticking clock. |
| YWC | Young without a clue |
| YPF | Young pressured by family |
| OWW | Older widowed women. |
| OSWs | Older separated women |
| VCOVs | Very conservative older virgins |

There is always a chance that you can meet these women by luck in your day to day routines.  However, some of these women may be hard to find as they may live outside the city and may not circulate that much. Your best chance is through networking. Try to get involved in some hobbies or activities where you have day to day contact with locals who you can befriend. Try to be friendly with your neighbors. Let it be known that you are single and available. Give out your cell number freely. People want to help you. Filipinos love trying to be match makers.

If you are religious, or at least don't mind being in religious environments, another possibility is to join a local church. Joining such a church and getting involved in some of the church activities is sure to give you instant status and recognition and establish you (in their eyes) as a good solid man (I'm not trying to imply that those of us that are less religious are not solid men!).

## Topic iii: *What's it Like to Date in the Philippines?*

It's a little bit like asking "What's it like to date in the USA?". The answer is, it depends on the type of woman you are dating. Because the Philippines appears small when looking at a map of the world people may tend to think that Filipinos are very homogeneous in their attitudes. This of course is very far from the truth! There are more or less 90 million people living in the Philippines and there are many sub cultures and attitudes in Philippine society. The attitudes run the gamut from extremely conservative to very liberal and westernized. So your experience in dating will vary depending on the type of woman you find.

College educated women and single mothers tend to be the most liberal. Uneducated women from the provinces tend to be the most conservative.

If you date a slightly older woman, say 23  or older who is somewhat liberal and westernized, your experience in dating should not be that much different than what you would expect in the USA.

More conservative girls, or even some girls that are not that conservative, but maybe a little nervous, may  insist on dating with friends or relatives at first. If you ask a woman for a date and she asks if she can bring a friend along, or her sister, mother or relative, well it's up to you how to proceed. I would say, if you like the girl,  go ahead and allow it. Of course you will be expected to pay all expenses, including those of the chaperones. For me personally, if they would ask to bring a friend along it was ok with me, but asking their mother to come along was a bit more than I could take. At any rate, don't allow this situation to continue for more than one or at most two dates. If by the third date she is not willing to see you alone, I would say it's time to move on.

By the way, this whole issue with friends coming along on the first date can also help you to gauge her character. For example, if she asks you for permission to bring friends along, that's a good sign. If she shows up for a date with friends having not asked you for permission, that to me shows a lack of character, understanding and trust.

Also, observe how the friends behave and what they order. If they buy the most expensive things on the menu and seem to be taking advantage of you, that is not a good sign. If they are conservative in how they order, that shows they are really along just to help out and protect their friend.

What about the issue of sex? How soon should you try? How long should you be patient if they don't want it?

Well again, this depends a lot on you and how liberal the girl is. Sexual attitudes among reasonably liberal Filipinas are not really that different than in western countries. I read a study about dating in the USA where the study determined that many new couples seem to have sex on the third date. This sort of makes sense. The first date is just to see if you like each other. The second date you try to get to know each other a lot better. The third date you get down to business ha ha.

Well anyways, for girls who are not virgins, girls that have already experienced sex, the third date rule is a reasonable rule of thumb. Of course it is not written in stone. Some girls, especially DOEs, will be willing to have sex on the first or second date. Others will want to wait a bit longer.

The situation is different with virgins. Virgins in the Philippines will usually tell you that they don't want to lose their virginity until they are married. However it is only a small percentage of these girls that really mean it. Only the very conservative and very religious girls will really insist on waiting for marriage to experience sex. So how do you know if they mean it or not? Well instinct and observation. But you do have to be a little more patient with an inexperienced virgin.

First just get them comfortable being alone with you, being affectionate and kissing. Then if you want to do more they may say something like, "I want to keep my virginity until I am married." The easy way around this is simply to promise you won't have intercourse. Tell them you will just have fun together, touching each other, playing, but you promise not to have intercourse. It's amazing, but most of them readily accept this as a compromise.  Then keep your promise. Do everything but intercourse, including oral sex. After a few sessions like that most will break down and allow you to have intercourse with them.  Even if they keep to the "everything but" rule, many men can live with that.

If you do however run into the small percentage of women who are serious about not having any  sexual fun until they are married, well what you do is up to you. For me, time to move on!

# Chapter 11: Buying a Cell Phone in the Philippines

If you plan on coming to the Philippines one your very first tasks should be to get yourself a cell phone that is compatible in the Philippines. Until you do, you will be at a huge disadvantage. Be aware that most cell phones used in the USA, Europe, or Australia will not work in the Philippines, or if they do work there will be large roaming fees associated with each call and text. Much better to just get yourself a cell phone designed for use in the Philippines.

Even if you only plan on being here a couple of weeks, you should still buy a cell phone. Cell phones are completely ubiquitous in the Philippines, even the poor girls have them. It's hard to explain the phenomenon if you have not witnessed it, but cell phones are used for so much more than just basic communication. They are used for entertainment, games, flirting, texting with friends even when there is nothing important to say, and on and on. For example some Filipinos are obsessed with downloading different ring tones. They will spend hours downloading and changing their ring tones. Many girls seem to be attached to their phones like they are part of their body, seemly always doing one thing or another with their cell phones and never putting them down. Sometimes it can get quite annoying, actually.

Cell phones, and the way they work and are used in the Philippines, are such a basic part of the fabric of society that if you are ignorant about it, Filipinos may find it hard to imagine what it is exactly you don't understand, and may have a hard time explaining it to you. Sort of like a Filipino asking a native Alaskan to explain snow. The Alaskan might find it impossible to understand how someone can't know about snow, and might not know how to explain it.

I had an experience like this the first time I arrived in the Philippines and was told I should buy a cell phone. When I asked questions about how the phones worked to the sales lady, she answered using terminology I was unfamiliar with, and when I tried to ask detailed questions to have her explain what she was talking about she got flustered and annoyed. I found out later she said to one of her co-workers in Visayan "He asks too many questions".

So that you don't have a similar experience, and so that you don't have to waste time figuring out how it all works, I will tell you everything you need to know.

## Topic i: *Do You Really Need a Cell Phone?*

YES!!! Please! Don't even think of not getting a cell phone Especially if you are interested in meeting women. A cell phone is standard equipment in the Philippines. An Expat without a cell phone is like a car without wheels, a boat without it's rudder, a horse without legs, a plane without wings, whatever! You get the idea!

## Topic ii: *Pre-Loaded .vs. Pay Later*

When you buy your phone you can choose the way you want to pay for your phone service. Pay later is the typical way it is done in the USA. You call and text as much as you want and at the end of the month you are sent a bill.

Pre-loaded means you buy credit for your phone ahead of time, and as you use the phone your credit is reduced. When it runs low you can add more. If you run out of credit your phone won't work until you add more.

There are many ways to add credit (or what they call "load") to your phone, but a common way, for example, is to buy a card for 300 peso containing 300 peso of credit. You scratch the card (like scratching a lottery ticket) to reveal a password. You call a special number and enter the password and the credit is automatically added to your phone. In reality, what this means, is that the database in the computer controlled by the carrier is updated to contain your new credit. In other words, the credit is known by the network, and not physically contained inside your phone. Your credit is associated with a specific phone number, and thus if you change your SIM card, you will also be changing your available credit  (See discussion of SIM card below). You can determine your credit remaining by activating a menu choice on the phone which will then request the information from the network and display it on your phone.

As an Expat getting settled in your new country, you really don't have to think much about this choice between pre-paid and pay later. In fact, almost everybody, even the locals, choose the pre-loaded option, as there are many advantages. You don't have any billing. You don't have any contract. You don't have to worry about cancellation. You can easily switch providers or change telephone numbers. You don't have to worry about changing your address, and  because there is no billing it is also more private, as there is no association between your telephone number and your address. You also don't have to worry about somebody stealing your phone and secretly running up a huge bill since you typically only load a small amount of credit at a time on your phone.  The advantages to the pay later method is increased convenience and lower cost for high volume users. In my opinion these advantages do not even come close to offsetting the advantages of the pre-paid method. I only mention the pay later option so you won't get confused  when you go to buy a phone. The sales person may offer you this choice simply as a matter of formality. Don't give it any thought.

### Topic iii: *Phone .vs. SIM Card*

Philippine cell phones have two main components, the phone itself, and the SIM card. The phone itself contains most of the hardware, the buttons, the battery, some of the memory and the basic features that are standard across all "carriers" or "service providers". The phone itself is not associated with a particular carrier or service provider.

The phone itself is useless without the addition of a SIM card. Think of the SIM card as the customizing agent. You could make the analogy to a computer and an operating system. A computer without an operating system is useless, the computer has all the hardware, but the operating system, like windows XP for example, adds the brains. The analogy is not perfect because unlike the computer, the phone already has some brains, but it needs the additional brains of the SIM card to actually function. Physically a SIM card is a tiny integrated circuit printed on a piece of plastic about the size of a dime (1cm x 1cm). The SIM card plugs into a socket inside the phone.

As I said before the phone is designed to be independent of the service provider used. The SIM card on the other hand is service provider specific. By choosing a SIM card you are choosing a service provider. A particular SIM card is associated with a particular service provider, and is designed by the service provider as an interface between the phone and the network system provided by the service provider. The SIM card also contains additional memory and features not contained in the basic phone.

Thus, when you go to buy a phone you really have two choices to make. What basic phone to buy, and what SIM card to buy to make the phone function.

When you choose your SIM card, you are adding the following to your phone.

- The service provider decision

- The telephone number of your phone

- Additional features designed by the service provider that are added to your phone

If you have two identical phones side by side, but one has a SMART SIM and one has a GLOBE SIM, you will find that they don't work identically. As you go through the menu items and features on the two phones, you will find that some are identical and some are different. The features that are identical come with the phone. The features that are different are specific to the SIM.

Sims are relatively cheap to buy, and some people even buy more than one SIM for a given phone. They do this so that they can avail of specific offers and discounts that are only available between people using the same service provider. It is however a nuisance to keep on switching different sims in and out of your phone. It is also common for people to just throw away a SIM and buy a new one, and by doing so get a new telephone number. They might do this, for example, if they have some friends turned enemies that they no longer want to communicate with.

So what kind of SIM should you buy? Well there are probably five or six different ones to choose from, but I strongly suggest you choose one of the two big ones most common in the Philippines, namely SMART or GLOBE. I can't really recommend one of over the other as they both have their defenders and detractors. You might find that in specific areas of the country Globe is more popular, and in other areas Smart is more popular. I suggest you buy the SIM that is most popular in your area.

## Topic iv: *All About Load*

To use a pre-paid type phone you need to add credit or load to your phone. The concept of load is actually a bit more complicated than you might at first think, since there are a number of ways to add load, and a number of different types of load.

### ♦ How to Add Load to a Phone

There are basically four ways to buy or obtain load. As described earlier you can buy a card with that you scratch with a coin to obtain a password. You then call a certain number and enter the password and the load is added to your phone.

You can also go a store (many different stores provide this service) and pay the clerk some money (anywhere from 20 to 150 pesos). The store will use a special service on their phone to call in your load. Using this method you can add load to any phone, your own, or somebody else's, as all you need provide to the clerk is a phone number and money. After the clerk calls in your load, two verifying messages will be sent out by the network provider. One will be sent to the phone of the clerk, one will be sent to the phone receiving the load.

The third method of obtaining or giving  load is a method called pasa load.  This is used between people that have the same type of service provider or SIM. Suppose you and your friend are both using SMART as your service provider. You can send a special message to a special number which will subtract load from your phone and transfer the load to your friend's phone. An additional peso will also be subtracted as a service fee.

The fourth way of obtaining load is thru your ATM card. Some banks have agreements with service providers so that you can go to an ATM and add load to your phone via the ATM. The cost of the load will be subtracted from your bank account.

### ♦ Different Kinds of Load

There are actually several different kinds of load you can add to your phone. There is standard load which can be used for either making voice calls or for sending text messages. There is text only load, which can only be used for  to send text messages, and there is special promotion load.

Special promotion load is specially discounted load that can typically only be used between phones with the same service provider. For example, for about 20 pesos you can buy a text only promotion that will allow you to text unlimited for 24 hours, but only to phones using the same service provider as you are using.

### ♦ Service Costs That Will Reduce Your Load

A simple text message to another cell phone costs 1 peso.

A voice telephone call to a phone with the same service provider as yourself costs about 7 pesos a minute. To another service provider costs about 9 peso a minute. To a land line about 11 peso a minute. An international call costs about 20 peso a minute.

One annoying thing about the way the calls are charged is that they only charge by full minutes, with partial minutes charged as full minutes. Even a 1 second call will be charged as a full minute. Sometimes this can be really annoying when your phone call is initially connected but then dropped by the network. You will still be charged for a full minute. Forget about calling some operator and requesting your money back, ain't gona happen!

By the way, in the Philippines all costs for messages and calls are born by the initiator. It never costs you any money to receive a message or phone call. This is different than some plans in the USA where you are charged for service time even if you were just the receiver of a call.

## Topic v: *What Brand of Cell Phone Should You Buy?*

Well there are many brands available, and some of the no name brands offer you phones at very low costs. However, if you don't want to think, or get stressed out by this decision, simply buy a Nokia. Nokia has a proven track record here in the Philippines. Most people buy Nokia. They are very dependable and very easy to use. If you have a problem figuring out how some feature works, it will be easy to find help if your phone is a Nokia. If you have some less popular brand you may have to figure out how to use it on your own.

## Topic vi: *Features and Costs*

Filipinos love their cell phones. An expensive cell phone is a status symbol in the Philippines. Filipinos that have a bit of money will rarely buy basic models. They want to buy a more expensive model for both fun and status.

### ◆What Features Do You Really Need?

All cell phones allow you to make voice calls and send text messages.

The suggested basic features are described below:

**Color Display**: A color display, although not really needed, is nice to have. A color display used to be a high cost addition, now it is available on all but the very cheapest models.

**Phone Lock**: For privacy and security you should be able to lock your phone so that nobody can turn on your phone without a password.

**Keypad Lock**: This is a feature where, if you don't use the phone for a while, the keypad locks up, and you need to enter a password to unlock it. Phone lock is manual and only applies to turning on the Phone. Keypad lock can be made to be automatic.

**Dictionary**: This is a feature that allows you to create text messages in English using less key strokes than the standard method. I will describe dictionary in more detail in the section titled "Texting Vs Calling". Some people like dictionary, some don't. Even many basic phones have the dictionary feature.

**Sent Message Log.** This is a feature where the phone keeps a list of, and saves the contents of all sent messages. The way the phone is designed you can't fake the sent message log. In other words you can't have it look like you sent a message to a particular person when in fact you didn't. The phone is hard wired so that only messages that were actually sent are placed on the log. Your only ability is to delete messages from the log, you can't edit or manually add messages to the log.

The sent message log is important for several reasons. Sometimes you don't remember if you sent a message or not. You can look at the log to remember if you sent a particular message to a particular person. You might also forget what you said to a particular person. You can also look at the contents of the message to see what you wrote. Finally, sometimes people claim that you never sent them a message. You can prove that you sent them the message by showing them the message on the sent message log. Even many basic phones have this feature. Make sure you buy a phone with this feature.

### ♦ What Advanced Features are Available?

My god so many, the most advanced models are almost like notebook computers. Here are some of the advanced features available.

**Polytonal sound**:  The ability for the phone to play basically any sound like music or voice. Phones without this feature can only make sounds like beeps and dings and dongs.  This feature is a prerequisite  for other features like music and voice recording. Using this feature you can also engage in a silly activity that many Filipina find fun. That is the ability to download or create your own ring tones. For example you can make it sound like a baby is crying every time somebody sends you a message. I know somebody that actually did this, and god was it annoying!

**Digital Camera**: The ability to take pictures with your phone. The more expensive  versions allow you to send the pictures to other phones or download the pictures to your computer.

**Internet access**: The ability to access certain cell phone friendly internet sites, and to get and send email on your phone.

**Digital Video Camera**: Some phones function as a full feature video camera with both video and sound. After recording, your video can be downloaded to your computer.

**Blue Tooth**: A wireless interface that allows your phone to communicate with your computer.

**Radio**: Use your cell phone as a radio.

**MP3**: Download songs to your phone in MP3 format, and play them on your phone.

**Recorder**: Use your phone as a sound recorder, so you can record conversations between you and other people.

**Enhanced screen**. Bigger display screen making it easier to display information, and better for displaying photographs.

**Enhanced keyboard**. Most phones are set up with buttons like a standard phone. A single button shares a number and several letters. For example one key shares the number 2 as well as the letters A, B and C. This makes it more time consuming to enter text. A phone with an advanced keyboard is set up more like a notebook computer with one key for each separate letter. This makes it much easier to enter text, but causes your phone to be much more bulky.

**Personal assistant**: More or less turns your phone into a small personal computer.

#### ◆ How Much Should You Spend?

Phones have come down in price drastically in recent years. You can get a decent basic Nokia phone that has all the features listed in the "what features do you really need" section for about p2000 ($40).

On the other hand you can spend as much as p40,000 ($800) for a full featured phone with all the bells and whistles.

So how much should you spend? Well if you have money to burn and you love toys, by all means buy yourself an expensive phone. On the other hand, if you like saving your money buy yourself a basic Nokia phone. There is no need to buy yourself anything more than a basic phone. A basic phone will allow you to do all the things you need to do.

There is one more reason to buy a basic phone as opposed to an expensive phone. An expensive phone is the target of theft. Usually thieves do not bother to steal cheap phones unless you give them an easy opportunity.

## Topic vii: *Texting*

### ♦ Texting .vs. Calling.

Most people in the USA are used to voice calls. Texting seems like such an arduous and time consuming task, and guess what? Not only does it seem it, but it is! If you are not used to texting it can be excruciating. That being said you will have to realize that texting is the way that most Filipinos communicate. The reason for this is simple. Calling is expensive, text messages are cheap. Voice calls cost at least 7 pesos a minute. This can add up quickly. Text messages on the other hand cost 1 peso or less.

### ♦ Special Deals for Texting

Normally text messages are one peso each. They can cost less than one peso per message because the service providers offer special deals when texting between people using the same carrier.

For example, suppose you want to communicate with a prospective date, and both you and her are using SMART. You can spend P40 (p20 for her and p20 for you) to buy something called 24 hour all text. With 24 hour all text you can text as much as you want for 24 hours so long as you text to people using SMART. This is a pretty good deal. For only p40 you can exchange messages all day long. This is a good way to make a prospective date feel comfortable with you before actually asking her to meet you. This is also why people sometimes buy multiple SIMs from different carriers. If you know you will be texting a lot to a particular person over the course of a day you can load your phone with the same type of SIM as the person you want to communicate with and then avail of the special "24 hour all text" deal. Some people actually buy multiple phones so they can do this without switching out their normal SIMs. This used to be a bit extravagant but with the costs of cell phones dropping so drastically it can actually make sense to have multiple phones. Personally I would feel like a nerd carrying around two or more cell phones, but people do it! Another solution is to get what's called a dual SIM card. For some brands of phone you can purchase a little electronic addition to your phone that allows you to plug in two SIMs into a single phone. Every time you turn your phone off and back on again, it switches SIMs. The problem with this method is that only one SIM at a time is active. Still, this a reasonable solution.

### ♦ Why Texting is Difficult

As mentioned before, one of the things that causes texting to be so difficult is that a standard phone does not have one button for each letter, and thus a given key shares a number and several letters. Also the keys are small and hard to see if you are a middle aged man with less than perfect eye sight. So, given that you will have to accept texting as a way of life, how can you make this task easier for yourself? Well unfortunately there is no way to make texting a walk in the park, but I can offer some tips to help you learn to text more efficiently.

### ♦ Practice Without Looking at the Phone.

You have to practice texting without looking at the keypad; the equivalent of touch typing on a standard key board. You have to have the keypad in internal memory inside your brain. If you can do this, your texting will be a lot easier.

### ♦ Standard Mode .vs. Dictionary Mode

Using a standard phone with a standard keypad there are two different ways to text. You can text in standard mode or, assuming you are texting in English, you can text in dictionary mode.

Standard mode, which I will describe in more detail below uses a technique of hitting a single button multiple times to get the exact letter you want. Most Filipinos choose to text in standard mode, even when texting in English.

Dictionary mode, which I will also describe in more detail below, uses computer logic to "guess" which word you are typing. Most of the time it guesses correctly and reduces the total number of key presses. Many native English speakers prefer the dictionary method.

There is no consensus about which method is better. They each have their advocates and detractors, their advantages and disadvantages, as I will describe below.

### ♦ Standard Texting Mode

In standard mode you have to press a key multiple times to get the letter you want. Consider the word FOX. The keys to type the word FOX are labeled as follows:

[def3], [mno5], [wxyz9]

In this case you have to press the first key rapid fire three times to get to the letter F, you will have to press the second key rapid fire three times to get to the letter O, and you will have to press the third key rapid fire twice to get to the letter X, a total of 8 presses! In addition, if you press the keys too slowly the phone will think you are pressing the key to get two separate letters instead of the second or third choices of the key. For example

Consider the word ACT

First you will press the [abc2] key once

Then you will have to wait a second or two so that the phone understands your next key stroke will be the second letter of the word, and not a second choice of the button [abc2].

Then you will press the same button [abc2] rapid fire three times to get to the letter C

Finally you will press the button [tuv8] once to get to the letter T.

What a pain in the neck!

There are, however, advantages to using standard texting mode. You don't have to worry that you correctly spell the word. You don't have to keep on switching in and out of dictionary mode, and most importantly you can use abbreviations. There are many abbreviations that people commonly use.

For example:

"I hv 2 go now b4 im L8 to 8" = "I have to go now before I'm late to eat"

You can even get clever and make up your own abbreviations like MrB8.

#### ♦ Dictionary Texting Mode

If you are texting in English you can put the phone in Dictionary mode, where the phone will use an internal dictionary to try to figure out which word you are typing.

For example suppose you press (only once per key)  the three keys

[def3],  [abc2],  [tuv8]

If you are in dictionary mode the phone will guess you meant to type the word EAT. The phone might have guessed right, or you may have meant to type the word FAT, in which case you will have to press the scroll button to scroll to the word FAT.

Much of the time there is only one choice and the phone will definitely pick out the right word for you. For example consider the following three key strokes:

[def3], [mno5], [wxyz9]

In this case the word FOX is the only possible choice. In general the longer the word the more chance the dictionary will guess correctly what you are trying to type.

Theoretically dictionary mode saves key strokes. However there are disadvantages. You have to know the correct spelling of a word, you can't use abbreviations and if the word is not in the dictionary you will have to switch out of dictionary mode into standard mode, type the word you want and then switch back into dictionary mode.

Sometimes you run into the following very annoying situation: You think you know how to spell a word, but you don't. Then you are confused, why didn't the phone know which word you were typing? You may have to erase the word and try again with a different spelling, or you may wind up giving up and switching out of dictionary mode.

### ♦ Enhanced Key Pad

You can buy a phone that has an enhanced keypad, with one key for each letter, sort of like a mini regular computer keyboard. This will make it a lot easier to text. However such phones are usually bundled with other expensive features and are quite costly. In addition the enhanced keyboard makes the phone more heavy and bulky.

### ♦ Using a Web Site

There are various web sites that allow you to type in a message in the computer and have it sent out over the cell network. A recipient can even associate their phone to Yahoo Messenger so that you can type a message in Messenger and they will receive it on their phone. I have not had good experiences with these sites. Either they have limits on how many messages you can send, or they are costly or they have large delay, or something. But feel welcome to try one.

### ♦ Using a Computer Interface

Some expensive phones have computer interfaces so that you can connect your phone to the computer, type your messages into the computer, and then have the messages sent out from the cell phone. Of course you have to be home next to your computer to use this method.

# Chapter 12: All About Money

In the introduction I touched briefly on the concept of Philippine currency. In this section I will discuss all aspects of money as it relates to both travelers in the Philippines for only a short period of time, as well as Expats living permanently in the Philippines.

### Topic i: *Philippine Peso Revisited*

As discussed in the introduction the Philippine peso is the unit of currency in the Philippines. One peso is worth about 2 US cents. Or putting it another way, one US dollar is worth about 50 pesos.

The peso is divided into 100 parts called centavos. Thankfully 1 centavo coins no longer exist. The smallest coin is the 5 centavo piece, followed by the 10 centavo piece and the 25 centavo piece. All of these coins are pretty useless, as even the 25 centavo piece is only worth about half a U.S. cent. Getting to the peso coins, we have a 1 peso coin, a 5 peso coin and a 10 peso coin. The lowest paper money is the 20 peso bill, followed by the 50, 100, 200, 500 and 1000 peso bills.

### Topic ii: *How to Handle Money for Your Short Term Visit*

The money strategy for a short term travel visit is always challenging. You have to balance convenience, security and cost (fees). You have a number of options as discussed below.

#### ◆ Cash

Cash is of course your most convenient option. When you bring cash make sure it is either in U.S. Dollars or Euros. These are the two commonly accepted currencies in Philippines. If you try to exchange other currencies you will probably not get a good rate, and in some cases you will get a terrible rate. If you try to exchange currencies from third world countries in many cases you will not be able to exchange them at all, and if you can exchange them you will probably lose about half the value in the exchange. If you come from some place having currency other than US Dollars or Euros you will probably do better if you exchange your money for U.S. Dollars in your own country, and then exchange the U.S. Dollars for pesos when you arrive in the Philippines. If possible try to avoid exchanging money at the airport where you will get a poor rate. Exchange your money a little at a time until you feel comfortable that you know what the fair rate is. If you want to make sure you do not get ripped off, go to a bank. I recommend BPI banks as a good honest straight forward bank. The rate you get from a bank may not be your best rate, but it will usually be ok.

Avoid black market exchangers. A black market exchanger is a person, often in a tourist area, who will come up to you and offer to exchange pesos for USD or Euros. Although most of them are ok at least in the sense that they won't run off with your money, they will however try to rip you off in the exchange rate if they feel you don't know what you are doing. There are also cases of scam artist exchangers who do run off with your money. Honestly I can't ever see any reason for going through a black market exchanger unless you are in dire need of money and no other exchanger is available. You are much better off going to a reputable exchanger with an office, or a bank. I don't even know how or why these black market exchangers exist.

If you didn't have to worry about loss or theft, cash would be your best solution. Unfortunately you can't ignore the danger associated with cash. If you lose it you are out of luck, if it's stolen you are out of luck.

If the wrong person sees that you are carrying a large amount of cash you could become a target. There are many stories of foreigners carrying large amounts of cash that are robbed. If you are carrying large amounts of cash, do not flash it. Keep most of your money hidden, and transfer just a little at a time to your wallet when you are in a private area.

I wouldn't recommend bringing more than $500 or at most $1000 dollars in cash.

### ♦ATM Card

When I first came to the Philippines in 2000 international ATM cards were just getting started. It was very hard to find an ATM machine that accepted my American ATM card. ATM cards have come a long way in recent years. It is now quite easy to find an ATM machine that will accept your international ATM card. Make sure your ATM card is set up as an international card. Most are these days.

The way it works is this. Your American ATM card may normally be used with Dollars but when you put it in a Philippine ATM machine you will request and get pesos. The money will be subtracted from your account in Dollars. The exchange rate is usually fair. ATM cards are an easy and convenient way to get money.

There is however a catch. There is usually a large transaction fee for each international transaction. Typically these fees are $5 to $10 dollars per transaction. Since the fees are transaction based and NOT a percentage of the money you withdraw, it is best to withdraw as much money as possible at any given time. However, even armed with this knowledge there are problems.

The first problem is you will not know what the maximum withdrawal amount is. They never tell you. Thus it is better to start high. If you request too much money, the request will be rejected, but there will be no fee. So start high and work your way down until the request is accepted. Of course this might be quite annoying to the people in back of you if there is a long line at the ATM!

The second problem is that the cash withdrawal limit for an international withdrawal is often quite small. Sometimes as low as P5000 peso or about $100 dollars. If you are paying a $10 fee for each $100 dollar withdrawal, this is pretty steep.

Not all banks have the same upper limits, so if you are not happy with one machine try a different machine at a different bank. BPI and BDO banks are a reasonable place to start.

### ◆ Credit Cards

Outside of Manila credit cards are still not that widely accepted. They are accepted at some large department stores and supermarkets as well as some of the fancier restaurants, however they are not accepted at most run of the mill stores and restaurants. Also make sure you know your credit cards policy for international purchases - many add an international transaction surcharge.

Finally, unlike in the USA or other western countries, there is no rule that they can't charge extra for credit card purchases. Many establishments add a 5% fee for using credit cards instead of cash.

In an emergency you should be able to find a bank that will give you a cash loan from your credit card. Of course you will be charged a hefty interest fee. Again you might want to start with BPI and BDO as places you can get a credit card loan.

It's worth taking a credit card with you, but you can't rely on it.

### ◆ Banking and Electronic Transfer

The problem with electronic transfer from your bank in the USA is that you need a bank in the Philippines to transfer the money to. If you are planning to be at a single location for a few weeks or more and you have any thought that you might be back to the Philippines again I would suggest setting up a Philippine bank account. The problem is, many (if not all) Philippine banks have residency requirements. Notice I did not say permanent residency requirements, I just said residency requirements. This means you need to have a permanent address. If you plan on being in one location for a while I suggest that one of the first things you do is go to a local bank and find out exactly what the requirements are for opening a bank account. Once you have a bank account you can have money wired from your USA bank into the Philippine bank. There is no problem transferring U.S. Dollars into a Philippine peso account. When the Philippine bank receives the funds they will simply convert it to pesos at the prevailing rate and deposit it into your account. When you leave the Philippines simply take out all your money except a few hundred pesos. If you never go back then no big deal, you lose a few Dollars. If you do go back then the next time you go to the Philippines you can wire money from your USA account to your Philippine account and have the money waiting for you when you get there.

If you are worried about the exchange rate you can also set up a Dollar or Euro account in your Philippine bank. Then when you transfer money, the money will go in as Dollars or Euros and you know exactly what you have. The problem is that the minimum amount for opening and maintaining a Dollar or Euro account is usually much higher than for a peso account.

Now, on the subject of electronic transfer there is one **very important** item I must mention. It is not always possible to initiate an electronic transfer from your American bank account to your Philippine bank account while you are in the Philippines. Some American banks require that you set up an international transfer agreement prior to your trip to the Philippines. The details of these agreements differ from bank to bank. Some banks may allow you to set up a general agreement that allows you to choose your foreign bank at a later time. Other agreements may require that you specify the particular bank and account number that you will be transferring money to.

If the latter is the case it presents a problem. How can you set up the transfer if you have not yet been to the Philippines? At least in this case you can set up the Philippine bank account on your first trip to the Philippines. Make sure you record all relevant banking information including the international routing numbers. Then when you get back to the USA set up the transfer agreement. Then the next time you are in the Philippines you will have no problem initiating a transfer from your American Account to your Philippine account.

### ◆ Can You Cash a Personal Check from Your USA Account?

Well not really. Personal checks from foreign banks are pretty much useless. The only thing you can do is deposit them into your Philippine bank account and wait between one and two months for them to clear. This obviously does you no good if you are on a short trip. However if you live permanently in the Philippines personal checks can be a convenient and cheap way to transfer money. More about this in the following section "How to handle money for the Long term".

### ◆ What Will You Do, What Will You Do?

Some of you may remember an old commercial for American Express travelers checks with the actor Karl Malden. In the commercial there is a happy traveler who all of the sudden gets robbed. Panicked she realizes she has nothing, no cash, no credit cards. She is stuck in the middle of a foreign country with nothing.

The voice of Karl Malden comes on in a voice over, "What will you do?, what will you do?"

Well it's best to give this scenario some thought before you leave. Here are some suggestions.

There are many Western Union offices in the Philippines. Set something up with a trusted friend or relative who can wire you money in the event of an emergency.

Leave an extra ATM or credit card with a trusted friend or relative. In the event of an emergency they can federal express it to you which will take two or three days.

Contact your credit card and ATM companies and ask what services they offer in the event that your card is lost or stolen in a foreign country.

By the way, I don't recommend travelers checks. Do they still even exist? I have not seen them in years here in the Philippines. Even if they do exist, I'm sure if you had them lost or stolen it would be nightmare to have them replaced here in the Philippines in a timely manner.

## Topic iii: *How to Handle Money for the Long Term*

Money for your Philippine vacation is one thing, but if you are an Expat living permanently in the Philippines you will have a whole different set of problems to overcome.

The first problem to consider is where to keep your money. Do you want to keep most of it in the United States and only transfer a small amount of it at a time to the Philippines? Do you want to transfer it all to the Philippines? Do want to spread out your money in a number of places including international banks?

The second problem is how to transfer your money to the Philippines when you need it. So let's explore these issues.

### ◆ Keeping Most of Your Money in the USA

The majority of Expats choose to keep most of their money and financial assets in their home country, at least initially, and only transfer the money to the Philippines as needed. Within the USA you can usually set things up either on line or with agreements so that you can transfer your money among different Banks and financial institutions within the USA. The problem comes when you want to transfer the money to the Philippines. When you are on vacation the ATM card is a reasonable method to transfer your funds. However, because of the high fees associated with each transaction, this method does not make sense for Expats living in the Philippines, it's like throwing money in the garbage.

There are two better ways to transfer your money. The first is with Electronic transfer. An electronic transfer typically costs about $30, but there is no limit to the amount you can transfer, so the $30 fee is reasonable.

For example, suppose you are using an ATM card. In the best of cases you will be able to transfer about $200 dollars at a time with a $5.00 fee. It is very likely you will not do this well. Maybe you can only transfer $100 at a time with a $10 fee. Even assuming the former if you transfer $5000 dollars over time, it will take you  25 transactions and cost you $125 dollars. Assuming the latter it will take you 50 transactions and cost you $500 dollars. In either case you would be better off taking out the $5000 dollars with one $30 dollar transfer.

Please keep in mind that you may have to set up a transfer agreement with your bank in the USA prior to coming to the Philippines, as described in the section titled "Banking and electronic Transfer" in the topic titled "How to handle money for your short term visit.

The second way to transfer money is with the simple personal check. Make sure you take an ample supply of personal checks with you when you are planning your move to the Philippines.

The personal check is often overlooked as an effective means of transfer because of the time involved. A personal check from a USA bank will take between one and two months to clear. If you bank at BPI,  which I recommend as a good bank, they guarantee that your personal check will clear in one month. You will have to open a dollar account as you can't deposit a dollar check into a peso account.

The good thing about a personal check is that it costs you basically nothing. It is free to deposit a personal check, or at most there is a very small service fee.

The bad thing is the time delay. However, if you are living permanently in the Philippines and you set things up right, the time delay need not be a problem.

For example, suppose you determine that your monthly expenses are about $1000 a month. For your first check transfer $5000 dollars so that you will have a buffer. While you are waiting for your first check to clear you live off your ATM card.

Then, once the $5000 dollar check clears, every month write a check to replace the money you used the previous month. This is the method I used for quite some time and it worked perfectly.

### Topic iv: *Transferring All (Or a Large Percentage) of Your Money to the Philippines*

#### ♦ The 10,000 Dollar Maximum Non Rule

You are likely to hear from people that you can't transfer more than $10,000 dollars at a time from your USA account to your Philippine account. You are likely to hear that if you want to transfer a large amount of money to the Philippines you have to do it $10,000 dollars at a time perhaps waiting one month between transfers. I certainly heard this rumor many times. Guess what. It's false. I don't know how this rumor has gained so much momentum because it simply is not true.

What is true is that if you want to transfer more than $10,000 dollars at a time to a particular bank, that bank has to do some additional paperwork explaining the circumstances of the transfer. Since perhaps the banks don't like to do this additional paperwork they are likely to tell you it's "better" if you just transfer $10,000 dollars at a time.

#### ♦ The FBAR: Uncle Sam Wants to Know

If you have more than $10,000 dollars in accounts outside the United States you have to file an FBAR report.  It does not matter if your money is in one account or spread out over many. The key is the total amount of money invested in all of your foreign accounts. If you have 1000 dollars invested in 10 different Philippine accounts you still have to file an FBAR.

FBAR is the nickname for the REPORT OF FOREIGN BANK AND FINANCIAL ACCOUNTS. FBAR is not only an acronym, but it's an acronym of a shortened version of the real name of the report, which is kind of weird.

FBAR stands for "Foreign Banking Accounts Report " Which is not the real name of the report. Regardless, everybody calls it FBAR. You have to file an FBAR every year that, if in the PREVIOUS year at any time your foreign holdings were $10,000 dollars or more. The FBAR is not part of your income tax return. It is a separate report that goes to a different department.

The FBAR report, also known as  Form TD F 90-22.1,   must be mailed on or before June 30 , NOT to the IRS, but rather to the US Department of Treasury, P.O. Box 32621, Detroit Mi, 48232-0621, You can download the FBAR forms from the internet.

The FBAR report basically specifies what accounts you own outside the USA, the institution, the account number and the amount of each account.

When I first learned of the FBAR requirement I was quite annoyed, as many Expats are. It feels like an invasion of privacy. I even toyed with the idea of not filing the report. However I, like almost everybody,  comes to the conclusion that the risk of not filing is not worth it.  The penalties can be severe including large fines and/or jail time.

### ◆ Why Might You Decide to Move Most of Your Money to the Philippines?

Well there might be several reasons. You might feel that this is now your home, so why should you have your accounts in the USA which is inconvenient.

You might want to lock in the peso rate so you can plan your future more accurately. As long as your money is in dollars you are subject to fluctuations in the exchange rate. When you change to pesos then you know what you have.

You might want to invest in Philippine investments.

And finally there is one other possible very good reason to get your money out of the USA which may apply strongly to some people and not at all to others. As long as your money is in American accounts it is relatively easy for someone with a grievance against you to have their lawyer petition the court for a freeze of some or all of your assets. If you are in some situation where you feel somebody might file a civil case against you for a large amount of money it is better for you to get your money out of US banks.

Now does getting your money into a foreign account protect you 100%? No. Theoretically the lawyer could petition the court of the country where your bank does business, but doing this is astronomically more expensive and difficult than if the account were held in a US bank. Foreign courts are not likely to grant a freeze of assets requested by a foreign lawyer unless the circumstances are extreme.

One other thought about getting your money out of the USA. Some people might believe you don't have to pay income tax on profits of Foreign investments. This is not true. You will still have to report all income and file a United States income tax return if you made sufficient money.

As far as hiding money so you can illegally avoid taxes, I highly recommend you don't try this! The odds of getting caught are too high and the penalties too severe.

### ♦ Is Your Money Secure in a Philippine Bank?

Well I think so, but who can ever say for sure? Who knows what will happen in this world? But it seems like the Philippines has been reasonably stable now for a good while. Many of the more reputable banks have been around for quite some time now, and as far as I know the big ones have never defaulted. I have read and been told that the bank I use, BPI, is very stable and liquid.

As I write these words in November of 2008 the world is in the middle of a terrible financial crises. Many financial institutions world wide have collapsed while others are on the verge of collapse, or need bailout help to prevent them from collapsing. Yet the Philippines seems to be weathering the storm quite well, because only a very small percentage of the Philippine investments were in international toxic bad debt instruments. So for now it seems Philippine banks are safer than US banks!

### ♦ What About Deposit Insurance?

Look for a bank that is accredited to have deposit insurance. All the big name banks do. Some of the little banks may not. Deposit insurance is only P250,000 peso ($5000) per account. However, if you trust your wife you can have up to three accounts per bank, one in your name, one joint and one in her name, so it's possible to have up to P750,000 ($15000) insured in a given bank. As of this writing there is some discussion going on about raising the insurance limit to P500,000, but it has not happened yet. I wouldn't worry too much about having your accounts insured if you put your money into one of the big banks. The three biggest banks in the Philippines are Metrobank, BDO and BPI in that order. If one of these banks fail then the

Philippines is already in deep trouble and I'm not sure the deposit insurance will help you anyway.

### ♦ What About Investing?

I'm afraid I can't offer you very good advice! I've always been terrible at investing, which is why I'm writing this book, because I need more money! Of course there are all the usual investments opportunities in the Philippines like land or business, but you are on your own about that.

I do however want to pass on one investment opportunity.

First I have to explain the concept of a Philippine Rural Bank. A Rural Bank is a bank that specializes in making loans to people living in rural areas such as farmers. Often these loans are at very high interest rates. They banks usually demand high quality collateral and may loan only a relatively small percentage of the value of the collateral there by securing the loan.

Rural banks are always in need of cash flow and will pay very good rates for short, medium and long term certificates of deposit. The really interesting thing is that some of the rural banks are accredited to have deposit insurance. This means that your high interest CDs are actually insured by the Philippine government so long as the amount of the CD is P250,000 or less. You can buy three of these CDs per bank, one in your name, one joint and one in your wife's name.

A few years ago when I inherited some money I did a lot of research and talked to a lot of people on ideas on how to invest my money. One of the people I talked to was an Expat living in the Philippines who urged me to invest in long term CDs from accredited rural banks in the Philippines. At that time many of the rural banks were offering a 5 year CD paying an annual interest rate of 20%, tax exempt! My friend argued, it's insured! How can you lose! His investment plan was to invest in a number of different accredited rural banks buying long term CDs up to the maximum insured value.

My reaction was, if it seems too good to be true it probably is. I just couldn't get myself to do it.

So instead I invested in a portfolio of international stocks and bonds. Although I'm not an economist I had a funny feeling the USA was in trouble so I decided to invest in international instruments rather than US instruments. For a while I did very well, then the financial crises of 2008 hit and I lost a lot of money. Hey, I was right, the USA was in trouble, but guess what, it didn't help me very much. The USA brought down the rest of the world including my portfolio of international stocks and bonds.

Meanwhile the investment that I thought was too risky is continuing to hum along quite fine! Not only did my friend make out on the high yields of the CDs, but he also made money by virtue of the money exchange rates. During the last few years the Philippine peso went up and the dollar went down.

Well to sum up, I'm not advising you to invest in Philippine Rural Bank CD's, I'm only making you aware of the option. You will have to assess the risk yourself.

[Editors note: A few of these rural banks did eventually fail during the financial crises and were taken into receivership by the Philippine government. The deposit insurance was honored, but some earned interest was lost]

## Topic v: *Spreading Your Money Among Several International Banks*

Suppose you don't want to leave all your money in the USA for some of the reasons discussed earlier. But suppose you also don't feel comfortable moving all your money to the Philippines. There is a third choice. Spread your money among several international banks. This way all your money is not tied to a particular country or currency. Look on the internet to find a number of international banks that allow you to do your banking on line or with telephone calls. But please, be careful! Don't get scammed!

One possibility is HSBC which is a huge international bank. The good thing about HSBC is that they have some offices in the Philippines. There are other international banks with offices in the Philippines as well, particularly in Manila.

# Chapter 13: About Visas and Permanent Residence in the Philippines

If you are an Expat wanting to live permanently and legally in the Philippines you basically have three choices.

- You can continually renew your travel Visa

- You can get married to a Filipina citizen and apply for permanent residence

- You can get a Special Resident Retirement Visa (SRRV)

I will discuss each of these options below.

## Topic i: *Continual Renewal of Travel Visa*

The rules have recently changed and the new immigration laws make it easy for foreigners to stay in the Philippines basically forever on a simple travel visa, so long as they keep shelling out the cash and as long as they don't do anything bad that will cause the immigration officer to not want to renew the visa.

When you first enter the country your travel visa will be for 21 days. Before the 21 days expires you may execute your first extension which will cost you about p3000 and give you an additional 38 days for a total stay of almost two months.

Before the 59 days are up you may extend your visa for an additional two months, and keep on extending every two months up to a total of 16 months.

After 16 months you may continue to extend two months at a time but only with permission of the chief of immigration up to a total of 24 months.

After 24 months you may continue to extend two months at a time forever  but only with permission of the commissioner.

Now,  what does it entail to get permission of the chief or the commissioner? I have no idea. I don't know anybody who has done it. Maybe it is easy, maybe not. Maybe it just requires dishing out the right amount of green stuff.  In any case, it is not really a problem. If it is difficult to get special permission of the chief or commissioner, simply leave the country for a day and then re-enter and start the process all over again for another 16 months.

How much will it cost you? Well the fees are actually quite complicated and vary from renewal to renewal based on when certain  provisions and penalties kick in. It would be nice if they just said something simple like, 6000 for each two month extension, but this is not the way it works.

Well never mind the exact details, it will cost you more or less p3000 per month to stay in the Philippines via continual renewal of your travel visa. In other words about p6000 for each two month extension.

If you plan on living permanently in the Philippines this method of continual travel visa renewal presents two issues, namely convenience and cost.

As far as convenience goes, most decent size cities in the Philippines have an immigration office, so you will probably not have to go too far to find one. On the other hand, if you choose to live in a remote location it could be a major pain in the neck to visit an immigration office every two months.  Typically you will spend a couple of hours or less in the office each two months doing the paper work to renew your visa. At the end of 16 months (assuming you don't get special permission) you will have to leave the country, and since the Philippines are islands, you can't just drive a car or take a bus over the border. You will have to travel somewhere by plane. Hong Kong is the easiest and quickest place to go, with Malaysia, Indonesia, Thailand, Vietnam and Singapore being reasonable alternatives.

As far as cost goes, if you want to think in dollars, figure on $60 a month for the immigration fees and $600 every 16 months for a short vacation. Thus your monthly visa cost is somewhere around 60 + (600/16) = more or less $100 a month. Of course if you tend to leave the country anyway every year or so for a vacation or to visit your home country you need not factor in the travel cost.

## Topic ii: *Marriage and Permanent Residence*

On the other hand if you are married you can apply for a permit resident card (Alien Certificate of Residence or ACR card). Applying for this card is a fair amount of work and will also cost a fair amount of money (20 to 40 thousand peso), but once you get it you never have to leave the country. You will, however, still have to report to an immigration office once a year and pay a small yearly fee. A lawyer who has contacts within the Immigration office can help facilitate the application. However, be careful not to get ripped off. Negotiate a fixed fee, and try to reserve the final payment for when the application is approved.

## Topic iii: *Special Resident Retirement Visa (SRRV)*

### ♦ What is an SRRV?

The SRRV is a type of Visa that encourages people from outside the Philippines to retire and invest in the Philippines. The SRRV allows a Expat to gain permanent residence in the Philippines WITHOUT having to marry a Filipina citizen. If you are already married to a non Filipina citizen, or if you are not married, but don't want to get married, and you want to live permanently in the Philippines, this kind of Visa is probably your best option.

I will go into the SRRV in considerable detail below, but for now I just want to describe it in it's simplest terms. The SRRV is under the jurisdiction   of the Philippine Retirement Authority (PRA), whose main office is in Makati Manila.

The PRA has defined certain kinds of investments, and has a list of partners offering such investments,  such that if you agree to invest in a PRA approved investment they will give you an SRRV.

So to simplify even more to it's most simple essence, it's basically this:

**Invest money in the Philippines, get an SRRV visa**  - it's that simple

### ♦ How Much Will You Have to Invest?

The minimum investment to obtain an SRRV depends on your age and circumstances. The PRA lists three cases, each case having a different minimum investment. These cases are described as follows:

**Case 1:** Applicant is under 50 years old

Minimum investment: $50,000

**Case 2**: Applicant is at least 50 years old, but has no qualifying pension. Minimum investment: $20,000 dollars

**Case 3:** Applicant is at least 50 years of age and has a pension of at least $800 per month (single) or $1000 per month couple.

Minimum investment: $10,000 dollars

### ♦ Types of PRA Investments

The PRA lists the following categories of investments which may qualify:

- Purchase of condominium unit

- Long term Lease of a house and lot, condominium or townhouse

- Construction of a residential unit on a leased parcel of land;

- Purchase of Proprietary Membership/Golf shares in golf clubs;

- Deposit into a PRA approved bank

### ♦ Living in a PRA Approved Residential Community

Please keep in mind that you can't just purchase any condominium, or construct on any leased land, it must be a PRA approved investment.

For practical purposes what this really means is this: You pick out a residential community/facility approved by the PRA and you buy a share or lease a condo, which allows you to live and play in this community. Different communities have different arrangements. But in all cases the bottom line is this: You have to fork out some good money, usually at least fifty and more typically one hundred thousand dollars or sometimes even more.

What are these communities like? Typically they are very upscale gated and guarded communities on the outskirts of a major city. They usually contain a golf course, tennis courts, a swimming pool and other facilities such as work out room, a restaurant and a bar. Basically it amounts to living in a country club.

If you want to live in a city without living in a country club type atmosphere, there may also be PRA approved condo units. Again, talk to a PRA office for details.

#### ◆ Country Club Share

This category is officially listed as "Purchase of Proprietary Membership/Golf shares in golf clubs" on the PRA web Site. Suppose you want to avail of the SRRV without committing yourself to living in a PRA approved community. What if you want to play at the golf clubs and tennis courts of such a community without actually living there? Many of the communities allow you to buy a "use of facilities" share. What this means is that for a certain amount of money you buy a share in the community which allows you to use all the facilities without having to live there. A typical share at a decent community with golf, tennis and swimming might cost in the neighborhood of $10,000 Dollars.

There is one problem however. That $10,000 investment may not be enough money to qualify you for the SRRV. As described earlier, depending on your circumstance, the minimum investment is 10, 20 or 50 thousand dollars. If you are in case 3 as described above your minimum investment requirement is only $10,000 and the "use of facility" share may be perfect for you. However, even if your minimum investment is (for example) $20,000 dollars, there is no reason you can't invest $10,000 in your golf share, and another $10,000 in some other PRA approved investment.

#### ◆ Bank Deposit SRRV

The PRA gives you another option, for those that **don't** want to live in a PRA community or buy a PRA approved country club share. Simply open up a special PRA bank account in a PRA partner bank and deposit the appropriate amount of money.

For example, suppose your minimum investment is $20,000 dollars because you are over 50 but have no qualifying pension fund. Simply open up the PRA approved bank account, deposit $20,000 into this account and the SRRV is yours! So very simple! Later on if you decide you want to buy into golf shares or live in a PRA approved residential community you can transfer your bank account investment into your new PRA approved investment.

#### ♦ Upside and Downside of SRRV Visa

What is the downside of an SRRV visa? Actually, if you leave money out of the discussion, there is no downside. The SRRV visa is a wonderful great fantastic thing. Extremely easy and quick to obtain and no reason to feel pressured into marriage!

Of course not everybody can leave money out of the discussion. The problem with the SRRV is that you have to put money aside and that money is basically untouchable so long as you want to keep your SRRV.

If you buy into a golf share, or you live in a condo in a residential PRA approved community you can argue that your money is being used towards a good purpose. However if you use the bank account method then that money is just sitting there, basically in escrow, and you can't touch that money so long as you want to keep your SRRV.

What happens if you really need that money? Can you get it? Yes, but perhaps not immediately. You have to go to a PRA office and file an application for release of the funds. Once the release is approved you lose your SRRV. So basically, in the case of a bank account, if you want to live in the Philippines the rest of your life, it's the equivalent of buying an SRRV for ten or twenty thousand dollars. I guess the bank account does make some interest, but I don't think this amounts to very much.

In the case of a golf share or residence in a condo, if you want your money back you have to do two things. You have to find a buyer for your share, and you also have to file an application for release of your investment once a buyer is found. Of course, as in the case of the bank account, you will lose your SRRV.

There is one other way to get your money back without losing permanent residence. Suppose you come to the Philippines as a single man and invest, for example, $20,000 in a PRA bank account.

Now suppose at a later time you fall in love and decide to marry a Filipina woman. Having an SRRV visa does not prevent you from also applying for a spousal permanent residence visa. Once you get the Spousal permanent resident visa you could withdraw your money from the PRA bank account. You would lose your SRRV visa, but it would not matter because you would still be entitled to permanent residence via your Spousal visa.

### ♦ Why Don't Most Expats Avail of the SRRV?

Certainly a large number of Expats do avail of the SRRV. However, all in all, compared to the total Expat population, the SRRV holders only represent a small percentage of the total.

Why is this?

Well certainly part of the reason is the money considerations. There are many Expats that just don't want to put aside the money required to obtain an SRRV.

However, I think money considerations is only part of the answer. The other part of the answer has to do with mindset. It takes a very together type of person to have the right mindset. The right mindset implies someone who really knows what they want from the get go. Someone who says to themselves, I want to retire in the Philippines and I'm going to investigate the best way to do it.

For most Expats this is not the way it happens. Most Expats, like myself, get sucked in slowly. Maybe they take a trip to the Philippines, they like it, so they schedule a second longer trip. Maybe after the second trip they schedule a third trip and on this trip they meet a woman and fall in love and decide to get married. They never even think about the SRRV. It never comes into their mind. Then maybe a year or two later they learn about it and say to themselves, hmmm, why didn't I do that?

Well hopefully this book will help you to think about this ahead of time, so you can make the best decision concerning your visa.

### ◆ What Are the Steps for Obtaining an SRRV Visa?

Basically the process starts with you contacting a PRA office. From everything I have heard the staff at the PRA offices are extremely well trained and helpful, and will hold your hand throughout the whole process. I have even heard they will pick you up from the airport or your hotel and bring you to the office.

Once at the office you will start the application procedure. Of course make sure you have all needed documentation such as passports, bank account information, proof of pension, etc etc etc. Don't error on the side of not bringing enough. Bring everything with you that could possibly be of use in the application procedure.

As part the application procedure you will also have to take a medical exam.

If your choice is simply to get an SRRV via bank deposit they can help you to do that immediately, and the SRRV can be in your hands in a relatively short period of time. If your choice is to find a golf share or residence they can probably help you with that as well.

### ◆ PRA Contact Information

For more information see the PRA website at www.pra.gov.ph

The PRA has a number of offices as listed below

(For information about how to dial from the USA to telephone numbers in the Philippines see the earlier section titled: **Use regular phone to have voice conversation)**

**MAIN OFFICE**

Philippine Retirement Authority
4/F Citibank Center 8741 Paseo de Roxas
Makati City 1227 Philippines
Tel. No. : 02 - 848 -1412 to 1416
 Email: inquiry@pra.gov.ph


**BAGUIO SATELLITE OFFICE**
Address: DTI-CAR NERBAC, PTA Compound
PCCI Bldg; Gov. Pack Rd., Baguio City 2600
Direct Line : (074) 423 - 3123
Mobile Number : 0928 - 551 - 0953
Email : baguio@pra.gov.ph


**CEBU REGIONAL OFFICE**
Address: Shop No. 7, 2nd Level, Waterfront Hotel
No. 1 Salinas Drive, Lahug, Cebu City
Direct Line : (32) 238 - 5693
Email : cebu@pra.gov.ph


**DAVAO SATELLITE OFFICE**
Address: DTI-NERBAC, Monteverde st., Davao City
Cell phone No. : 0928 – 551 - 0954
Email : davao@pra.gov.ph


**SUBIC / CLARK SATELLITE OFFICE**
Contact City Tourism Office, Ground Floor, Olongapo
Convention Center
Old Hospital Road, East Tatinac, Olongapo City, Zambales
Telephone/Fax No. : (047) 224 -1471
Cell phone No. : 0918 – 924 - 0585
Email Address : carloponti_zialcita@yahoo.com

# Chapter 14: Your First Trip

Unless you are absolutely sure you want to live in the Philippines, and you are sure you know where you want to live, I don't recommend that your first trip be a permanent move.

Your first trip should just be to explore, have fun and learn about the country. Try to travel light. Perhaps a small carry on backpack and one medium sized piece of luggage with wheels. It's nice to be mobile and travel easily.

Of course where you choose to travel within the Philippines will depend on the time you have available, your particular tastes, and also possibly on the women you met on the internet and plan on visiting. However I will give you some ideas

Since you will be first landing in Manila it makes sense that you stay there for at least a day or two or three. You may not like it. You may be overwhelmed by the size, traffic and pollution. I suggest you consider Makati as your first taste of Manila. Makati has many fine restaurants, malls and night life.

After a few days in Manila proper you may want to consider visiting a suburb south of Manila. I suggest Paranaque as one of the nicer suburbs of Manila. Paranaque is not nearly as crazy as Manila proper yet offers many fine restaurants and night life. If you are a tennis player there is also a nice tennis club in Paranaque. If you have any interest in the SRRV visa then you might want to visit some of the PRA approved facilities available in Paranaque and neighboring areas such as Alabang. If the SRRV is really your first choice for long term visa, you might also want to consider visiting Tagaytay, a mere two hours drive south of Manila. Tagaytay is not an exciting place, but it has many beautiful PRA approved facilities, and it's located several hundred meters above sea level, so it's a bit cooler than most of the Philippines (but not like Baguio).

If you are interested in visiting one of the famous night life areas you might consider Angeles about two hours drive north of Manila. Angeles can be a fun place for some people, but it's not for everyone.

If you hate hot weather and you like the idea of living in Baguio high up in the mountains you might want to take a trip there. For only about  p500 you can take a bus from Manila to Baguio. Better to go at night when it's cool and the traffic is not so bad. A night trip from Manila to Baguio takes about six hours. A day trip can take up to 8 hours. There is also air service from Manila to Baguio for about P3000. However I don't suggest visiting Baguio during the rainy season which extends from May through September, as Baguio has a notoriously bad rainy season.

After you finish exploring Luzon it is time to explore some other Islands. Most foreigners choose to visit Cebu. Cebu seems to be the center of the Expat community in the Philippines. There are many Expats living in Cebu. Cebu also has a reputation for having among the most beautiful and friendly women in the Philippines, affectionately known as Cebuanos. Cebu is a big city, but not nearly as crazy as Manila, and a lot less expensive.

From Cebu, if you like the idea of visiting a smaller city with a sizable Expat community you might want to consider visiting Dumaguete which is located just south of Cebu island.  From Cebu city you can either take a fast boat to Dumaguete (about three hours ride) or you can take a bus which travels down the length of Cebu island and then crosses over to Dumaguete via short ride on a ferry boat. The bus trip takes about four hours and is about half the price of the fast boat.

If you want to visit a vacation resort area you might consider visiting Puerto Galera or Boracay.  Boracay is definitely one of the more fun places in the Philippines.

# Chapter 15: The Best Places for Expats to Live

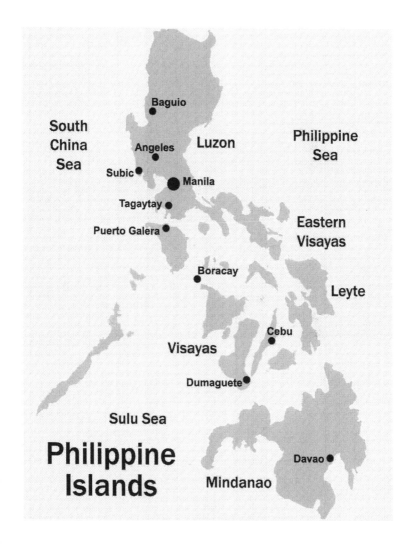

## Topic i: *General Discussion*

Expats are spread out all over the Philippines. Go into any city just about anywhere in the Philippines and there will usually be at least a few Expats living there. There are even Expats living in the middle of nowhere, deep in the provinces, far from the cities.

Nevertheless, it is my strong opinion that you will be a lot better off and feel a lot more comfortable if you choose a location where there is a sizable Expat population. There are a number of reasons for this.

First of all you won't feel like an alien from another world. I have been to places in the Philippines where they rarely see foreigners, and it's not pleasant to have everyone stare at you and call you Joe. If you live in an area where there are many Expats, the locals are used to it, and used to dealing with Expats. You are not a big deal.

Also, it's good to have fellow Expats for support, to ask questions, to get advice, or to have friends from your own culture. There is also some protection from living in a popular Expat community. If something goes wrong at least there are people watching.

In general, if there are many Expats in an area, it means the local government and politicians encourage Expats. If this was not the case, there probably would not be so many Expats living there. Go to a place where they are not used to foreigners and you might not be received with the same open arms attitude.

So in this section I list the main Expat areas. This section is not intended to give detailed information about the various places listed. It is rather to give you an intuitive feel about what these places are like. Where you will visit and live is of course one of the big choices you have to make. Hopefully this section will give you some ideas. For details consult travel books and the internet.

## Topic ii: *Manila*

**Band performing in Makati**

There is not much for me to say about Manila for the simple reason that there is too much to be said about Manila. I can't possibly do it justice in just a few paragraphs. Manila is a huge sprawling city. It has many areas with many different flavors within the city. It has everything. But it is huge and crowded and crazy. The traffic is a nightmare. Also the cost of living is at least 50% higher in Manila compared with other parts of the country. In my opinion Manila is a better place to visit than it is to live. If you want excitement and nightlife Manila is of course a great place. Makati is sort of the center of Manila and is sort of like the Manhattan of Manila. From what I understand there is an Expat population living in Makati. If you like Girlie bars Makati has a large selection with the most beautiful women. The prices reflect this. Personally I can't see living in Manila proper. It's just too crowded and crazy. Of course Manila has everything including the best medical facilities in the country. If you want to be near all of this without being in it, perhaps you might consider South Metro Manila (see below).

## Topic iii: *South Metro Manila*

There are a lot of Expats that want to be near Manila without being in it. They feel comfortable being near a city where everything is available. Also, of major concern to many Expats is the availability of a top notch hospital. Manila has several hospitals that are supposed to be world class (see the medical chapter). No other place in the Philippines really has top notch medical facilities. For this reason alone many Expats choose to live in the Manila area.

Some of the South Metro Manila areas of interest include Paranaque, Alabang and Muntinlupa City Some of these areas have expensive communities, gated with guards and complete with golf and tennis courts. Many wealthier Expats choose to live in these areas. Many of these areas are PRA approved.

## Topic iv: *Cebu*

**SM Mall in Cebu**

Cebu is the second largest city in the Philippines. Cebu is big, but not nearly as big as Manila. Cebu has bad traffic, but not nearly as bad as Manila. Cebu is a complete city with much to offer, but it still can't be compared to Manila. Despite this, or because of this, Cebu has a large Expat population. I think it's fairly safe to say that Cebu is the Expat center of the Philippines. Why? Well I think people like a complete city, but most people feel Manila is just too much, thus Cebu is a good compromise. Also the cost of living in Cebu is much lower than Manila and Cebu has a reputation for friendly people and beautiful women.

That being said, Cebu is not the prettiest city in the Philippines. There are many dirty and ugly sections of Cebu, as I guess there are in most large cities. Another negative thing about the Cebu area is there are no nice beaches near by. If you are a beach person, Cebu may not be the best place for you. You might hear some people say there are nice beaches on nearby Mactan island. Don't believe it. There are some nice hotels and resorts there, but no nice beaches.

## Topic v: *Angeles*

**Typical Girlie Bar in Angeles**

Angeles is famous for a few reasons. First it is the home to Clark Special Economic Zone, formally an American Air Force Base, the last military base held by the Americans until agreeing to leave in 1991. Second it's famous for being utterly destroyed by the 1991 eruption of Mt. Pinatubo, which was the second largest eruption in the world in more than the last 100 years (Second only to Mt. St. Helens). Third it has a popular gambling Casino and finally it is famous for having one of the most notorious red light districts in the Philippines.

Angeles has a fairly large Expat community and it's easy to understand why. Angeles is a full city in it's own right with all the full city amenities like hospitals, malls, restaurants and shopping centers. For those that like to gamble Angeles has the Casino. For those that enjoy Girlie bars and hard core entertainment, there is the famous Angeles red light or "entertainment" district. For those that like country clubs and upscale facilities there is the Clark Special Economic Zone.

Angeles is also only two hours travel from Manila, and the now completed Clark-Subic highway allows you to get to Subic bay and the nice beaches located there in only about an hour.

The "Entertainment District" is located along the length of Fields Avenue and it's surrounding side streets. It's almost like a city within a city and of course has a very different flavor than the regular part of Angeles. To be fair, the entertainment district is more than just a bunch of prostitutes in sleazy girlie bars. It also has many nice normal bars, karaoke clubs and restaurants. If you have the right personality it's actually a pretty fun place.

On the negative side, the city of Angeles proper is not a pretty city. It is a sprawling, traffic congested, air polluted and often dirty city. Many Expats don't want to live there because they feel that because of the Casino and the Entertainment District Angeles attracts the wrong kinds of elements. Angeles is land locked and there are no beaches in the immediate vicinity. The nearest beaches are more than an hour away in Subic Freeport.

## Topic vi: *Subic/ Olongapo*

Located just one hour South West of Angeles along the now completed Clark-Subic highway (no small motorcycles allowed) is the Subic Bay, Olongapo, Subic Bay Freeport (SBF), Barrio Barretto, Subic town area.

If you read about this area or look it up on the internet you are likely to get quite confused. I certainly did before I visited the area. So that you won't be as confused as I was, I will now explain each of the areas listed above.

### ♦ Subic Bay and Surrounding Area

Subic Bay refers to the large geographical bay around whose shores are all the other areas listed below. Subic Bay is approximately 6 km (4 miles) wide and 12 km (8 miles) long.

### ♦ Subic Bay Freeport (SBF)

SBF special economic zone is the area that was formerly a US naval station before being released back to the Philippines in 1991. SBF is a huge area consisting of approximately 67,000 hectares (670 sq km, 258 sq miles). SBF itself can be categorized into several areas.

Near the entrance is the town of SBF, if you want to call it that. It is where all the stores, restaurants and services exist. Beyond that are the country clubs and residential communities, some of them PRA approved. Beyond that are the beaches and the airport. Some of the beaches are fairly decent. Beyond that are vast stretches of undeveloped land, much of it jungle.

SBF has a very different feel from most of the Philippines. Here for example traffic laws are actually obeyed and rules are followed. It's much stricter and tightly controlled than what you typically see in the Philippines. It's a tightly run ship if you will (to borrow terminology from it's Naval base past).

In SBF, at least near the entrance where the town is, police are a very visible presence, and unlike the police in most of the Philippines, they will enforce small infractions.

If you like the idea of living in a more tightly controlled, more rule oriented location with a western feel to it, then SBF is for you.

### ♦ Olongapo

If you want to escape the confines and restrictions of SBF visit nearby Olongapo city, which is your typical mid size Philippine city. Olongapo used to have a sex industry that served the US military when SBF was a naval base, but this was abolished shortly after the naval base was closed down.

### ♦ Barrio Barretto

Barrio Barretto is a small town several miles north of Olongapo, which has a number of hotels, restaurants, and what's left of the sex industry in the area. The sex industry here is a very distant and poor cousin of Angeles.

### ♦ Subic Town

Subic town is a place not to be confused with SBF or Olongapo. Subic town is located many km from SBF/Olongapo and is not of much interest to the typical traveler or Expat.

## Topic vii: *Baguio*

**Burnham Park in Baguio**

Baguio is located in Luzon a about 350 KM north of Manila. Baguio is a land locked city located high up in the mountains at an elevation of over 5000 feet (1500M).

The main reason for an Expat to choose Baguio is because of its cool weather. Baguio is the only major city high up in the mountains and the only major city to have consistently cool weather. If you hate hot weather and you want to live where there is an Expat community, and in a city, Baguio is really your only choice.

However not everything about Baguio weather is good. During the good part of the year from October through April the weather is spectacular. Wonderful perfect sun filled days in the mid 70s (24c), followed by pleasant, even chilly (but not cold) evenings.

However Baguio has an exceptionally long and difficult rainy season extending from May through September. During this time it rains almost every day, often heavily and often for long periods of time. Baguio is also prone to major storms and typhoons during the rainy season. Baguio is also located on a fault line and is in danger of a major earth quake. The last major earth quake occurred in 1992 and more than a thousand people died. Of course no one knows when the next major earth quake will occur.

Because of the huge difference in weather quality between the dry and rainy seasons the population of Baguio shrinks and swells dramatically between the rainy and dry seasons.

Another problem that pertains mainly to down town Baguio and the major streets is the air quality. Baguio has a large number of diesel powered jeepneys (small buses), and these jeepneys spew out large quantities of black diesel smoke. The Philippines is supposed to have emissions control and testing, but obviously it is not enforced very well.

Above and beyond the weather and air quality Baguio is a reasonably nice and clean city. It is fairly complete having nice restaurants, night life, sporting facilities and a major SM mall. If you are a tennis player it has a wonderful government run tennis club where you can just show up to play, and they will set up the match for you. If you are a golfer there are two nice 18 hole golf courses.

If you travel outside the city there is some spectacular mountain scenery that is truly breath taking. Also outside of town is a nice country club and a living/sporting facility known as Camp John Hay. These are where the golf courses are. If you are a person of means you can live in Camp John Hay or the country club which are upscale PRA approved facilities.

There are a reasonable number of Expats living in Baguio, but not as many as you might think. I guess, unless you really hate hot weather, and that is major factor for you, there are better choices. Many Expats don't want to live here because they want to be near the ocean. Baguio is very isolated and going somewhere else (like to Manila) involves either taking a plane, or taking a long and arduous car or bus trip. Many people don't want to live permanently in Baguio because of the long and difficult rainy season.

There is one other problem with Baguio. It is not something you will notice as a casual visitor, but something you will definitely notice if you live here for a long period of time.

The population of Baguio is made up of about half people that have immigrated from other parts of the Philippines and half indigenous mountain people. A large group of the indigenous mountain people are from a tribe called Igorots. These people make up a large percentage of local government and the legal system. Igorots are different from other Filipino groups. They are not as easy going and relaxed as most Filipinos. Igorots have a history of tribal feuding and revenge and unfortunately some of this has spilled into modern society. Igorots have a very short fuse. They are quick to anger and slow to forgive. Just keep in mind you have to be very careful when dealing with Igorots.

## Topic viii: *Dumaguete*

**Rizal Blvd, along the ocean, downtown Dumaguete**

Dumaguete, the capital of Negros Oriental, just south of Cebu island, used to be a small city, but it is growing rapidly and now must be put in the category of medium size city. In just the three years I have been here I have seen a considerable increase in population and traffic. Dumaguete now has a McDonalds, and sometime in 2009 the first major mall (Robinsons) will be open for business. It might be kind of funny to mention McDonalds as a big deal, but McDonalds and Malls are kind of the water markers for a growing city in the Philippines. With the opening of McDonalds and the Robinson Mall you could say Dumageute has arrived as a real city.

The rap against Dumaguete used to be that it was lacking in some areas. Lacking in good night life, lacking in good restaurants, lacking nice movie theaters and lacking a mall. As Dumageute is growing this is changing and Dumaguete is becoming more of a dynamic and complete city. The opening of the Mall in 2009 should help a lot.

Dumaguete, a coastal city, also has a number of beaches and beach resorts in the area. Some of the resorts are quite nice, but the beaches themselves are nothing to write home about. Dumaguete has a number of "ok" beaches but no great beaches.

If you are a sports minded person there are also a number of tennis courts, golf courses and badminton facilities available. The golf courses, although available, are far from world class and if golf is your main hobby Dumaguete may not be the best place for you.

As far as night life goes, well Dumageute has a few "ok" places but it is not the place to be if night life is a big priority for you. If you are interested in DOEs, well Dumageute has them, but they are not of the same beauty or quality as in places such as Cebu, Makati, Angeles or Sabang.

Dumaguete has a surprisingly large Expat population and this is because there are a lot of good things about Dumaguete. Dumaguete is known as the "city of gentle people", and I think there is some truth to this. By and large the locals are friendly and laid back and avoid confrontation and trouble. The police here are also very good about avoiding confrontation and not making big deals out of little deals. The police here are interested in preventing major crimes, not in hassling the common person.

Dumaguete, because of some quirk of nature which I don't understand, has probably the best weather in the Philippines. Unlike other locations in the Philippines there is no real rainy season here. It rains all year round, but seldom too much. When it does rain, it tends to rain mainly at night, or in quick afternoon bursts. It's almost like there is a rain God here in Dumaguete and he (or she) is very polite. It is also extremely rare for a typhoon to pass over Dumaguete.

Dumaguete also has, unlike some cities in the Philippines, an abundant supply of pretty decent water. Most of the locals have no qualms about drinking tap water, although most Expats still shy away from this practice.

Dumaguete is a university town and has a number of universities including Silliman University which is considered a fine school. Dumaguete also has two decent medical centers that are fine for normal everyday medical problems but definitely not fine for major or unusual medical problems.

Dumaguete is also known as the motorcycle capital of the Philippines. Probably because of the mild weather motorcycles are very popular here and make up the majority of the traffic. If you enjoy riding a motorcycle you will feel right at home here.

To summarize, Dumaguete is a fine and pleasant place to live with a large Expat community. If you want a pleasant place to live Dumageute is a good choice. However if you are into excitement, fine restaurants, great night life and world class golf courses, Dumaguete is not your best choice.

## Topic ix: *Davao City*

When people talk about living in Davao City the first thing that usually comes up is the "rumor" about the vigilante system in place. Before I go on let me give a disclaimer. I have no proof whatsoever that what I am about to tell you is true. That being said, I have heard the story so often from so many different people that I would be surprised if it were not true.

According to the rumor Davao City has an active and strong vigilante group in place. They don't tolerate bad people such as drug dealers, drug addicts or other types of trouble makers. In most cases they give people a warning. Get out of Davao City within a week or ELSE. In extreme cases they may not give any warning. From talking to people I don't get the sense that the vigilante group is out of control. They only act when they are sure of the circumstances. They are not interested in hassling the normal law abiding citizens. They keep a low profile.

Well is this a good thing? Well morally it's up to you to decide. But I can tell you that most of the citizens of Davao City are very happy with the system. Davao City is one of the safest cities in the Philippines.

Besides being safe, Davao City is clean, well run and complete. By complete I mean it has all the amenities like malls and nice bars and restaurants, sporting facilities, etc. Personally I think Davao City is a very nice place to live.

There is, however, a problem. Davao city is located in Mindanao. Davao city itself is a Christian city. However, much of Mindanao is Muslim and these areas are dangerous for foreigners. Thus if you live in Davao City you may feel like a prisoner trapped within the city. If you want to travel and explore you will have to take a trip to another island.

## Topic x: *Puerto Galera/Sabang*

Located about 150 km south of Manila on the island of Mindoro is the town of Puerto Galera. Of all the places listed in this "best places for Expats to live" chapter, Puerto Galera is the only one I have not visited. I hope that will change in the next version of this book! Anyway, I can't talk from personal experience but I have heard a lot of good things about Puerto Galera. It's supposed to be very beautiful with many nice beaches and water sports. Some people consider it the diving and snorkeling capital of the Philippines. One of the beaches, Sabang Beach, is supposed to have an X rated night life scene rivaling that of Angeles. From what I understand there is a  small but growing Expat community living in Puerto Galera.

## Topic xi: *Tagaytay*

Tagaytay is located about 70km south of Manila. Tagaytay is basically a large mountain of volcanic origin with a large flat top about 600 meters high and a large crater in the center. At the bottom of the crater is a lake, and in the center of the lake is a volcano. It's this volcano that gave birth to Tagaytay, but this volcano is sunk down below the surrounding area of Tagaytay. Geologically speaking it very unusual and beautiful.

Advertisers promoting Tagaytay as a vacation or living destination often like to say it has a cool climate similar to Baguio. This is an exaggeration. While it is definitely true that Tagaytay is a few degrees cooler than the lowlands, it is nothing like Baguio in terms of average temperature. It still gets hot in Tagaytay, it rarely gets hot in Baguio. Still, even the few degrees difference between Tagaytay and the lowlands is significant in terms of comfort.

Tagaytay is not an exciting place. In fact it may be exactly the opposite. But Tagaytay is a beautiful place, particularly near the top. From an Expat's point of view the main attraction to Tagaytay is the numerous exclusive upscale PRA approved residential communities located near the top. These communities typically have all the "fixings" like golf courses, tennis courts, etc, etc. If you want to live in a nice, quiet, cool, beautiful and safe upscale PRA approved facility not too far from Manila you may want to take a look at Tagaytay.

One thing to keep in mind is that the volcano located in the center of Tagaytay at the bottom of the crater is still classified as active. The last eruption was as recently as 1977. The last major eruption was in 1911 and killed over 1300 people. This may be an issue when considering whether to fork over a large amount of money for your beautiful PRA approved residence.

## Topic xii: *Boracay*

**White Beach Boracay**

Boracay is a small island off the North West tip of Panay Island. There is no commercial airport on Boracay. The quickest way to Boracay is to take a flight to nearby Caticlan on North West Panay Island. From there take a shuttle boat to Boracay. Boracay has one proper pier, but this pier can not always be used. Depending on the time of the year and the weather the boat may have to disembark on the side of the island opposite the pier and you may have to jump out of a boat into two feet of water and walk the last 20 or 30 meters to the island. There are porters to carry your luggage, and if you are not embarrassed, you can even choose to be carried yourself so that you don't get wet.

Boracay is only a small island about 7km long and 1 to 2 km wide. Despite it's small size Boracay is probably the most famous and popular vacation destination in the Philippines.

Boracay is a great place to play and have fun. The most popular spot in Boracay is White Beach, a strip of white sand beach about 2km long. Along the entire length of white beach, 50 meters or so inland, are hotels, restaurants, bars and entertainment.

On the beach itself many water sports are available such as para sailing, wind surfing and jet skiing. Other parts of the island are known for it's snorkeling and diving locations. There is a certain electricity about Boracay. It is a vibrant place.

Visitors to Boracay include a nice mix of foreigners and wealthy Filipinos. Boracay is mainly intended as a vacation spot, but there are a small percentage of people living there, including a small Expat community. If you love the beach and the party life style, and you have the money to do it, you might consider Boracay as a place to live.

# Chapter 16: What Kind of Domicile?

The following is a general guideline as to how you might want to acclimate yourself relative to your living situation. The general idea is take your time and don't rush to commit yourself. Hold off on commitment. Thus I recommend an approach of slow increasing commitment.

This is just a general guideline, it is by no means written in stone. If you feel secure going into a situation, by all means ignore the advice. Just be careful not to get yourself into a situation you regret.

## Topic i: *First Week*

When you arrive in a new location, especially after a long journey it's very tiring to look for the best deal in a hotel. I suggest the first night you just take the first reasonably acceptable facility you find. Pay for one day only. You have no idea if you are getting a good deal or if you are in the location of town you want to be in. You can use one of the standard travel books to try and have a couple of choices picked out ahead of time. Resist the taxi or pedicab's advice as to where you might want to stay. They have no idea what you really want. If they offer a particular place most likely it is because they get a commission for bringing someone to that hotel.

The next day search for a good deal in a normal hotel. It's so much easier when you are not dragging around luggage, when you are not exhausted and when you can see things in the light of day.

## Topic ii: *Short Term – One Week to Two Months*

A hotel is ok for a short period of time but it adds up to a lot of money over a longer time, plus it's very confining. If you look around you should be able to find a little apartment or apartelle that you can rent by the month. In particular you can try to make a deal with the owner of an empty unit. This is usually good for them, they can at least get some income while trying to find somebody for the long term.

## Topic iii: *Medium Term – Two Months to a Year*

Find yourself a decent apartment or house to rent. The cost is so much lower than a hotel, and so much lower than a similar unit in the USA. The cost, of course, varies by location but in most locations except Manila you can get a small but comfortable apartment for as little as P6000 a month. For p15000 a month you can rent a house or large apartment in good condition in a good area. The important thing is, rent first. Don't rush into buying a house or property to build on. Make sure you are acclimated and know what you are doing before making that kind of decision. I've seen a lot of people rush into buying a house and/or property and then regret it.

## Topic iv: *Long Term – A Year or Longer*

### ◆ Renting an Apartment or House

Even if you plan to live permanently in the Philippines there is no need to rush into buying or building a house. There are a lot of advantages to just renting. Renting is inexpensive in the Philippines and of course if your situation changes or you decide you want to live somewhere else you won't be saddled with the burden of trying to sell your house. For me, unless your heart is really set on owning a house, I think it's just more prudent to rent. Even if you like living in a house you can usually rent a very nice house for about P20,000 ($400) a month.

### ♦ Buying or Building a House

**Typical Expat Dream House**

No matter the dangers, no matter the disadvantages, there will always be people with their heart set on buying or building a house. Well it's understandable why this is so tempting. For about $200,000 dollars you can build a dream house -a house that might be worth close to a million dollars in a decent area in the USA. Even for $100,000 dollars you can buy land and build a very nice house. Even for $50,000 dollars you can buy land and build a respectable house. If you want to buy a house you can do even better. I will discuss the reasons for this later.

Buying or building a house may seem like a wonderful thing to do but it is fraught with dangers. The main problem is this: you can't buy property in your own name. In the Philippines foreigners are not allowed to own property. This mean you will have to put the house in your Wife's name. Now everybody wants to think that their relationship will be perfect and last forever – or until we die, but we all know this is not always the case. Things change. Relationships change. Things don't always work out. If your relationship goes south you will be at a big disadvantage when it comes to your house and property.

Now you might ask, isn't there any way to protect yourself? The answer is yes, there are all sorts of schemes to protect yourself. There are fancy things you can do like set up corporations or you can own the house on the land but not the land itself. The most simple and common means to protect yourself is to set up a long term lease. For example the house is in your wife's name but you immediately execute a 50 years lease allowing you to live in the house for 50 years. A 50 year lease is the longest lease a foreigner can execute allowed by Philippine law. I won't go into all the schemes because frankly I don't understand them all. You should and must talk to a reputable lawyer to protect yourself as much as possible. Despite your most careful precautions, these protections only go so far. Let me give you an example. As I mentioned the most common scheme to protect yourself is to have your wife own the property, but for you to sign a 50 year lease on the property giving you the right to live there for at least 50 years. Now, suppose you your marriage turns bad. Well you have the right to stay there, but probably not the right to kick your wife out of the house. Thus it can turn into a nightmare scenario where your estranged wife brings in her relatives to live there with her and your life is miserable. Having a 50 year lease does not give you any rights to sell the property. It's not like in most western countries where you can get a divorce and the property is split. In the Philippines there is no divorce, so there is no settlement of property. It is not uncommon to see foreigners with marriages turned bad just walk away from their investment. I've seen it happen on more than a few occasions.

Now in addition to the nightmare scenario of having your marriage turn completely bad, there is also a more subtle effect resulting from putting the property in your wife's name, namely this: it shifts the balance of power. A marriage between an older, wealthy (at least wealthy by Philippine standards) foreigner and a young sexy Filipina does not have the same dynamics as two people the same age of the same culture falling in love. I know it's hard to stomach the reality, you want to believe otherwise, but you have to accept that these marriages are somewhat of a contract, with each party getting what they want. The man gets the companionship and sex of a young sexy woman and the woman gets to live a much better and comfortable life. Hopefully there is also love there, but whether you want to admit or not, that underlying implicit contract is the glue that keeps things together.

Now, in this arrangement it's the man that normally holds the balance of power. This is because it is the man that controls the money. Suppose, for example, that the man has an affair and is caught by his wife. Well there might be some screaming and shouting and broken furniture, but ultimately, what can the wife do? She can't divorce him, because there is no divorce. She does not want to leave him because she does not want to go back to her former life of being poor. So, ultimately she has no choice but to accept it.

Now suppose that the man spends $200,000 dollars to build his dream home and puts it in his wife's name. All of the sudden the balance of power shifts dramatically. Now she has this over him. Now for example, if she catches him in an affair she can do all sorts of things, from filing legal proceedings to have him extradited to his own country to more simple horrors like inviting all her relatives to live in the house.

So I'm not saying don't build or buy your dream house. Many Expats do and sometimes it works out just fine. I'm just saying be aware of the dangers and don't do it unless you feel very secure in your relationship.

Another issue to consider is what happens if your wife dies before you do. Do you then own the property? The answer is no, and unless you are careful and set it up properly, the property may pass on to Filipino heirs of your diseased wife. There is however a way to protect yourself from that. Make sure that the buying contract has your name on it, and that it states that you are the one providing the funds for the purchase. Of course you must see a lawyer for details. If you do this, then under Filipino law, you have the right to live in the house for "a reasonable amount of time" after your wife dies, while trying to sell the property. The proceeds of the sale will go to you. What the definition of a "reasonable amount of time" is, I have no idea.

So far I have discussed the negative practical and social aspects of buying property in your wife's name. There is also a more positive social side to buying a house in your wife's name. This is a gift to her and her family. Most likely you will die before her. Maybe you are 60 and she is only 22. She will probably have a long life ahead of her after you die. If you love her, or at least care about her, you will want to set something up so she is provided for once you die. One of the best ways to do this is to buy a house in your wife's name.

In addition to the social implications involved in buying a house you must also be very careful about the property deed and make sure you are not scammed. There are several levels of property deeds, ranging from the low level quit claim type deeds, all the way up to government backed and guaranteed deeds. Again, make sure you get a reputable lawyer.

### ♦ Buying a Ready Made House

There are some very compelling reasons for buying a ready made (already built) house. For one thing you don't have to worry about the possible nightmare scenarios associated with dishonest or incompetent builders. Above and beyond this you can often get a much better deal buying an existing house than building your own. This is especially true for high end houses. This is because there are a lot of foreigners that come to the Philippines and build their dream houses. Then circumstances change. Maybe the man dies, or they need money, or the marriage falls apart, whatever. They need to sell the house. Now when these high end houses are put up for sale there is a very limited market for them. This is because very few Filipinos can afford them and many foreigners will have their heart set on building their own dream house rather than buying a house. Low demand of course drives the cost of the house way down. Often you can buy an existing high end house at a much lower cost than what the original owner spent to build it. If you buy a house for a good deal then there is a much better chance that if you decide to sell it you will get your money back or even make a profit.

### ♦ Buying Property and Building a House

First off, as I mentioned above, don't go into the project thinking you can make a profit if you have to sell. Unless you are very lucky chances are, that if you have to sell, you will lose a lot of money.

Second, be very careful about each step of the process. Make sure the land deed is solid. Make sure you get a reputable architect. Make sure you get a reputable builder. Of course use a reputable lawyer to make sure the land deed is good. When choosing an architect or builder look for another Expat or wealthy Filipino who recently built a house and is happy with the result. Use the same architect and builder. Make sure the architect is willing to be on site a large percentage of the time.

Finally, and in my opinion this is very important, be involved in the process at every step of the way. Don't just go about living your life in a separate location and expect that the job will get done right. Unfortunately Filipino workers are very prone to take advantage if they feel they are not being watched. It is best if you are on site almost all the time while they are working. Ask questions, tell them how you want things done, get involved. The more you understand about the process and the more you question, the better. Keep everybody on their toes. Make sure there is somebody there that can translate between English and their local language. It's very hard if nobody can speak English. Your spouse can help you in this regard.

As far as construction goes, I am not a builder but I can point out a few things that you should watch out for.

I suggest you avoid wood as much as possible. Of course it will cost more but if you expect to live there for a long period of time it is worth it. A house made of wood will be eaten alive by termites and other insects. The termite problem is very bad in the Philippines. The termites are very clever and ravenous. Even if the foundation and walls are cement if the floors and roof structure is wood the termites will find a way. They will even attack wood doors, cabinets and moldings.

When designing the interior and exterior try to avoid any holes that allow access to insects or rodents. This means all places where pipes and wires enter or exit should be properly sealed. If there is a way in the insects and rodents will find it.

Another thing to think about in your design is air conditioning and insulation. Most foreigners need air conditioning. The Philippines is a hot country. You need a place to escape. Unless you are rich I don't suggest central air conditioning, it will be very expensive. Thus it is best if you give some thought to how much air conditioning you plan to have. Is just your bed room sufficient? Perhaps a bedroom and a small study/TV room? Something like that. Now something that most people don't give much thought to is the concept of insulation. Insulation is more commonly associated with cold climates rather than hot climates. However, insulation can make a huge difference in your air conditioning efficiency. It's well worth it as you can buy a smaller air conditioner and run it for a lot less money. You will make your money back from the cost of insulation quite quickly. I have personal experience with this as I bought a decent size AC for my room and was disappointed to find that in the day time it could not keep the room cool. I added insulation and it made a huge difference.

Prior to the construction of your mostly concrete house I suggest you educate yourself about concrete. Sometimes the words concrete and cement are used interchangeably, but they are not the same. Concrete is a mixture of sand, gravel and cement. Cement is the glue that holds it all together. Learning about concrete is (in my nerdish opinion) actually pretty interesting. I used to think all concrete was created equal. Nothing could be further from the truth. I have literally seen some structures dissolve during a flood because the sand level was too high and the cement level too low. Filipino contractors often like to try and save money my keeping the cement level (the most expensive part of the mixture) low. Make sure you specify the quality of concrete.

Well, to sum up, there are many dangers and problems associated with buying a lot and building your dream house, but that does not mean you should not do it. Many do, and many are very happy about the result. You can build a fantastic house for just a small percentage of what it would cost you in the USA.

### ♦ Philippine Retirement Authority (PRA) Approved Residential Communities and Condos

Earlier, in the section about Visa's and permanent residence, I discussed the basics of the Special Residential Retirement Visa (SRRV) and PRA approved residential facilities.

In that section I describe how the SRRV might be a good choice for those Expats that either can't or don't want to get married to a Filipina woman.

But now let's put aside the questions about visas and permanent residence. Instead let's explore what it's like to live in a PRA approved community and if you will enjoy it there.

Depending on the kind of person you are, you may love living in such a community, or in fact you may hate it. It is very different than living in a normal Philippine city or neighborhood.

There are a number of different legal vehicles that PRA communities use. You may be purchasing a condo, or in fact you may just have a long 50 year lease. There are other options as well. But basically they all amount to the fact that you dish out a minimum of $50,000 dollars and more likely $100,000 or even more, and then you get to live the rest of your life in the PRA community, assuming nothing goes wrong, like war, earth quake, political upheaval or the community goes bankrupt.

What if you want to get out of the community, can you get your money back? Basically it is like any other investment. You have to sell it to get your money back. The value might go up or down, and you might have a darn hard time selling it at what you feel is a fair price. If you do sell your investment you also lose your SRRV visa.

These PRA accredited communities are typically upscale. You will get to live in a nice house, in a gated area, with 24 hour security. The grounds are usually well kept up and very beautiful. You will get to enjoy all the amenities of the community which will usually have a golf course, tennis courts, a club house, swimming pool, restaurant, work out area and various other amenities.

So, sounds pretty good, any problem? Well for the right kind of person it is pretty good. If for example you love golf and want to play every day and you are content to just hang out all the time with your Expat friends, well it's a pretty good life.

However, some people they may find this life a bit boring after a while. These communities are nothing like the "real world". It's basically a community of rich or semi rich people (at least by Philippine standards) that have isolated themselves from the rest of Philippine society.

Of course there is nothing to say you can't leave the community and go have fun at the nearest city. You are not locked inside! But the problem is most of these communities are a bit of a distance from the city. Some more than others. Of course the ones that are most near the cities are going to be the most expensive.

As I see it there are a couple of other problems associated with these communities. If you do wind up either marrying or living with a Filipina girl she might be quite unhappy in one of these communities. She might feel like she is out of place, that everybody is very high society, and that she does not fit in.

The final problem is that your beautiful home in your beautiful community can't be handed down after you die. You should talk to the PRA office to understand all the rules associated with this topic. It is likely your wife can continue to live in the area after you die, but after that, that's it. This would be especially and obviously true in the case of the 50 year lease. In any case, even if the unit did go over to your wife after you died she probably could not do very much with it except try to sell it. These communities usually have very strict rules about who and how many people can live in the unit. Your wife will not be able to invite her family clan down to enjoy the good living. Ain't gona happen. So if you are going to marry a Filipina woman, and you want to leave her a gift of house and property after you die, this is not the way to go.

For the right person, this is a good deal. For me, I would rather live in or near a city and be part of the Philippine society. If I was not married and wanted to avail of the SRRV, I would rather buy a "use of facilities" share and enjoy the golf and tennis and live somewhere else.

If you want an SRRV, and don't need to live in a residential type country club community you might also be able to buy a PRA approved condominium within a city. Again, talk to the PRA office for details.

# Chapter 17: Maids (Helpers)

**Filipina Helper**

One of the great conveniences of life in the Philippines, available to anybody reasonably well off, or even of modest means, is the availability of low cost maids (or - more politically correct – Helpers).

A wealthy Filipino family might easily have four helpers running around. One for taking care of the kids (yaya), one for cooking and buying food at the market, one for cleaning and laundry and a man for driving and simple house hold maintenance chores. So a typical wealthy Filipino family household may consist of four generations of family, plus a few single brothers and sisters and four or more helpers.

The typical Expat can't handle such a zoo. The western Expat needs more privacy. Some Expats choose not to have a helper due to privacy or other issues. However, most Expats, especially those married or living with a steady girl friend, do avail themselves of a helper. Most Expats choose to have only one helper. A small household consisting of only an Expat and his Filipina wife only needs one helper.

A Helper is one of those conveniences  you never knew you needed until you came to the Philippines. Then after you get used to a helper, they are hard to live without. Need a glass of water? Why bother to get up and get it, call the helper. Have a craving for a candy bar but there are none in the house and it's raining? No problem, have the helper run down to the local store and buy one. Finished eating? No need to clean up after yourself. Just leave the table and the helper will clean up. Yup, having a helper is part of the good life in the Philippines.

So, what is the cost of a helper? Well, monetarily, not much. Typically a helper's salary is around p1500   ($30) a month, perhaps a little more in a bigger city, a little less in the provinces. In addition, of course, you will have to buy for her all items necessary for normal day to day living such as food and toiletries. As far as food goes you are not expected to share your expensive "western" food with her. She is happy to eat dried or local fish, a little pork, a few vegetables and a lot of rice. Typically, all things considered, salary and expenses, figure a helper will cost you around p3000 to p5000 ($60-$100) a month. That's not a lot of money for all the convenience you are getting. Helpers start their careers as young as age 16 and can continue into old age. Most Expats feel most comfortable with younger helpers in their late teens or early 20s.

So why are these helpers willing to work for next to nothing? Well, several reasons.

First of all, what else are they going to do. Typically these girls are uneducated and not able to land normal jobs. If they stay at home they are just a burden to their family.

Second of all, they usually lead a more comfortable and healthy life as a helper than they do at home. These girls are typically from very poor families often living in bamboo homes without electricity or running water. By working for a wealthier family they get to live in a comfortable home with better food, running water and electricity and watch TV when they have finished working.

Finally, even though their salary is so low, they still take pride helping their family. Typically a helper will only keep 500 or so of their salary for themselves and send the rest home to their family. Basically the helper needs no money for herself as all normal living expenses are paid.

The quality of life for a helper depends greatly on the bosses she works for. Most bosses realize that these people are human beings and deserve some quality of life. In many cases these helpers almost become a part of the family. However, some "masters" take terrible advantage, basically treating their helpers as slaves, forcing them to work long hours with no time off and treating them with disdain. Interestingly (if that is the right word) many of these girls accept this fate and continue to work in these circumstances – it is sad to see.

As an Expat used to western thinking your idea might be to treat your helper so well and with such respect that they will be grateful to you, and thus work hard and be loyal and honest.

Unfortunately such thinking does not usually work well in the Philippines. This is a good time to say something about the attitude of bosses towards low level workers, and the attitude of low level workers towards their bosses. Low level workers in the Philippines do not think the same way as their counterparts in western countries. The appropriate cliché is, "give'm an inch, they'll take a foot". In Filipino culture if you give a worker a chance to take advantage of you, they probably will.

As a boss, (both for Filipino and Expat bosses) there is a constant balancing act. Of course you want to be reasonable and treat your employees with appropriate respect, and not make their life miserable. On the other hand if you treat them too nice, or you don't work them hard, they will lose respect. This is a hard concept for most Expats to assimilate and many Expats make the mistake of treating their help "too nice".

Anyway, getting back to the subject of household helpers, is there any down side to having a helper? Well unfortunately, the answer is Yes.

Let's start with the obvious, loss of privacy. Many Expats feel a distinct loss of privacy by always having a helper around. What if you want to have hot sex with your wife on the living room floor. You can't, you have a helper! Even in your own bedroom your wife might feel embarrassed to let loose with a scream during orgasm because you have a helper. Sex is definitely one of the areas that can feel constrained by always having a helper. One way to reduce this factor is to buy, build or rent a house or apartment with an upstairs and downstairs. Make it clear to your helper that she is only to go upstairs with permission.

Another fact of life about helpers is that you can never find one that's perfect. They don't exist. Maybe they work hard, but they are not honest. Or they are honest but they don't work hard. Or they are honest and work hard but are unpleasant and always have a scowl on their face. Or maybe they are honest and work hard and are pleasant, but they are dumb, and always making mistakes. There's always a problem and you have to accept some level of imperfection. If these girls were perfect, they wouldn't be maids.

If you have to fire a helper this can be an awkward process. You have to consider the reason for her being fired. If she is just incompetent and did nothing grievously wrong and you feel she is honest, then make up a story that has nothing to do with your dissatisfaction, and give her a month or two warning. Then give her at least one month severance pay.

If there is a serious problem that requires her immediate dismissal, such as you catch her stealing something, then just be firm and have her leave immediately. You will still have to pay expenses for her to get back to her province. You should probably still offer her a month severance pay based on the condition that she leave immediately and not cause any problem. Don't hand her the severance pay until she is packed, has handed you her keys and is out the door. You may want to consider changing the locks.

Another problem with a helper is the sense of responsibility you have towards her. For example, suppose your helper develops a major medical problem. What do you do? You have no formal obligation to spend large amounts of money to help her, but on the other hand, what is your alternative? Just send her back to her province to fend for herself knowing perfectly well she doesn't have the money to get healthy again? Knowing that perhaps she could even die? You hope something like this does not happen but if it does it can put you in a very difficult position.

Ok, so suppose you have considered all the positives and negatives of getting a helper and you decide to go ahead and hire one. How do you find one? Well it's usually by word of mouth. Let all your friends and neighbors know you are looking for a helper and you are sure to get numerous recommendations. The problem is, how can you possibly know the quality of your helper before meeting them? Sometimes they have to make a long trip from the province and they don't want to come for nothing. Even if you talk with them, sometimes you can't tell their quality until they actually start to work for you. You don't want to commit yourself to a helper only to find out a few days later you can't stand them. If you fire them after only a couple of days it's terribly embarrassing and everybody loses face.

After making a couple of mistakes in this regard I have developed the following technique which seems to work well and which I suggest you might want to use.

When somebody wants to recommend a helper and after discussing her circumstance you feel you might want to try this helper, instead of just saying yes, give the following story:

*"Well I would like to hire her but somebody else is already requesting the job. I'll tell you what. Since the other helper can't be available for another week why don't you have your helper come down for a one week tryout. I will pay her transportation from the province to here and back. In addition I will pay her salary for a week. After the week your helper will go back home and I will try the other girl. Then I will make a decision."*

Of course the "other helper" is make believe. If after a week you like the helper, just have her stay. If you don't like the helper tell her that her one week tryout is over and you will let her know your decision next week. Since you paid all her costs and gave her a salary and told everybody ahead of time what would happen, nobody loses face. Of course she goes home and that is the end of it. In Philippine culture you would not contact her to let her know she did not have the job. You would just never contact her and she would get the idea.

# Chapter 18: Dangers in the Philippines

## Topic i: *Physical Danger*

The Philippines has been listed for many years on the US State Departments list of dangerous places to travel. This is a little unfortunate because as a result many people get the impression the Philippines is a dangerous place to travel. To be honest I really don't understand this listing. I realize there are some dangerous places in the Philippines like Muslim controlled areas of Mindanao, or out of the way isolated mountain regions. The answer to that problem is simple. Don't travel in the dangerous areas.

In general I find the Philippines to be a reasonably safe place. I have been here for eight years and personally have not had any problem. I have never been robbed or accosted. No one has ever pulled a knife or gun on me. Nobody has ever thrown a punch at me. The worst thing that ever happened was that I had my cell phone pick pocketed. Most Expats will tell you that the Philippines is safe. In general Filipinos are not a violent people.

Now, that being said, it's a reality that no place is 100% safe. Of course you will hear the occasional horror story. Of course you have to behave in a prudent way. Don't go alone to isolated spots by yourself, especially at night. Don't flash large amounts of money or wear expensive jewelry. Don't be antagonistic and cause arguments and tensions.

Speaking about flashing money, there is one story I have heard repeated many times. It concerns withdrawing large amounts of cash at a bank. Supposedly there are sometimes "spies" at the banks watching to see if anybody withdraws a large amount of money. If they see anybody doing so they message their partners who then follow the foreigner hoping for an opportunity to rob them. In general you should never carry a large amount of cash with you.

When you choose a place to live, don't choose an isolated house or apartment in the middle of nowhere with no neighbors around you. Such places are targets for thieves. Choose a place within a community with neighbors who get to know you and will watch over you.

Of course bad things occasionally happen everywhere. You hear plenty of horror stories about bad things that happen in the USA. The point is this:

It's not that the Philippines is completely safe, it's that in my opinion the Philippines is no more dangerous than the USA, perhaps less so. For me, physical danger is not an issue when considering a trip to the Philippines.

## Topic ii: *Scam Artist Danger*

Unfortunately some Filipinos look at Westerners as a means to extract money. There will always be people who try to scam you out of money. It's up to you not to be naive and not be fooled.

Here is an example of another non physical danger. Suppose you are involved in a traffic accident and a Filipino gets injured. Suppose the accident is not even your fault. Still many Filipinos will see this as an opportunity to extract money, and in many cases they are successful to at least some degree. For example suppose the accident is clearly not your fault but regardless they file a suit against you. Many foreigners would rather just settle for a few thousand dollars rather than be dragged through the Philippine legal system. I will describe this kind of danger at length in the section titled "Laws, the legal system and staying out of trouble".

# Chapter 19: How Much Does it Cost to Live in the Philippines

### Topic i: *General Discussion*

People are always asking, "How much does it cost to live in the Philippines?". Can I live on $500 a month? Can I retire there with only $100,000? Well unfortunately there is no definite answer. The answer is, it depends. It depends on exactly where you live in the Philippines and it depends on the kind of life style you want.

I usually give people a general rule of thumb. If you are from a typical western country like the USA, calculate the cost of the life style you want in the USA, and whatever that is, divide by 3. However, this is only a very general guide.

What makes the calculation difficult is that you can't just apply a percentage to everything. You can't just say everything in the Philippines cost three times less than in the USA. If does not work that way. Some things, such as labor costs, are vastly cheaper in the Philippines. Other things, such as imported luxury items are actually more expensive.

Below is a table comparing the costs of some things in the Philippines to their costs in the USA. This of course is only ballpark since costs vary so much in both locations and they are always changing, but this table will give you a general idea.

| Description | Typical USA Cost $ | Typical Philippine Cost in $ |
|---|---|---|
| One hour labor to fix problem with Car | $80 | $4 |
| Beer at a bar | 3 | 1 |
| Hard drink at a bar. | 6 | 2 |
| Six pack local beer from a store. | 6 | 3 |
| Inexpensive bottle of wine | Same | Same |
| Bottle of high alcohol low quality rum or brandy | 5 | 1 |
| Pack of Cigarettes | 5 | 1 |
| Meal for two at medium quality restaurant | 30 | 10 |
| Small studio apartment in decent area | 600 | 80 |
| Large three bedroom apartment in decent area | 1400 | 250 |
| Rent nice three bedroom house | 2000 | 350 |
| Gasoline for car | Same | Same |
| Good quality tennis racket on sale | 100 | 200 |
| Haircut at medium quality parlor | 15 | 2 |
| Nice Tee shirt | 10 | 3 |
| Pair of no name Jeans | 30 | 10 |
| New Economy car | 14000 | 10000 |
| Minimum yearly insurance for a car | 800 | 60 |
| Minimum yearly insurance for a motorcycle | 300 | 20 |
| Miscellaneous cart load of typical groceries | 150 | 100 |
| Entrance to Movie theater | 8 | 1 |
| One hour massage | 60 | 5 |
| Decent quality name brand electronics goods | Same | same |
| Low cost Chinese electronic goods | Not avail | cheap |
| One Hour of tennis at a tennis club | 30 | 2 |

| | | |
|---|---|---|
| 18 holes of golf at a nice course | 150 | 30 |
| Buy a nice 3 bedroom house in a nice area | 300,000 | 100,000 |
| Buy a minimal house in a mediocre area | 60,000 | 10,000 |
| Buy property and build your dream house | 1,000,000 | 200,000 |
| One month of cable TV | 50 | 10 |
| Uninsured 15 minute doctors visit | 100 | 5 |
| Dental cleaning | 50 | 10 |
| Drugs and medication | Same | same |
| Appliances like Refrigerators and AC | Same | Same |
| One night at a low cost hotel | 50 | 12 |
| One night at a high end hotel | 200 | 60 |
| One night at a luxury resort hotel | 300 | 80 |

So to really figure out how much it will cost you to live you sort of have to figure out the kinds of things you want to do, and the relative costs of these things.

You might wonder why a new car costs less in the Philippines. There are several factors such as shorter distance from Japan and Korea (where most Philippine cars come from), lower labor and storage costs and different (less) safety standards. For example air bags are not required. A given model of new car in the Philippines will not be exactly the same as the corresponding model in the USA.

The other thing to keep in mind is that there are inexpensive alternatives that exist in the Philippines that don't even exist in a western country. I will give three examples

First suppose you want your monthly rent or residence expense to be extremely small. I don't even know how you would go about that in the USA. Rent a house with many people? In the Philippines they have a concept called "bed spacer". You are literally just renting a bed space in a room with other beds. The beds are typically bunk beds, or sometimes even triple beds.

You have a shared bathroom and a shared kitchen. Sometimes a shared TV room. It typically costs about P1000 ($20) per month to rent a bed space. There is no way you could reside in the USA for $20 dollars a month. The only thing that cheap in the USA is a place in the gutter. By the way, if as a Westerner, you tried to rent a bed space for yourself, I think you would be laughed out of Philippines!

A second example is low cost transportation. In many places in the USA it's hard to even exist without a car. Even in urban locations where public transportation exists the cost is not all that low.

In the Philippines they have the concept of pedicabs and jeepneys. Pedicabs are basically extremely low cost taxi's. They are motorcycles with side cars. jeepneys are basically informal buses where you just hop on any time you want and hop off any time you want, and pay only a few pesos for the ride. Jeepneys and pedicabs are everywhere in most cities and even in rural areas. It's much easier to get by without your own transportation in the Philippines than in the USA.

A third example concerns having your own permanent full time live in maid (or Helper - more politically correct). The concept as it exists in the Philippines does not really exist in the USA. Helpers were discussed in detail in a previous chapter. For about $30 dollars a month salary plus food you have a full time helper available to you at your beck and call. These women do it because their life as a maid with at least decent food and shelter is better than their alternative.

So the Philippines gives people the opportunity to live in inexpensive ways that do not exist in western countries. That being said, as a Westerner you are unlikely to want to avail of these opportunities (except for the Helper which you will probably want). As a Westerner you will want to live the good life, and even in the Philippines the good life costs money.

So how much does it cost to live in the Philippines? The best way to answer this is to give several scenarios and give an estimate for each scenario.

## Topic ii: *Cost Estimates for Specific Life Style Scenarios*

Please keep In mind that these estimates are only very ball park. They will vary according to your exact habits and tastes. Also, costs change. I can't promise that costs will be the same when you are reading this as when I wrote this. Even so. the following should give you a pretty good idea of how much it will cost to live in the Philippines for your specific life style.

### ♦ Extreme Minimal Existence

This is kind of a hypothetical because no Westerner could stand to live this way, but low salaried Filipinos can and do live this way. You rent a bed spacer for P1000 a month. You eat rice and a little low cost pork, fish or vegetables. You don't go to the doctor, you don't go to the dentist. You have no car or motorcycle. You don't ever pay money to have fun. All your clothes are from second hand shops.

Estimated Cost: $100/month

### ♦ Minimal Acceptable Existence for a Westerner Living by Himself

You rent a small but serviceable studio apartment for p4000. You have fan only, no AC. You don't own any transportation. You eat cheap foods. You only see the dentist or doctor in emergencies. Maybe you have a drink once in a while but you don't go out a whole lot, any fun you have is low cost fun such as going for walks or going to the beach.

Estimated Cost: $400/month.

### ◆ Reasonable Existence for a Westerner Living by Himself

You rent a small but decent place for about P6000 a month. You have an air conditioned room to escape to. You own a motorcycle. You go to the dentist and doctor when needed. You eat out occasionally. You eat decent food. You go to bars and have some drinks. Every once in a while you have some fun with a girl. Maybe you have a hobby like tennis or golf.

Estimated cost: $700/month

### ◆ The Swinger Living the Good Life

You don't want a wife or permanent GF, but you like women. Maybe you enjoy the occasional company of a doe, and you enjoy dating and giving women a good time. You live in a nice P12000 apartment in a nice location. You have a nice car and perhaps a small motorcycle. You eat out and frequent bars often. You don't have a helper because that would cramp your life style, but you have somebody come in a couple of times a week to clean and wash your clothes. You live a very comfortable life style.

Estimated Cost: $1400/month

### ◆ Low End Existence with GF or Wife

If you have a wife or girl friend your existence can't be all that low, or they will leave you! Even the existence I describe here will not be acceptable to many women.

You rent a small but livable place for P6000 a month. You don't have a helper. You don't own transportation. You have fans but no air conditioner. You give your wife or GF an allowance of only a few thousand peso a month. You eat out and go to bars occasionally. You eat decent but low cost foods. You go to dentist and doctor only when really necessary. You don't buy any luxury goods.

Estimated cost: $1000/month

### ♦ Decent Existence with GF or Wife

You rent a decent but small place for P9,000 a month. You have a helper. You have an inexpensive car or motorcycle. You give your wife or GF an allowance of $100 dollars a month to do with as she pleases. You see the doctor and dentist when needed. You go to restaurants and bars occasionally but not that often. You eat healthily but modestly. You air conditioning your bedroom only when you go to sleep. You don't buy luxury items like fancy soaps, conditioners or expensive clothes. You live a simple but comfortable life style.

Estimated cost: $1300/month

### ♦ Good Existence with GF or Wife

You rent a nice place for P12,000 a month. You have a helper. You have an inexpensive car and a motorcycle. You give your wife or GF an allowance of $200 dollars a month to do with as she pleases. You see the doctor and dentist when needed. You have hobbies. You go to restaurants and bars on a regular basis and in general have fun. You eat high quality food. You have air conditioning, phones and Internet hookup. You have cable TV. You buy some luxury items like nice clothes or fancy soaps for your wife.

Estimated cost: $1700/month

### ♦ High End Existence with GF or Wife

You rent a nice house for P20,000 a month. You have a nice car, or maybe even two. You have a small motorcycle. You have at least one helper. You give your wife or GF an allowance of $300 a month. You buy gifts and luxury items for your wife or GF. You have hobbies. You go to nice restaurant and bars often. You furnish your house with nice things.

Estimated Cost $2500/month.

### ◆ Luxury Existence with Wife and Family

You have a wife and two kids. You own a luxury home. Your kids go to privates schools. You have three maids and a driver. You have two dogs and a cat. The house has several air conditioned rooms. You have two nice cars and a motorcycle. You eat at fancy restaurants and have expensive hobbies. Your house is furnished beautifully. You host parties on a regular basis. You swim in your backyard swimming pool.

Estimated Cost: $5000/month.

# Chapter 20: What About My Stuff?  What Should I Take to the Philippines?

When you are finally ready to take the leap and make a new life for yourself in the Philippines, you will have to make some decisions about what to do with your old "stuff", your material possessions presently located in your home country.

In general I don't recommend bringing over large things. The shipping expense will be high, and you are subject to the whims and desires of the customs officials. I will describe all of this in more detail in the sections below.

### Topic i: *Customs Fees and Taxes*

If you try to bring over large expensive items you will probably be hit with large customs fees. I have heard  a lot of nightmare stories about customs officials and their arbitrary ways. If they see a large expensive item they are likely to feel that somebody should make some money from it. In some instances they may be looking for bribes.

### Topic ii: *Motor Vehicles*

I highly recommend that you do not try to transfer your motor vehicle to the Philippines. It's very likely to turn into a nightmare. I know of one case where a person was so discouraged about all the red tape and hassles they put him through that he just gave up and donated his van to the city, figuring he could at least get a little bit of good will out of the deal.

### Topic iii: *Electronic Equipment*

When traveling you are supposed to be able to bring over personal use electronics equipment such as cell phones, Personal Digital Assistants (PDAs), laptops and notebook computers.  As long as these items are yours, and have been in use prior to the trip, there is not supposed to be any custom fee's or taxes. However, if you are bringing over a brand new never used piece of equipment they are allowed to charge customs fees and taxes. Sometimes the amount can be quite significant.

Well, good that I'm telling you this, because now you won't be surprised and you will know what to do if you want to bring over a brand new piece of equipment. Take it out of the box and throw away all the packing. Make it look used. If it's a computer, transfer some personal files to the computer. Dirty it up a little. Don't give them any excuse to claim it's a new piece of equipment.

## Topic iv: *Luggage*

If you are in your own country and you already have a permanent address in the Philippines, and you are going back to that address, I recommend you use your  full allowed luggage limit to bring back as many items as you can. It might even be worth it to go over the limit and pay the penalties. Check your carriers web site for the international luggage limits and penalties as the policies are always changing.

One thing to keep in mind is that most domestic carriers in the Philippines have a much smaller weight limit than international carriers. However if you are on a domestic flight, but can prove you just recently arrived on an international flight, most local carriers will honor the international limit.  However, suppose you arrive in Manila, spend a week vacationing there, and then board a flight to Cebu. Most likely they will not honor the international limits and you will have to pay the penalties.

## Topic v: *Balik Bayan Boxes*

The Balik Bayan box policy was enacted to give overseas Filipino workers a break when sending items back to their families in the Philippines. Those US cities with active Filipino communities such as Los Angeles, NY, Boston and many others will have a Balik Bayan Agent. If you can track down some

Filipinos in your home city they can usually give you the telephone number of the Balik Bayan Agent.

The way it works is this: You contact your local Balik Bayan agent and tell them you want to send one or more boxes to the Philippines. The agent will tell you when the next shipment is going out, and will usually deliver the box or boxes to your home. Balik Bayan boxes come in several sizes but the most economical per unit volume is the biggest box, which is the six cubic foot size (24"x24"x18") . Most people choose this box.

The cost of sending the box to the Philippines varies according to exactly where you are in the USA, and where the box is going in the Philippines. A typical cost for a six cubic foot box is about $120.

After you receive your box you usually have a number of days, or even weeks (until shortly before the next shipment goes out) to stock your Balik Bayan Box. There is no practical weight limit to the box. You can and should jam pack your box to the limit. The box must be addressed to a Filipino residential address.

Shortly before the shipment goes out the agent will come to your house, collect the money and take your box away to be shipped. Obviously there is economy of scale because many hundreds if not thousands of Balik Bayan boxes are shipped at once.

Typically it takes in the vicinity of 8 weeks for your Balik Bayan box to reach it's destination. There is nothing more exciting for a Filipino family than to receive a Balik Bayan box from their overseas family member. The sender of the box usually takes great care in stocking the contents and makes sure there is something for everybody.

Balik Bayan Boxes, from what I am told, are rarely checked or hassled by customs officials. The policy was designed for overseas Filipino workers, but for the life of me, I can't see how they can prevent anyone from using the boxes, so long as they have a Filipino residential address to send the box to. If you have some trusted Filipino friends in the Philippines I don't see any reason why you can't use the Balik Bayan Box as an economical way to send your stuff to the Philippines.

## Topic vi: *Container Vessels*

If you really have your heart set on sending all your stuff, furniture, appliances, clothes and tools etc to the Philippines, it can be done, but it will cost you. Besides the cost you pay for shipment expect to pay large custom fees to have the items released.

The most economical way to send your stuff is to rent a container, put your stuff inside the container and send it on a container vessel. Containers come in 10, 20 and 40 foot sizes. For example a ten foot container has an interior space of approximately 16 cubic meters. You can get the exact size of various containers by looking up the information on the web or contacting your shipping agent.

When investigating exactly how to send your stuff I suggest you DO NOT start by calling up shipping companies in the USA or your home country. Instead start backwards by contacting the largest container shipping company in the Philippines, Namely "Aboitiz 2GO", the web address for this company is www.2GO.com.ph". Whatever company your container starts with, it will almost certainly end up in the Philippines with Aboitiz 2GO, so your most efficient means of finding the most economical carrier is to contact them first in the Philippines and ask for the appropriate agent for your local area.

## Topic vii: *Your Best Strategy*

All in all I don't suggest you try and bring any big items from your home country to the Philippines. I think your most economical strategy is to bring as much as you can on each trip to the Philippines, possibly make use of the Balik Bayan boxes and buy the rest of what you need here in the Philippines.

# Chapter 21: Laws, the Legal System and Staying out of Trouble

## Topic i: *General Discussion of the Legal System*

The Philippines has many laws. In fact they have many good laws. A lot of their laws are based on American laws, which makes sense because before the Philippines was a free country they were occupied by the USA for many years.

The trouble is, not that they have bad laws, but that the laws are inconsistently enforced and that corruption is rampant.

Although a lot of the laws are similar, there are also some very fundamental differences between how the legal system is set up here compared to the USA.

First of all, there is no jury system here in the Philippines. Your fate is determined by a judge. The judge is in complete control. Your life is in his hands. There is the concept of appeals, but at any given level a single judge is in control.

Another difference is that the distinctions between Civil and Criminal cases are often blurred. There is the concept of a civil case and a criminal case, but often criminal cases can be dismissed if there is a monetary settlement between the perpetrator of the crime and the victim.

For example, suppose somebody is operating a vehicle while drunk and he drives into a little girl and kills her.

In the USA there is criminal proceedings against him. Nothing can prevent him from going to jail if he is found guilty. If the victims family wants to collect money, that is a separate issue governed by a separate civil trial.

In the Philippines, in many instances, a person can avoid criminal proceedings if he can come to an agreement with the victim (or if the victim is killed, with the victims family). Consider the case of the little girl killed by the drunk driver. If the drunk driver has money he may offer the family several million pesos to forgive him. If the family accepts the case is over. If the driver has no money or the family refused to accept the offer, the case goes to trial and the man could go to jail. In most cases if the perpetrator of the crime can offer a reasonable settlement the family will accept. What good does it do to send a man to jail if you get nothing out of it? Of course the family could later file a civil suit against the driver, but then it will turn into a long ugly drawn out affair with lawyers. In the Philippines if you don't have money it's hard to win your case.

Is this a good system? Well there are arguments on both sides of the issue. On the good side consider this: The man does not have to go to jail, society is spared the expense of supporting a prisoner, and the family is compensated with money. Everybody is happy, what's the problem.

Well unfortunately there are lots of problems. The drunk driver is free to drive drunk and kill again. The rich get away with anything while the poor go to jail. That does not seem right.

And finally this system encourages false accusations and the filing of criminal complaints for the sole purpose of getting money. To explain how this works I have to give you some more background.

In the Philippines anyone can accuse anybody else of a crime. You simply have to go to the Fiscals office, fill out a complaint and pay a small filing fee. When a fiscals office gets a complaint they will send out a courier to the accused notifying the accused of the complaint and giving the accused ten days to respond to the complaint. The accused has to sign a statement that he received notification of the complaint.

So what is a Fiscal? A Fiscal is like a junior attorney. Their job is to process the criminal complaints. Their job is to take each complaint, do due diligence to see if the complaint has merit, and then to either dismiss the complaint or continue the case to the courts. First of all, if the accused does not answer the complaint by filing a counter argument explaining their side of the story and why they are not guilty, then it is automatically considered that the case has merit and it is forwarded to the courts.

Now assuming the accused files a counter argument, as they surely must do if they are not crazy, then the Fiscal is supposed to review both the complaint and counter complaint. They are supposed to review all the evidence and conduct interviews if necessary. Usually the process takes several weeks or even longer.

While the Fiscal is deciding whether to forward the case, you are under no restrictions. The key here is that the criminal complaint was initiated by a citizen, not the police. If the police are the ones to initiate the complaint then you will be immediately arrested and have to post bail. However since a citizen initiated the complaint you are under no restrictions unless and until the case is forwarded to the courts. In fact, if you think the case has significant merit and you are worried about the result, now is a good time to get out of the country. Either that or negotiate with the plaintiff to dismiss the case. However with most cases concerning foreigners this is not the situation. It is usually the case that somebody is filing a complaint in a marginal situation for the expressed purpose of extorting money from you. Even so, if you think the case has even limited merit it might be in your best interest to negotiate with the plaintiff at this point, to have him dismiss his complaint. However if you think the case is completely bogus it's hard to do this. You are likely to let the situation continue in the hope that the Fiscal will dismiss the case.

If the Fiscal dismisses the case, it's over, finished. If the Fiscal decides to forward the case, it does not mean you are yet guilty, but it does mean your life is about to get a whole lot more stressful.

As soon as your case is forwarded to the courts you are subject to arrest. Now if you have a good lawyer and he has been properly monitoring the situation your lawyer should know that the Fiscal is about to forward the case. Your lawyer should have the bail all set to go, so that you never have to spend any time in jail. All but the most grievous of crimes are bailable. Typical bail for a non violent crime is one or two hundred thousand peso ($2,000 to $4,000 dollars).

Now if your lawyer is amiss, or some funny business is going on, you may never get any warning. The police may show up at your door and arrest you. Typically a bail hearing is scheduled for the next day. If you are arrested on Friday afternoon you will have to spend the weekend in Jail. Most judges will not sign arrest warrants for Friday afternoon unless there are special circumstances.

**VERY IMPORTANT**: if you have a criminal complaint pending against you make sure you have liquid cash available. If you don't and you can't pay the bail, you will have to stay in jail.

Now let's revisit the situation of a Fiscal.

It is a Fiscals duty to conduct an honest investigation with due diligence to determine whether or not to continue the case to the courts. The problem is, fiscals are underpaid and overworked. They don't possibly have time to conduct  a thorough investigation for all their cases. This leaves them open to bribes. It is pretty much commonly known that a significant number of Fiscals take bribes. Unfortunately for you it is much easier for a Filipino to bribe a Fiscal than for you. The Filipino usually has the right contacts and knows the Fiscal and whether he is open to bribes. As a foreigner it is very dangerous for you to attempt to bribe the fiscal, and I don't recommend it. If however, you still want to attempt this approach, **NEVER** approach the fiscal directly yourself. You must use a trusted Filipino go-between.

Now when a Fiscal is considering whether or not to accept a bribe, they have to be somewhat careful. If they dismiss a case that clearly has merit they are open to a lot of criticism and flak and could even lose their job. Similarly they could be open to a lot of criticism if they forward a case that clearly has no merit whatsoever. They may incur the wrath of the judge who wonders why this ridiculous case was forwarded.  This leaves the marginal cases that are susceptible to hanky panky. It is also the marginal cases that are the most difficult to do due diligence on. Thus the Fiscal may be happy to take a bribe in a marginal case and thus remove the case from his caseload. If the bribe is for the purpose of having  the case continued to the courts the Fiscal probably rationalizes to himself  that he did not find the defendant guilty, he merely continued the case to the courts so that the court could make a proper decision. This rationalizing does not take into effect that the Fiscals forwarding of the case is usually the beginning of a nightmare for the defendant.

## Topic ii: *The Foreigner Extortionist (FE)*

Now this whole business of citizen initiated criminal complaints and bribable Fiscals has spawned a despicable type of Filipino that I will call the "Foreigner Extortionist" (FE). An FE is usually a local person who has lived there a long time if not all their whole life. They know the system, they know the Fiscals, and they know which ones can be bribed.  They look for situations in which they think they can extort a foreigner. The FE never attaches their name to anything. They stay on the sidelines encouraging someone to file a criminal complaint and telling them how much money they can make out of the situation. They offer advice, knowledge and encouragement, and sometimes some up front money to do such things as file the case. If everything works out for the FE and their client the FE, of course, gets a percentage of the money. If it case blows up in the face of the plaintiff the FE simply washes their hands of the situation. They never get legally involved.

The existence of FEs is one reason you should NEVER have sex with an underage girl. Let's explore this further. Honestly the police probably couldn't care less if you have sex with an underage girl, assuming of course that the encounter was completely consensual, and that the girl was not overly young. Such cases will usually only come to court from a citizen filed complaint.

The legal age for consensual sex in the Philippines is 18. Now suppose you have sex with a 17 year old girl. The encounter was completely consensual, in fact the girl encouraged you. Now suppose the family finds out. Maybe the family is only mildly upset. Maybe they are really more upset with their daughter than they are with the foreigner. Maybe they just happen to explain, just in passing, what happened to some of their friends, and somehow an FE finds out about it. The FE may approach the family and tell them how they can make hundreds of thousands of pesos by filing a criminal statutory rape complaint.

In this kind of case you are really in trouble. You really did break the law. Your two choices are to either leave the country before the cases is forwarded to the courts or to settle with the family.

## Topic iii: *Two Real Life Examples*

I will now give two real life examples which I have personal knowledge of. This first concerns a completely bogus claim, the second concerns a highly marginal case, but one in which the foreigner nevertheless did something stupid to get himself in trouble.

### ♦ The Traffic Accident – A Mild Example

The first real life example concerns a traffic accident. A foreigner driving a car was stopped in traffic, completely stationary. A Filipino who was very drunk and driving a motorcycle rammed right into the back of the car. The car was slightly damaged, the motorcycle was totaled and the Filipino driving the motorcycle was injured, although not in any life threatening way.

When the police arrived it was very clear that the man was very drunk (although the police don't use breathalyzers, so there is no conclusive evidence). The police understood the situation and talked to the parties. The foreigner was willing to not press charges or file a claim even though his car was damaged. The Filipino was happy to be alive and not have anyone hassle him for driving while drunk. The man dragged himself off for medical care and it looked like the whole thing would just go away.

The an FE got hold of the situation. The FE encouraged the accident victim to file a claim for reckless driving. In the claim he claimed that the foreigner was backing up on a main road at the time of the accident. It was completely made up and bogus.

Even though he felt he was in the right, the foreigner did not have the stomach to fight it. He wound up paying to replace the motorcycle, for the mans medical care and some additional money for pain and suffering.

### ♦ The Business Deal Gone Bad – A True Life Horror Story

The second real life example concerns a business deal gone bad. A foreigner and his wife had a small business, namely a hair and facial saloon. The business was more or less breaking even and the couple was tired of it, and wished to sell it.

Since the business wasn't 'really making any money they couldn't really sell it for a lot of money. Finally they made a deal with a "friend" of the wife. They agreed to sell if for only p150,000 ($3,000) which more or less just covered the cost of the equipment and furnishings, or not even. They agreed on a deal where the buyers would pay P50,000 down, and then P20,000 a month for five months until the full P150,000 was paid. They agreed that the buyers would take over the running of the business immediately and that after the full amount was paid an official transfer of name would take place. Until the full amount was paid the business would remain in the name of the original owners. The agreement was written and signed, but since they thought they were all friends they did not get any lawyers involved, figuring they would get the lawyers involved only at the time of the official transfer.

The new future owners paid the initial P50,000 as agreed, and then took over the running of the business. After that they never paid another peso. Of course the original owners kept on asking about their money and were constantly put off, the usual stuff, we don't have the money now, but we will have it soon.

Months went buy and the original owners continued to pressure the buyers. Finally the buyers told the original owners that they had the money. The buyers were told to meet at the saloon at a given time and collect the full P100,000 and sign a receipt that all the money was now paid.

When the original owners arrived at the saloon at the designated time the buyers were nowhere to be found. Instead the employees of the saloon told them the buyers had left P10,000 (ten thousand, not one hundred thousand) and a note. The note read something like the following: As agreed upon in our telephone conversation we are handing over the remainder of the money owed, namely P10,000. Please sign this paper agreeing that you accept this P10,000 and that now all payments are complete and the business will be transferred to our name.

The husband was enraged. Instead of signing the note he grabbed the 10,000 and in addition started putting some of the small equipment, like scissors, conditioners and colorings, hair driers, music CDs etc, in plastic bags. The employees, who used to be their employees, did nothing but watch uncomfortably. After collecting what they could carry the original owners, husband and wife left. What the husband did was understandable, but it was a BIG mistake.

The husbands thought was that he was going to force the buyers to negotiate properly. It never occurred to him what might happen.

When the original owners tried to contact the buyers to continue negotiations they found that the buyers were no longer interested in talking. A few days later they received a notice by currier from the Fiscals office informing them they had been accused of "robbery with intimidation", and that they had ten days to reply.

The original owners were shocked. They never dreamed that the buyers would get the law involved. The wife in particular was shocked, as she thought the woman buyer was her friend. Again they tried to contact the buyers who again were not interested in talking. What they didn't know, of course, was that an FE had become involved.

A day later the buyers contacted the sellers and said ok, they were now willing to negotiate. They agreed to meet at a restaurant. When they arrived they were shocked to see a whole entourage, including the husband and wife, "witnesses", and of course the FE who was introduced as a friend of the family. The FE (a woman in her 50s) did all the talking. It very quickly became clear they had no intention of negotiating in reasonable manner. They basically said give us several million pesos to drop the case.

As a result the owners were forced to find a lawyer. That's when they made their second mistake. Instead of asking people in the Expat community for a good lawyer, somebody that had proven themselves in the Expat community, the husband chose a lawyer he was friendly with at his golf club. The lawyer claimed that he new the fiscal well, had grown up with him, and was still friendly with him. He implied that this would improve the odds that the complaint would be dismissed.

In any case, the lawyer promised his clients one thing. Don't worry, no matter what, you will not go to jail. If the Fiscal is about to forward the case he will tell me, and we will get the bail all set up.

The lawyer charged them a retainer fee of  p200,000 ($4000) which seemed like a lot to the couple, but the husband did not really question it, since he figured it was worth it if this lawyer could really help him. They later learned that the retainer fee for this kind of case was usually more in the ball park of p50,000 ($1000) or even less.

So with the help of their lawyer the sellers wrote their counter reply to the Fiscal. How could they be robbing the saloon if the saloon was still in their name? Essentially they were robbing themselves. As for the P10,000 that they took, this was simply partial payment for the P100,000 still owed to them by the buyers.

They submitted their reply and then waited. The husband was surprised that the Fiscal never called them into is office for an interview. He had been given the impression that this was standard procedure for a fiscal doing due diligence. After a couple of weeks he went to the Fiscals office to introduce himself. He asked the Fiscal if he wanted to interview him. The Fiscal seemed taken aback.  The Fiscal replied no, he was just going to consider the case from the evidence of the written materials.

So the husband left and they continued to wait for the Fiscals decision. Then one Thursday evening around 5pm without any warning about a half dozen police came to arrest them. Since it was already too late to arrange bail they were put in jail. The poor couple was in utter shock. The wife was hysterical. When the lawyer came to visit them in jail, they asked how could this happen? I thought you would not let this happen.  The lawyer replied that he too was in shock, and very angry at the Fiscal for not keeping him informed. But don't worry the lawyer replied, tomorrow we will have a bail hearing. Bail for a simple case like this is very standard and always granted. The lawyer informed them that bail for a robbery case without violence or weapons was P100,000 ($2000) each.

The next day the police escorted them to the court for the bail hearing. After waiting a while the lawyer informed the husband that the Judge wanted to talk to him. When the husband approached the judge, the judge started screaming at him. "I hate Americans. I hate all you people. You think you can just come to our country and do anything you want. You have no respect". Etc. Etc. After listening to the judges rampage for about a minute or so, the husband could not stand it anymore, and he simply turned and walked away. This sent the judge into a further rage, and he started screaming, BAIL DENIED, BAIL DENIED, take them back to jail.

The wife fell down to the floor in hysterics, crying and screaming. The husband started shouting, we have to inform the American Embassy. We have to get the American Embassy involved. He screamed this over and over again very loud.

The police were all set to take them back to jail, but the lawyer begged the police to wait while he tried to talk to the judge. The lawyer went with the judge inside the judges chambers. When the lawyer came out he informed the husband that the judge wanted to talk to him again inside the judges chambers, and please be respectful and remain calm no matter what, if you want to avoid jail.

When the husband sat down inside the judges chambers he found that the judges' demeanor had changed completely. The judge was completely calm and reasonable. He talked to the husband to confirm his knowledge about the case. The judge then said, this is a ridiculous case. It's not a criminal case, it's a civil case. I don't want to see you again. I want this case negotiated. The judge then granted bail.

Buy the time the husband emerged from the judges chambers the poor wife was a complete basket case. It hardly even registered with her that bail had finally been granted. She was expecting to go back to jail.

After this the couple, no longer trusting their lawyer, fired him, and retained the services of another lawyer who they researched and found to have an impeccable reputation. After hearing the story the new lawyer said he would talk to the lawyer of the buyers and get back to them.

A day later the new lawyer informed the sellers that the buyers were willing to drop the case if the sellers agreed to sign over the business and pay them an additional P100,000 ($2000) dollars.

Totally exhausted and stressed out the sellers agreed. The next day the papers were signed and the case was over.

Now, the sellers will never know exactly what happened, but let's try to analyze this situation and guess what might have happened.

It's almost a 100% certainty that the Fiscal was bribed. If he had not been bribed he would have done due diligence and interviewed the parties, and probably would have tried to broker a settlement for this case that he must of known was a waste of the courts time.

As far as the lawyer of the sellers goes, it's a little harder to figure out. Clearly this lawyer was interested in extracting as much money from his client as possible. But why wasn't he aware of the Fiscals decision? Usually the lawyer of a client has a relationship with the Fiscal, and usually the Fiscal lets the lawyer know if he is about to forward the case so that bail can be arranged. This is just normal professional courtesy. It's especially strange since the lawyer claimed to be a friend of the Fiscal.

There are two possibilities. The first is that as part of the bribe to the Fiscal, the Fiscal agreed not to inform the lawyer of his pending decision to forward the case. This would seem a little strange, because if they really were friends, this would jeopardize the friendship. The second possibility is that the lawyer also received a bribe to allow his clients to be arrested. If this is true you might consider that the lawyer was completely corrupt and totally working against his clients, or you might consider that the lawyer was only partially corrupt, figuring, so what if they spend one day in jail, I'll take the bribe, then I'll get them off. Any way you look at it, it's hard to figure out what went on with the lawyer.

Now let's consider the police that arrested the couple. Most likely they were also bribed. Most court ordered arrest warrants are issued in the morning. It is common practice to arrest somebody  in morning or early afternoon, so they can arrange bail. The police were probably bribed to wait until 5pm so that the couple would be forced to stay in jail for the night.

Now let's try to figure out what happened with the judge. This one is very difficult to figure out, there are numerous possibilities.

The most evil possibility is that the judge was also bribed to deny bail. Then when the husband started screaming about the American Embassy maybe the judge had second thoughts knowing it would be very difficult to justify denying bail for such a marginal case. Of course had bail really been denied then the buyers and FE would be in a great position. The sellers would have been sent back to jail for at least a couple of months while awaiting trial. The FE could have then negotiated a very steep price to agree to drop the case. This undoubtedly was their very big hope.

The second possibility is that the husband had the unfortunate luck of meeting the judge when the judge was in a very bad mood. The judge went on a tirade, but then later calmed down and did the right thing.

The third possibility is that the whole thing was just grandstanding.  Maybe the lawyer was friends with the judge, and asked the judge to do it, so the lawyer could seem like a great person, saving his clients from jail. Maybe the judge got a kick out of scaring the shit out of the American. Maybe they later had a beer and laughed about it.

Now let's consider what happened after the sellers obtained a new lawyer. By this time the FEs hand was played out. There was no threat of jail. If in fact the sellers lawyer was corrupt and taking bribes from the FE, well this lawyer was now gone, and finally the judge had already made it clear he didn't want the case tried. At this point the buyers and the FE knew they didn't have much leverage. Their only hope was to make a settlement for a small amount of money knowing the buyers wanted to avoid further stress.

Now let's consider who made out from this whole mess.

Not the sellers, ha ha ha. What a nightmare. All they ever wanted to do was sell their business for a small amount of money. Instead they wound paying about P400,000 ($8000) dollars in lawyer and settlement fees, spent a day in jail, and lived for more than a month under extreme stress.

The buyers and the FE also failed miserably. They were hoping to make a big score. Instead it is likely the money they got didn't even cover the combined costs of the bribes and legal expenses. Also, the sellers lived under considerable stress, specially from the many people that told them what they were doing was wrong and urging them to settle. The FE probably did not suffer that much. For them, it comes with the territory, you win some you lose some.

The ones that made out of course were the lawyers, especially the lawyer of the sellers, and probably the Fiscal accepting the bribe.

## Topic iv: *The Moral of the Stories*

The bottom line is don't do anything stupid that could subject you to an FE. In the second story the sellers were not bad people looking for trouble. They were not "robbers". But the husband did a very stupid thing by taking the law into his own hands and taking the money and items from the salon. He opened himself up to the FE.

So be careful. Weigh your actions at all times. Don't be rash. Avoid trouble at all costs. Remember you are in a foreign country with foreign customs and limited rights.

On the other hand, even if you try your best to avoid trouble, sometimes trouble comes looking for you, as in the case of the first story. In such a case you have to decide whether you want to fight it. It's hard for most people to give in when they know they are right. It's up to you what you do, whether or not to fight. But this chapter will hopefully give you some idea of the dangers and what to look out for.

## Topic v: *Get a Lawyer Ahead of Time*

Another moral of the second story is to have a lawyer ready ahead of time. In the second story the husband was forced to pick a lawyer quickly under duress, and the result was not good.

I know it's hard to think about finding a lawyer when you have no reason, but it's still a good idea to have some choices picked out ahead of time.

When Choosing a lawyer **DO NOT** ask your Filipino friends for a recommendation. The reason is that they might provide a lawyer that is good from a Filipino view point, but you will have no idea about this lawyers attitude towards foreigners. Some lawyers view foreigners as a money tree.

The only way for you, a foreigner, to find a good lawyer is to ask around in the Expat community. Find one or more Expats that have had a positive experience with a lawyer. Perhaps there is a lawyer that is well known in the Expat community for doing a good job for foreigners.

## Topic vi: *The American Embassy*

In the second story the husband yelled out, "We have to inform the American Embassy!". This brings up the question: how much can the American Embassy really help you? Well from what I have heard from many different people is "Not much". If you try to get the Embassy to help you they will simply tell you it is not their country and they don't have any power. They will tell you that you are in the Philippines and you are subject to their laws and legal system.

The most the Embassy can do for you is to write a letter on your behalf stating that they are aware of and are monitoring the situation. Can this help? Sometimes – a little bit. It can make the people involved aware that they are being watched and that they may be held accountable for their actions. It might help to force them to act in an appropriate and proper manner. But all in all, don't expect the American Embassy, or the fact that you are American, to save you.

# Chapter 22: Schools and Education

Most people reading this book are probably not interested in schools or education in the Philippines.   Most of you are divorced, single again, and alone, coming here to the Philippines to start a new life. However, maybe there are a few exceptions. Maybe you are marrying a Filipina woman with kids and you want to know how it works. Maybe you are a single dad bringing your kid here. Well that doesn't seem very likely. Anyways, just in case you are one of the exceptions I will quickly describe the education system here in the Philippines.

First of all, in the USA there is kindergarten and then 12 grades before graduating high school. In the Philippines there are only 10 grades. Students typically graduate high school at age 16. As in the USA education is mandatory for children, but only up to age 12 (as opposed to age 16 in the USA). However, unlike the USA where the law that children must attend school is enforced, here in the Philippines it is not really enforced. It is very common to see young children, especially young poor children who are not attending school. Some of theses children are taught how to beg and are out on the streets starting at around age six. It's very sad.

For most Filipino families, not having a lot of money, they send their children to public schools. The level of education is not very good in many of these schools. Yes, they learn how to read and write, they learn the most basic arithmetic, and maybe some rudimentary English, and that's about it. They really do not have a very good sense of history, geography, current events or the world around them. Ask them to describe the events that led up to world war two and  most likely they won't have a clue. Ask them to point out Australia on an unlabeled map, most likely they can't (hmmm, is that so different than American Children?). In many typical public schools the children are taught in their own language and learn English only from attending English class, like American children attending American schools and learning French from attending French class twice a week.

When I was a high school student I was forced to attend French classes for three years. I managed to somehow pass the classes and now as an adult I perhaps remember about ten words of French! It is a similar thing for many unmotivated students attending public schools that teach in the native language. Also remember that non native Tagalog students must learn two languages, Tagalog and English. In the end many of them wind up with only a very rudimentary knowledge of English.

Of course if a school teaches in English (that is, English is the standard language of the school) it's a very different story. In this case a student is forced to learn English. Middle class or upper class Filipino families with a bit more money will usually send their kids to private schools. Most private schools are taught in English and the level of education, while considerably higher than Filipino public schools, is still probably lower than a good school, even a good public school, in the USA or other western country.

For those people, both Filipinos and foreigners, who want to send their kids to the very best schools available in the Philippines, they will send their kids to an International School subscribing to the International Baccalaureate program. There are a number of such schools available in major cities throughout the Philippines. The Baccalaureate program or standard is an international standard of course work and achievement designed to prepare a student to attend a good university anywhere in the world. The Baccalaureate schools, unlike other schools in the Philippines, are based on a 12 grade program, as in the USA.

Private schools in the Philippines, of course, cost a lot less than private schools in the USA. Even a top notch Baccalaureate school will cost considerably less than a typical private school in the USA. If you are a foreigner with your own children you will most likely want to send your children to an international Baccalaureate school.

# Chapter 23: Medical Situation

Unfortunately, if you want top notch medical care, the Philippines is not the best place to be. If you are unhealthy and have complex medical problems, or need state of the art surgery perhaps you don't want to retire here (with the possible exception of Manila, as will be discussed below).

On the other hand, for run of the mill medical problems you will probably be ok. The medical care available here is not great, but it is also not terrible. They won't inject you with dirty needles! They don't practice voodoo medicine.

Let's explore all this in more detail by examining different areas of the medical system.

## Topic i: *Dental Care*

I have found the dental care here to be just fine. They do all the standard procedures such as caps, crowns bridges and root canal and they do it at vastly lower prices than in the USA. They may not have all the latest state of the art dental equipment but they seem to have what they need to do most standard dental work.

## Topic ii: *Drugs, Medicines and Medications*

The good news is that most drugs are available at your local drug store.

The bad news is that the price of the drugs is more or less the same as in the USA. Almost all the drugs are imported and as such there is no great price reduction. Some of the drugs are marketed at a somewhat reduced price compared to the USA. The Philippines does produce some generic drugs and those drugs that are produced in the Philippines are of course much cheaper than their imported counterparts.

The controversial news is that almost all drugs are available without prescription. Only a few drugs such as Morphine, Percidan and Valium are restricted and require doctors prescription. Almost everything else is available simply by asking for it. Personally I like this system so much. It's a pain in the butt to always have to go to a doctor for a prescription, even when you know perfectly well what you need. Whether you agree with this system is up to you, but for better or worse, that's the way it is.

Make sure you go to one of the large reputable drug stores to get your medicine even if it costs a bit more. I have heard rumors of counterfeit medicine. I have no idea if the rumors are true.

Besides regular drug stores, Chinese drug stores offering Chinese medicines are also popular. Some of these medicines really do work. In particular a number of different kinds of "Chinese Viagra" are sold at a small fraction of the cost of regular Viagra or Cialis. Some of these "Chinese Viagra" medicines definitely work, or so I have been told (wink wink). I have no idea of the long term effects of these medicines. For that, you are on your own.

## Topic iii: *The Cost of Medical Care*

Labor in the Philippines is cheap. This is reflected not only with low level workers, but also at the professional level. Doctors in the Philippines don't make anywhere near as much money as their counterparts in first world countries. A typical 15 minute consulting visit at a doctors office usually costs about P300 ($6). Similarly doctors making rounds at hospitals and performing surgery also get far less money than their first world counterparts.

A room at a hospital in the USA can cost as much as $500 dollars a day or more. In a typical private hospital in a typical city (not Manila) there are usually three levels of rooms. Group rooms with many beds and one bathroom, usually not air conditioned. Semi private rooms with four people to the room and one bathroom, sometimes air conditioned and sometimes not, and private rooms with a private bathroom, a TV and air conditioning. Amazingly even these private hospital rooms only cost about P1500 ($30) a day.

So, the room is cheap and the doctors fee's are low. However, the medicine basically is the same cost as in the USA, since almost all the medicine is imported. This results in a "interesting" situation where the typical hospital bill is often dominated by the cost of drugs.

For example, suppose you spend a week in a hospital getting treated for some kind of blood infection. You might find that the base hospital charge is p15,000 ($300). The doctors consultants fees might typically be around p10,000 ($200), but the charge for drugs and medicine is P50,000 ($1000). Still, your total bill for one week in the hospital, $1500 in this example, is still far less than a weeks stay in an American hospital.

## Topic iv: *The Doctors*

As far as the doctors themselves go, many of them seem to be decent. Some of them have even been educated at western medical colleges. It's hard for me to exactly compare how good these doctors are compared to their counterpart in western countries, since I am not a doctor myself. My intuition is that many of seem ok and know what they are talking about.

One thing I have noticed is a definite difference in philosophy concerning medicine. Taking a pill is the preferred way of solving a problem in the Philippines. Sometimes when a particular test is not available at the local laboratory the doctor will prescribe medicine based on his guess rather than go through the expense, trouble and delay of having the test done where it is available, which is often only in Manila.

## Topic v: *Medical Care Without Money*

Supposedly a person without money can go to a government hospital and get free care. This is pretty much a joke. Yes they can go to a government hospital and a doctor will see them and offer advice. Yes if they are really sick they will stick them in a bed in a room jam packed with dozens of other beds. But that's about it. They won't do any tests, buy any medication or do any procedures unless you have the money to pay for it. Basically, In the Philippines, if you are seriously sick and you don't have money or medical insurance, you die. Hmmm – is that so different than the USA?

## Topic vi: *The Laboratories*

Most decent sized private hospitals have their own lab. These labs are fine for the normal and common blood and urine tests. However they usually do not perform the more advanced state of the art tests available at a top notch hospital or lab. It is not uncommon to be told, that if you want a certain test done, you will have to go to Manila.

## Topic vii: *The Hospitals*

There are several levels of hospitals in the Philippines. Basically they can be categorized into three main categories, as described below.

#### ♦ Government Hospitals

Government hospitals are where the poor people go. You get a free bed, and free doctor consulting, but not free medicine, lab tests or surgery. If your only exposure to hospitals are high quality western hospitals, then you will be shocked when you enter a government hospital. There are no private rooms or even semi private rooms in a government hospital. Many beds are crammed into a single area. Thirty or more people share the same bathroom which might only be cleaned once a day. It is usually filthy, has no toilette paper, and lacks a toilette seat. The hospital is hot, smells bad and is oppressive. Nurses care is at a minimum. Patients can usually only expect to see a doctor once a day. There is no privacy whatsoever. Personally I would rather stay at home and die than spend any significant time in a government hospital.

### ♦ Typical Private Hospital in a Typical City

Private hospitals are a definite big step up from government hospitals. They are cleaner, have more doctors and nurses, and the beds and equipment are better. As a Westerner you will almost certainly want to ask for a private room if available.

Even though a typical private hospital is much better than the government hospital, it's still  not nearly at the level of even an average hospital in a first world country. For one thing they will be lacking the most modern state of the art medical equipment. Second, they simply lack the experience and knowledge to perform complex medical procedures and surgery. If you have a serious or unusual medical problem you simply do not want to be at one of these hospitals.

Above and beyond the quality of the medical care you receive you will find the experience of staying in such a hospital to be far different than what you are probably used to. Things work very differently. Things that you would just take for granted at a western hospital you can't take for granted in a private hospital in the Philippines.

For example there are usually no CALL Buttons. None by the bed, and no emergency CALL buttons in the bathroom. How can this be? What if you are sick or weak and you need help? What if are sitting on the toilette and you can't get up?

Well the reasoning is that you are supposed to have a full time helper stay with you 24/7 to keep you company and provide for your needs while in the hospital. For most Filipinos this is not a problem. Most Filipinos are part of extended families, and most Filipinos that are wealthy enough to stay in a private hospital usually have at least one helper (maid). So the helper and the family members take turns keeping the patient company.

Unlike in western hospitals nurses are not involved in the routine care of the patient. The job of the nurses is to administer medicine, take temperatures and blood pressures, monitor the IV's and in general help the doctors.

If you are in such a hospital and you are very sick or weak, and have no one to keep you company and help you will have a very difficult time. You may have to hire somebody to help you. The only good news is that hiring such a helper will not cost you so much.

There are many other amazing differences as well. For example, most hospitals do not supply toilette paper. You will be asked to supply your own toilette paper. Sometimes you will be asked to supply your own knives, forks, spoons and glasses for eating. You will supply your own tooth brush, your own tooth paste and soap. You get the idea.

If the doctor prescribes medicine and that medicine is not available at the hospital – which it often isn't - you (actually your helper) will be asked to get the medicine yourself. If there is no helper to get the medicine, or you don't have the money to pay for the medicine, you simply won't be administered your medication, it's as simple as that. If you need a procedure such as an x-ray or ultra sound, they will ask you to pay for it first, before they will do it. In fact it's a constant hassle and stress, always having to worry about obtaining your medications and paying for procedures. This is not what you want when you are sick. What you want is to relax, have everything done for you, and at the end of it all, pay your bill. This is not the way it works in the Philippines.

### ◆ Best Hospitals in Manila

There are supposed to be several very good "world class" hospitals in Manila. St. Lukes is probably the hospital with the best reputation, followed closely by Makati Medical Center. There is also a new hospital, very beautiful with all the latest modern equipment, namely the "Asian Medical Center". This hospital however has not been around as long as the first two mentioned, so it's reputation is not yet fully established.

To be honest I have not had personal experience with these hospitals. There are some people who claim that these hospitals are world class hospitals as good as any in the world. There are others who say, that although these hospitals are by far the best in the Philippines, they are still not as good as a good western hospital.

I know of a Filipino named Tim, a fairly wealthy Filipino about 70 years of age. He recently related a story to me about him and his now deceased friend. It seems about 15 years ago, by coincidence, Tim and his friend were both diagnosed with heart disease at about the same time. Both were told they would need a bypass operation. Tim, having more money and contacts in the USA opted to go to the USA to have his operation. Tim's friend opted to go to one of the well known hospitals in Manila. Tim told me his friend died a couple of years after the operation, and here he was 15 years later still ticking. Of course, as a medical study, this story does not hold a lot of water. A test group of 2 is not exactly significant. The point of the story is that it demonstrates how some people, even Filipinos, are convinced that even the best hospitals in Manila are not as good as a good western hospital.

Even so, if you want to live in the Philippines, and you are concerned about the availability of quality medical care, then you may choose to live in or near Manila for this reason alone.

# Chapter 24: Food

Concerning food there is good news and bad news. The bad news is that most foreigners can't stomach most traditional Filipino food. The good news is that you usually won't need to. You will be able to avoid traditional Filipino food by either going to mid range or high end restaurants, or by buying and cooking food for yourself.

## Topic i: *Traditional Filipino Food.*

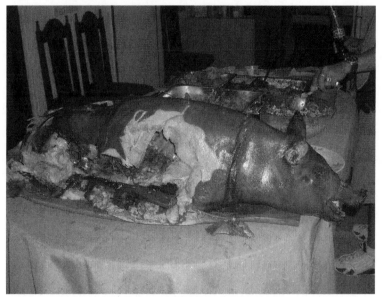

**Lechon – a Filipino delicacy!**

It's interesting to compare the countries of Thailand and Philippines when it comes to food. The people of both countries come from very similar blood lines. In fact when looking at a photograph it's often impossible to tell the difference between a Thai and a Filipino. Both countries are reasonably poor third world countries. Yet, for some reason, Thailand has developed a wonderfully varied cuisine consisting of interesting, spicy and healthy food, whereas traditional Filipino food is bland (or worse), has few spices and is loaded with fat and is terribly unhealthy.

Some of the traditional Filipino food you will probably not be able to eat includes things like dried and smoked fish, shrimp paste, fish heads, fish balls, chicken embryos, fried intestines, chicken feet, pig ears, beef and chicken liver, vegetables cooked with pork fat, and on an on. If you are a beef lover you will have to re-evaluate your love of beef. It might be possible to get decent beef in a larger city at some of the fanciest restaurants or specialty stores which offer imported beef at very high prices, but as far as the local beef is concerned, it's awful. One can see why when you look at all the sickly skinny cows running around. In America the growing of beef is a very technical undertaking using food science to help grow the tastiest beef. In the Philippines the cows just basically run around in fields eating grass.

Of course not all traditional Filipino food is so unappetizing to the Westerner. There are some traditional Philippine foods the Westerner can handle, foods such as rice, vegetables, chicken adobo, fried and barbequed chicken, pork chops, vegetables and eggs. Even so, go to a typical Filipino party and you will be lucky if you can find two or three foods you enjoy eating.

One food which is considered a fantastic delicacy in Philippine culture is what they call lechon. Lechon is a whole pig barbequed for hours over an open fire. No decent party of any stature is considered complete without lechon. The lechon is brought to the party in all it's glory, as a full pig, complete with head, nose, ears, mouth and eyes. Filipinos have no problem with this. By the time the party is over, nothing is left of the poor pig but a bunch of bones.

Actually many foreigners do enjoy lechon. However it is extremely fatty and unhealthy. For me, personally, I can't get past the image of the poor pig, cooked in it's entirety. I like to see my meat in little pieces that have no resemblance whatsoever to the original animal!

## Topic ii: *The Market*

All Filipino cities big and small have a traditional market where items are sold on the street and prices are haggled over. The freshest fish, meat and vegetables at the most reasonable prices can be found at the market. However, if you are not used to it, it can be a bit overwhelming, especially where fish and meats are sold. The smell is pretty bad. I let my wife go to the market and I stay far away!

## Topic iii: *Supermarkets*

Most larger cities have modern or semi modern supermarkets where the foreigner can shop without the un-pleasantries of the Market. Many western type foods are available at these supermarkets. The largest cities typically have the most modern supermarkets with the most variety. Some of the biggest and most modern supermarkets (for example those in the SM malls) are very similar to supermarkets in the USA. Many western type food is available, both locally produced and imported. The imported foods are quite expensive.

Some foods that you may be used to are simply not available in the Philippines at any cost. For example there is no fresh milk. What they call fresh milk is imported milk packaged in aluminum lined boxes and lasts many months on the shelf with no refrigeration. Actually this milk is not that bad. Fresh orange juice In cartons is also not available. The only orange juice available is no refrigeration needed, in cans or aluminum lined boxes. Also there is no frozen food section in the supermarkets. Do you love the taste and convenience of your frozen food dinners, a complete meal ready to eat after only 5 minutes in the microwave? Sorry – not available.

## Topic iv: *Restaurants*

You can more or less group restaurants into four categories. Those providing traditional Filipino food only at very low prices, those offering mostly Filipino food but offering a few international dishes, specialty restaurants offering particular types of food, like McDonalds, Pizza or Chinese, and International restaurants offering a wide range of international fair including some Filipino dishes.

In a typical city there are plenty of restaurants. All the cities previously listed as being good for Expats have plenty of restaurants suitable for Westerners, including specialty restaurants and international cuisine restaurants. Interestingly the pizza restaurants seem to be surprisingly good. Seems the Filipinos have really got the hang of making pizza.

# Chapter 25: How Do You Keep From Being Bored?

To keep from being bored do lots of drinking – ha ha ha.

I'm just kidding. Or sort of kidding. There are a significant number of Expats whose main hobby is drinking.

Gambling is another common vice here in the Philippines. Besides cockfighting and casinos (casinos are only available in a handful of cities) in most cities with a decent Expat population you can find a poker group with stakes ranging from low to high.

Assuming you don't want gambling or drinking to be your main hobbies, how else will you keep from being bored?

Well if you don't already have a wife or steady girl friend the hobby of looking for one, or dating, can take up a good amount of your time. Assuming you are already married or have a GF, this of course is not an option.

I strongly suggest you don't work. Besides the fact that it's usually not legal, the amount of money you make won't be worth a hill of beans.

What about starting and owning a business? First of all, the business won't be in your name, and second of all, it's really very difficult to make significant amounts of money in the Philippines with a business. Especially for Expats. If you want to start a business go into it with the attitude that it is more of a hobby than a business to make money. Some Expats enjoy opening a small bar or restaurant. It's a lot of work and not worth it unless you enjoy doing it.

At home you can help alleviate boredom with cable TV and an internet connection. Most areas offer cable TV, and it is relatively cheap, about $10 per month. Unlike in the US there are not 57 billion different options. You either have cable TV or you don't. A typical connection will have about 50 channels, with half being local Philippine channels and half being international Channels. Plenty of channels will be in English. Standard channels like CNN, Animal planet, National geographic and HBO are commonly available.

Most cities and surrounding areas now offer broad band internet connections such as DSL, cable or even broad band wireless. A typical connection will cost you between P1000 and p2000 a month. If you don't want the expense of your own computer and broad band connection you can always go to an Internet Café. There are many internet cafes in the Philippines. They are often crowded, uncomfortable, noisy and offer no privacy. Personally I hate them. However they are available if you need them. For me the cost of a computer and connection at home is very well worth it.

Some Expats look for excitement by building their dream house. The process of researching and buying land, designing and building your house is a process that can take many months and consume most of your time. If you are lucky and things go well it can be a rewarding and exciting process. I honestly believe that the reason many Expats choose to build a house is to have something exciting to do. I think when the house is finally finished there is often a let down, and they find that the process of designing and building the house was far more exciting than living in it!

If you are sports minded, golf, tennis and badminton are popular sports in the Philippines and there are many golf, tennis and badminton facilities.

If you are exceptionally fit you might consider joining a bicycling or hiking club, which are also popular in the Philippines. However most of the members of these clubs are young and most likely these are not for you.

VFW (Veteran of Foreign Wars) and Rotary clubs also are numerous in the Philippines. If you like volunteering and getting involved in "feel good" projects, you might look into joining your local rotary club.

Well you get the idea. There are ways to stay active and busy if you try.

# Chapter 26: Self Abuse, Prostitution, Karaoke Bars, Massages and Extra Services

### Topic i: *Low Cost Method*

The last chapter concerned how to keep from being bored. This chapter concerns how to keep from being horny ha ha ha. Well of course if you have been in the Philippines a while and want a girl friend, chances are you have a girl friend (or wife). But what if you don't. What if you have not yet found your GF, or you are between GFs, or whatever and what if all these gorgeous sexy Filipinas are driving you crazy, what can you do?

Well of course there is the old fashioned self abuse method, very inexpensive, reliable and safe – although I have heard that sometimes it can make you go blind. Ok, but you are tired of that, and your vision has been bothering you a lot lately! So what other options are there?

### Topic ii: *Prostitution*

Well of course you can hire a prostitute. Prostitution has been discussed in passing a number of times in previous chapters of this book. I don't know the official laws on prostitution, or whether it is legal, or where it is legal, but regardless it does not matter. Prostitution is de-facto legal in the Philippines. In almost any city it is easy to find a prostitute. In some cities it is more obvious than other cities. In some places you are hit over the head with it, such as in Sabang , Angeles or parts of Makati.

Well I guess it depends on your personality, but to me hiring a prostitute is pretty disgusting and degrading, and no, that has nothing to do with my moral attitudes. You hire somebody who pretends to like you for a little while, who wants to have sex with you as quick as possible, make you cum as quickly as possible, and then get their money as quick as possible and leave. There is no romance whatsoever, and you also have the thought that, where that "member" is going, many thousands of "members" have ventured before! If you do hire a prostitute, you had better use a condom or you are in serious danger of catching a disease.

So is that it? Self abuse or a prostitute? No other choices?

Actually there are a couple of other choices, and it my opinion these other choices are safer and more enjoyable than hiring a prostitute (or so I've heard!).

## Topic iii: *Karaoke Bar with Girls and VIP Rooms*

You can look for a karaoke bar with VIP rooms and girls that will entertain you and keep you company as long as you keep buying them a ladies drink. I have previously referred to these girls as entertainers, otherwise known as GROs or Guest Relations Officers.

Here is how it works, and how much it will cost you.

You walk into the karaoke bar, sit down and order a beer. The normal beers you order for yourself are usually quite reasonable, no more than a regular bar. Sometimes they will ask you right away if you would like company. Sometimes they will leave you alone at first. Regardless, you say you just want to relax and enjoy a beer. So you slowly sip your beer and observe. Look around the room and see if any girls catch your attention. Usually after about 15 minutes or so a waitress (or head Madame) will come back and ask you again if you want company. You have every right to say you just want to enjoy beer by yourself (for as long as you want). Sometimes girls will come up to you and ask you if they can sit down with you. You can either say no, you want to be alone for now, or you can accept. If you accept you usually have about 5 or 10 minutes to "sample the product". They will talk to you and entertain you for a little while. After a little while you can offer to buy them a drink if you like them. If you don't offer, they will ask you, "is it ok if you buy me a drink?" You can refuse if you want, and they will leave shortly thereafter.

If you notice a girl you think you might like you can call over the madam and request that the girl sit with you. Now if you are the one to call over the madam and request a girl, you must order a ladies drink right away.

A ladies drink will cost somewhere between about p150 all the way up to p400 depending on the city you are in, the quality of the bar, and the quality of the women. At a typical bar in a typical city figure about p200 for a ladies drink. In Makati figure p400.

Ok. So now you sit down in public with your girl, enjoy your drinks and talk. The girls are generally trained to make a ladies drink last about half an hour. If the girl is good, she will flirt with you, cuddle with you, touch you and act in a seductive manner.

After the girl finishes her drink, you have a number of options.

- You can pay your bill and go home.

- You can dismiss her and continue to drink by yourself.

- You can dismiss her and request a different girl to sit with you.

- You can order another drink for her and continue to sit with her in public

- Or finally you can request a VIP room.

By the way, don't worry about hurting these girls feelings. Unfortunately for them, that's just part of the territory. If you buy a girl a ladies drink and then decide you don't like her, don't feel bad about requesting a different girl.

Ok, now suppose you like the girl and you want to request a VIP room. As discussed previously, the girl does not have to go into the VIP room with you, they have the right to refuse if they don't feel comfortable. Usually they won't refuse since this is how they make good money.

Now supposedly a VIP room is simply a comfortable private room with a karaoke machine where the two of you can choose songs and sing along with a microphone. This is how they might get around any local laws that prohibit sex for money. In fact, some people, particularly groups of people, do rent these VIP rooms for the purpose of relaxing, drinking and singing songs with their friends.

However if you rent one of these rooms by yourself and your entertainer, it's almost always the case you expect something else to happen. A happy ending. Before I get to the happy ending part let me describe how much it will cost to rent the room.

Any money you spent on drinks for yourself or your lady prior to renting the VIP room is separate. Typically you will pre-pay the VIP room at a cost of between p1000 and p2000 depending on city, the quality, etc etc. This fee is almost always "consumable" meaning the cost of the room is deducted from your drink bill. Often they will ask what drinks you want ahead of time and serve them all at once so they don't have to bother you while you sit there in privacy with your girl. Buy the way the doors are never kept locked, but they will knock before entering.

For example, suppose the VIP room is p1500, the ladies drinks are p300. and the regular beers are p50. You might request 4 ladies drinks for your lady and six beers for yourself. This will come to p1500 and will cost you nothing over the cost of the room, since p1500 is "consumable". Now if it's a decent karaoke establishment that treats their customers properly and doesn't play games, they should put all the drinks on the table at once and then leave you alone unless they are called. Sorry but you will have to get used to either warm beer or beer with ice.

Now the question becomes – how long will they allow you to be alone with the girl. That should depend on how many ladies drinks you ordered. Normally you are allowed about a half hour per ladies drink. In the example above you ordered four ladies drinks, so you should be allowed to spend two hours in the room. Make sure you negotiate this ahead of time. Some less reputable establishments play a game, where they bother you after only an hour insisting you buy more drinks if you want to stay in the room. To say the least this is rather annoying and can ruin the whole mood. In Filipino tradition  (see cultural habits) they may simply choose to ignore you and not answer this question, or pretend they don't understand your question. Don't let them get away with this! Make sure it is clear exactly how much time you are allowed in the room before you are forced to buy more drinks. If you don't like their answer you can try to negotiate. If they won't negotiate it's up to you, either resign yourself to paying more, or walk away. Don't pay the p1500 fee until this is resolved!

Ok, so now let's assume everything is resolved, you paid the fee, the drinks are on the table, and you are alone with your entertainer. Now what?

Well exactly what you do, and your style is up to you. Typically you start out by just cuddling and singing together, and progress from there. Often they will touch you on your pants to see if you are hard or encourage you to get hard. In the end it usually comes down to either masturbation or a blow job. You should not expect sexual intercourse. The room is not set up for it, and the door is not locked.

You are not required to pay anything further, but if the girl was nice to you, entertained you well, and finished in a satisfying "happy" way,  you might want to offer her a tip of p200 or p300 peso,  or if you are really happy and generous, p500.

So how much did all of this cost you? Quite a bit actually. Assume you ordered two ladies drinks and two regular beers before going to the VIP room. That's p700. The VIP room cost p1500. Assume a p200 tip for the girl, and p100 for the madam. That comes to a grand total of p2500, or about $50. But on the other hand, by western standards it's still cheep, and if all goes well it's enjoyable and you won't catch any diseases.

You might be curious to guess how much the girl gets out of this. Typically they get 40 to 50 percent of the price of the ladies drinks. Since in the example above you ordered a total of six ladies drinks at p300 each, for a total of p1800, she would get somewhere between p720 and p900. This is a pretty good amount of money for a Filipino for just a few hours work. However you have to remember that it's not always easy for a girl on a given day to get a VIP customer. There are usually more girls than customers. The successful girls can make a lot of money. Some girls make nothing and have to give up. It's a commission based job.

## Topic iv: *Massage*

When foreigners first come to the Philippines they are often confused about massage. They see massage parlors or clinics in many places. They have heard about massage often being sexual. Isn't there clean massage? Or, if you want sexy massage, how do you make sure and not embarrass yourself? Well you are right to be confused. You are right because several variations of massage exist in the Philippines. I will describe the three basic variations below.

### ♦ Legitimate Clean Massage

Actually the majority of massage places in the Philippines are clean. They are legitimate massage places with trained masseuses and do not do offer any sexual extra's. If you are in such a place don't embarrass yourself and make the masseuse feel uncomfortable by asking for any sexual extra. Well, how do you know if you are in a "clean" massage place? If the masseuse is wearing a formal looking, nurse like uniform, that's usually an indication of "clean only" massage. Most clean massage places will make the customer wear shorts. However even some clean massage places allow the customer to be naked. However, in such a case the masseuse will take care to always keep your private parts covered with a towel. They will never look at your penis. When giving you a massage they may get close to your groin area, but they will never touch your penis or testicles. Also, if the room is only a curtained in area without real walls or a real door, they will not offer extra, as there is not sufficient privacy.

### ◆ Legitimate Massage with Extra

There are some massage places that offer legitimate massage with trained masseuses that will nevertheless offer "Extra Services", otherwise known as a "happy ending". By EXTRA I mean massage of the penis (masturbation) until the point of orgasm. Extra in a legitimate massage place does NOT mean oral sex or sexual intercourse. It only means massage of that "special area".

How do you know if you are in a place that offers extra? How do you know the difference between a clean only massage and a massage offering extra? Well it's usually easy to tell. The following signals are usually present when extra is offered.

- The room will be completely private with real walls and a real door. Curtained in rooms are not suitable for "extra"

- The masseuse will usually be wearing more casual or sometimes even sexy attire, not a formal nurse like uniform.

- You will be asked to remove all your clothes and the massage will performed naked

- The masseuse will not take particular care to avoid seeing your nakedness. For example you might be asked to turn over and she won't even bother to cover you with a towel

- She will not shy away from body contact while giving you a massage. For example she may get up on the bed and straddle you while giving you a back massage so that she can apply extra pressure. With clean massage the masseuse will usually stay on the floor and apply the massage from the side.

- While performing the massage she will get very close to your penis and testicles and sometimes even "accidentally" brush up against them. If you get hard she won't say anything and will appear not to notice.

Ok, so suppose you are getting a massage and you are pretty sure from the signals that "extra" is offered". The massage is coming to an end. What happens? What do you do?

The masseuse will rarely if ever offer an extra service. She will usually just say "finished". This is your cue to ask for extra. Simply ask, "Do you offer extra?" She will know what you mean.

She might say something like, "how much you give me", or she might say something like, You mean "masturbation?", or something like that to make it clear that it is just massage of your penis, and nothing more. Anyway, typically, if you are a foreigner and not her regular customer she will start by requesting P1000. You tell her that's too much and offer her P500. She will usually shake her head indicating "no". She is hoping that you are so horny you will simply give in. Instead simply say, ok, never mind and start to get dressed. Most of the time they will say ok and do it for p500. That's pretty much the standard fee. Think about it from her point of view. Five hundred peso is two days work for many Filipinos. She can get an extra five hundred for about three minutes worth of work. You think she wants to give that up?

Not all cities have massage places offering extra. Many cities crack down on this practice. For the life of me I can't understand why. They will look the other way when prostitutes are roaming the streets, but enforce the massage laws. In my opinion the practice should be encouraged. It's very enjoyable for the customer, and far more safe than prostitution, and although you could argue it degrades the girls, you could also argue that it gives these girls a way to make good money without putting their health at risk. Also, which is more degrading, massaging a penis or fucking ten strangers a day?

One place where this practice is common is in Manila. In Manila there are many upscale massage and spa places which will also offer extra. Also if you are in a hotel in Manila and request an in room massage, most of the time these girls will do extra.

If you request a hotel or home massage, how can you know if the girls offer extra? Use similar techniques as described above. If the girl arrives in a fancy professional looking uniform, that's a signal they don't offer extra. When the girl arrives you might simply ask, how should I dress? If she says "take off all your clothes", or she says "up to you" that's a sign that she offers extra. If she says please wear shorts, that's a sure sign that she does not offer extra. While she is giving you the massage observe the same signals as described above, in terms of whether she looks at your body and how she touches you.

### ♦ Whore House Masquerading as a Massage Place

The third type of place is one I suggest you avoid at all costs. It is a whore house masquerading as a massage place. Typically these places are utterly disgusting. When you walk in you will immediately feel something is wrong. It will not seem like a legitimate massage place. It is likely to be dirty and ugly. The next sure sign is that they will ask for the money in advance. Legitimate massage places do not ask for the money in advance. If you ask to see or choose your masseuse more times than not they will refuse until you pay the money. If you do choose to continue and pay the money they will then lead you to an ugly room with a dirty bed, and an ugly disgusting prostitute. The prostitute might not even pretend they are a masseuse, they might ask right away what you want. If you do say you want to be massaged, they might give you a half hearted massage for about two minutes and then say "finished. What you want now?". If you told them you paid for massage and all you want is massage they would be utterly confused and annoyed. They want you to come in, fuck them, cum, leave your money and go. They don't want to waste their time giving massage for no additional fee.

Well, do you still want to visit one of these places after the picture I just painted? If you do, you are a truly desperate man!

## Topic v: *Is She or isn't She? (A Prostitute)*

So far we have discussed quite a few different kinds of sex workers. There is the hard core prostitute with a pimp (bugaw), there is the prostitute working in a whore house, there is the self employed bar prostitute and there are the dancers and entertainers affiliated with bars.

There is however one other kind woman (Prostitute?) that I have not discussed yet. This kind of woman seeks out a few steady partners and is available when needed by her partners for a fee.

The most common example of this is students. There are a certain group of young women who desperately want an education but simply can't afford it. They have made a well thought out and carefully weighed decision (which they would describe as being practical) that trading sex for money (hence education) is the lesser of two evils. The greater of the two evils being that they get no college education and are doomed to the kind of life led by the non educated.

In one study where many college students filled out anonymous questionnaires almost 50% of Filipina college students admitted to trading sex for money at least once.

Of course many of them do it a lot more than once. Many of them obtain their whole education in this manner. These girls of course do not like to think of themselves as prostitutes. In fact they would probably consider it quite insulting if you thought of them in this way. It would pain them to admit that they were any kind of prostitute.

These kind of girls do not want to take just anybody and they do not want the stress of having too many partners or partners they do not feel comfortable with. They want to set themselves up with a few partners that can support their education and with whom (if they don't actually enjoy) they can at least not feel disgusting with. They also do not want to present themselves overtly as offering sex for money. They work in a more subtle manner.

So how does it work for these women and how do they get set up with their partners.?

One way is that they simply keep an eye out for prospective clients. If a foreigner for example shows interest in them, they will show interest back if they feel he is an ok guy. At some point they will let it be known that they are a student needing money. They will feel out their prospective client to see if he is the kind of guy they want. Still, they will not usually directly mention money.

If you do wind up having sex with them, they will expect money. If you don't offer it to them, they may ask, by saying something like "I need to buy some books for my classes, can you help me out?".

If you don't give them money, they will not be happy, but there is nothing they can do. However you will never see them again. If you do get the hint and give them a thousand pesos or so, they will be happy and available to you in the future. When you do give them the money they will be much happier if you say "here is some money because I want to help you with your studies" rather than if you say, "here is some money for having sex with me".

The other way these girls connect with their clients is through the grape vine. Maybe some guy mentions he has a friend looking, so one girl introduces her lover's friends to one of her friends. Sometimes there are people (usually gay) who specialize in setting up the arrangement. They will usually expect a good size tip for setting up the arrangement but after that you need never pay them again.

# Chapter 27: Expat Citizenship

**Expat hanging out with Filipino friends**

When I talk about citizenship I am not talking about the legalistic meaning which describes a citizen as "a naturalized member of a state or nation who owes allegiance to it's government and is entitled to it's protection". I'm talking about the more simple non legal definition in which a citizen is simply a member living in society, fitting in, acting appropriately and interacting with that society.

When discussing Expat citizenship in the Philippines there are two things to think about. The first is how to be seen as a good citizen. The second is how to accept your role as a second class citizen. I will discuss each of these topics below.

## Topic i: *Good Citizenship*

When you are living in the Philippines it's really important that you be a good citizen. Actually let me re-phrase that. It's really important that people think you are a good citizen. Appearances are everything. You might be a lousy guy behind closed doors that is mean to your wife and overworks your helper, but if in public you are smiling helpful and friendly and don't cause problems, that's what is important, at least in terms of your acceptance by other Filipinos. Conversely, you might have the best heart in the world, you might be a person that really cares about and helps people, but if you sometimes get into arguments, lose your temper or in general cause problems your good heart will do you no good. All in all it's best that you satisfy both sides of the equation.

What happens if you get on the wrong side of Filipinos? Well in extreme cases this can cause you terrible problems, even your life. But let's not talk about extreme cases, let's just talk about your everyday run of the mill cases.

Filipinos hate foreigners that cause problems. If you get the reputation of being "not a very good guy", a guy that causes problems and gets in arguments, you will be ostracized by the Filipino community. You will feel it, and it will feel lonely. If you have a problem, and you need help, there will be no one willing to help you.

On the other hand, if they like you, and they feel you are a good guy, they will go out of their way to be friendly to you, and to give you help in the event of any problems that you might have. In particular it's helpful to make friends with some of the more influential Filipinos in your area, such as policemen, politicians or other high level professionals.

So how do you be seen as a good guy? How do you make the Filipino community like and respect you? Let's break it up into DOs and Don'ts.

### ♦ Don't Lose Your Temper

Filipinos hate it when you lose your temper. They are not at all comfortable with it. One loss of temper can cause you to loose a lot of good will. Strive at all times to manage your anger.

### ♦ Don't Get Into Arguments

Similar to losing your temper, Filipinos are not fond of getting into arguments. In general they don't handle it well and have trouble not getting angry. When you talk to your casual Filipino acquaintances keep the conversation light. Don't get into controversial topics, or if you do, be prepared to retreat at the first sign of trouble. If for example you are discussing the topic of birth control and the role of the Catholic church, and you feel them starting to get upset, simply say "well I understand your point of view", and then change the subject.

### ♦ Don't Disparage the Philippine Image

Philippines in general are proud of their culture and heritage. If they are playing the national anthem you should stand up.. Don't remain seated because you are Westerner. Never directly disparage the Philippine image or name. For example If you were to ever get in an argument and say something like "what do you know, you are just a stupid Filipino", that kind of talk could get you into a lot of trouble. Those are fighting words.

### ♦ Don't Treat Your Wife and/or Helper Badly

If it becomes general knowledge that you treat your Wife and/or helper badly people will lose respect for you. In extreme cases, if for example people found out your beat your wife on a regular basis, you could wind up dead. Filipinos are protective of their fellow citizens. Of course if you are the kind of person that treats your wife badly, reading this paragraph is unlikely to change your behavior!

### ♦ Don't Cause Problems

Let me give a concrete example here, about something that actually happens commonly. Namely that they permanently lock a fire door. Suppose you are in a restaurant or bar, and you notice the back fire door is permanently locked with a pad lock. Above the door it says "FIRE EXIT". In the USA this would be a pretty serious infraction, one for which they could get a hefty fine. In the Philippines it happens all the time. When an establishment is trying to get their initial license they have to make sure they pass the codes. After that no one usually looks, and if they don't like the idea of having a fire door, they simply lock it. Fire doors sometimes present a problem for management, as an unguarded fire door is a way for a customer to leave unnoticed, and a guarded fire door would be a waste of money and resources. Often they solve this problem by simply locking it. Of course they could add an alarm system to the door, but that would probably never even enter their thought process! Why should they do that when they can simply and inexpensively lock the door.

Suppose you notice this locked door and ask to talk to the manager. When the manager arrives you say in a nice way "I noticed that your fire door is permanently locked, isn't that dangerous?" So far, no real problem. There is nothing wrong in bringing it to his attention. He may be mildly annoyed but that's about it, no big deal.

The manager will thank you for bringing it to his attention and then proceed to utterly ignore your concern. Of course the manager knew the fire door was locked, it was probably his decision.

At this point, in keeping with being a non-problem-maker you need to just forget about the whole thing.

But what happens if you don't want to forget about it. What happens if you make a big deal about it. Let's explore what would probably happen if you went down this path.

Suppose two weeks later you were at the establishment again and you noticed that the fire door was still locked. Suppose you talked to the manager again and said something like: "I'm afraid I simply have to insist that you unlock your fire door, it's simply too dangerous. If you ignore my request I will have to report you to the authorities".

Such a statement would probably enrage the manager. He would probably control himself, but inside he would be seething. His attitude is: "why is this foreigner causing problems, it's none of his business, this is not his country". Almost certainly he would ignore your request. His pride alone would not permit him to honor your request.

Now suppose your make good on your threat and you go to the local authorities and report the problem. You might think that they will be receptive to you. You might think that they will be eager to investigate and  fix the problem. But this is not what is going to happen. The authority will also be thinking, "why is this foreigner causing problems". The authority will understand how the Manager will feel if he permits this foreigner to control the situation. Most likely the authority will pretend to thank you for bringing the problem to his attention and then he too will ignore you.

The more you pursue the issue, the more everyone will hate you for it. In the end you will be mightily sorry you ever went down this path.

So the moral of the story is this: "You're just a foreigner, you're just a guest in the country, don't cause problems!"

### ♦ Do Be Friendly

Filipinos appreciate if you are friendly, open and accessible. They appreciate it if you accept their offer to join them for a beer every once in a while. Now if you are not friendly, and avoid contact with Filipinos on a social level, this will not make them hate you, but neither will it endear yourself to them.

### ♦ Do Treat Everybody With Respect

Treat everybody with respect. Don't put down anybody and don't put down Filipino people, Filipino culture or the country of the Philippines. Avoid being negative.

### ♦ Do Treat Your Wife Well

If your wife honestly and truly loves you and believes you are a good guy, she can be your best advocate. People will always be asking your wife, "What's he really like? Does he treat you well? Is he a good guy?". If she is always building you up, this gets ingrained into peoples attitude about you. They are more likely to give you the benefit of the doubt and think of you as a good guy. On the other hand if your wife is always saying bad things about you, this will also color their view of you in a negative way.

### ♦ Do Be Generous (Within Reason)

Every once in a while it's appreciated if you treat Filipinos to some beers, or food, or whatever. This does not mean you should give away all your money in the hopes of being liked! In fact, they probably would not even respect you for that. But the right amount of generosity in the right situations can do a lot to build up their good will towards you.

## Topic ii: *Accepting Your Roll as a Second Class Citizen*

If you are a good guy, a good Expat citizen, Filipinos will accept you and be friendly to you. However never get confused and think you have the same rights as a Filipino. Filipino rights always take precedent over foreigner rights. I'm not talking about the written law, I'm talking about the de-facto law.

Consider the example above concerning the locked fire exit. Had a Filipino of decent standing made the complaint the manager probably would have resigned himself to unlocking the door (at least for a while). Or had the manager refused and the Filipino reported the problem to the local authorities, they probably would have felt obligated to investigate. Of course in real life this would rarely if ever happen. Filipinos themselves are not fond of causing problems.

Since I am an avid tennis player, I will give you some examples related to some of my tennis experiences.

At one tennis club where I belonged I Noticed a number of annoying problems which could be fixed for very little or no expense. For example there was a hole in the fence where the balls were always going through. For about 20 pesos they could buy some wire and fix up the hole. I wrote up a list of these easy to fix problems and handed them to the Manager. Of course everyone of them was ignored. It's seems their pride won't let them fix it because they don't want to be told what to do by a foreigner. Had a Filipino made the suggestions, some of them probably would have been followed.

Here is another example that occurred in a different town at a government run tennis facility. During the day time the court operated on a first come first serve basis. However, at night, under the lights, the courts were reserved. I inquired, how you go about reserving court time? I was instructed to go to the town recreation office where I could reserve time. When I arrived at the office the woman was friendly to me and told me, yes you can reserve time. Just pick out the time you want and pre-pay for the lights and court and I will give you a ticket. So I did exactly that.

When the time came for me to play and I arrived at the courts with ticket in hand, I was told that it was not my time. I was told the courts were already reserved, and the people playing, played at this time every week.

I protested, "but I was told you can reserve the court at the recreation office, I even have a ticket stating this is my time".

Despite my reservation they would not give up the court.

The next day I went back to the recreation office and told my story. The woman there said she would bring it up with her boss, a higher up government official, and that I should get back to her tomorrow.

So the next day when I was got back to her, she told me that her boss said I should bring up the problem with the president of the tennis club, and she handed me a name and a telephone number.

So later that day I called the President of the club and introduced myself. It seems he had already been made aware of the situation. As soon as he heard my name, he said, "I'm busy now, I'll call you back later". Of course he never did. I got the idea. I am only a foreigner, and the night time reservations are for Filipinos. At this point I gave up, which I can assure you was the right thing to do.

So the bottom line is this. Don't expect to be a first class citizen. You are not, you are a second class citizen. Accept this and you will be better off.

# Chapter 28: Potpourri of Living Related Topics

## Topic i: *Motels (Smotels)*

**Typical Motel (Smotel)**

In the Philippines a motel should really be called a smotel. Can you guess what the S stands for?

A motel in American English implies a hotel on a major highway with doors leading directly to the outside, so you can conveniently drive right up to your room and then go inside.

A motel in Philippine English has a totally different meaning. It is a special kind of hotel specializing in making it convenient, private and discreet for couples wishing to have sex.

The following types of couples may frequent a motel

- Men bringing prostitutes

- Young couples hiding from their parents and friends

- Men having affairs with their mistresses.

- Any couple that does not have a private place to have sex.

The way it works is this. You drive your vehicle into the motel complex. A motel worker or guard will appear and open a garage door for you. You enter the garage and without a word being spoken the worker closes the garage door behind you. From the garage you enter directly into the room which is connected to the garage.

There is typically a telephone in the room which if picked up will go directly to the office. If you want something like a snack or beer or a condom you can pick up a phone and call the office and somebody will deliver the items to your room. If you don't pick up the phone nobody will bother you. So go ahead and have fun. If you so desire not a word will be spoken to you by the staff from the moment you enter the complex until you are ready to leave. The room charge is by the hour, typically something like 300 pesos for the first two hours and 100 peso an hour after that.

There is no checkin or checkout, nothing to sign, you never leave your name. When you are ready to leave pick up the phone and tell them you are ready to go. Shortly thereafter a worker will appear with your bill. After you pay it, the garage door will be opened and you can leave.

What a wonderful Philippine invention!

## Topic ii: *Popular Sports in the Philippines*

Sports are quite popular in the Philippines, and there are many good athletes. I think the only reason there are not more Filipino athletes performing at the international level is that their diminutive size hurts their chances. In sports such as boxing and billiards where size does not matter they do have some world renowned athletes.

The following sports are available to the casual athlete and spectator.

- **Basketball**

Basketball is perhaps the most popular sport in the Philippines. There are many basketball courts all over the Philippines, even in poor areas. Many of these courts are not in the greatest condition, but that doesn't stop the Filipino kids, teenagers and young adults who love to play. Unfortunately for you, basketball is a young persons sport, and since readers of this book are most likely 40 or older, you probably won't be participating in much basketball.

- **Tennis**

Tennis is also very popular and available in most cities throughout the country. Tennis is popular among young and old alike. There are basically three flavors of tennis courts available, namely government run tennis clubs which are subsidized and very inexpensive, private clubs which are more expensive but still very reasonable compared to the USA and town owned tennis courts which are free. Town owned tennis courts are almost always hard court and available on a first come first serve basis. Private and Government courts are sometimes hard court and sometimes clay. Most tennis courts always have kids hanging around who will serve as your ball boys and scorers. It's not considered polite to reject their services. The cost is very low, typically 20 to 40 pesos per set (divided between two or four players). Most foreigners initially feel uncomfortable having a ball boy and scorer but they quickly get used to it and learn to like it.

- **Golf**

Available at many upscale, often PRA approved facilities and locations, throughout the country. If you enjoy golf there are plenty of places to play and the cost, while extremely expensive by Filipino standards, is still much less than in the USA.

- **Boxing**

Filipinos love watching boxing and have some world renowned boxers. Manny Pacquiao is considered pound for pound one of the best boxers in the world and is a national hero in the Philippines.

- **Billiards**

Billiards is very popular in the Philippines and can be found in many locations in a typical city. Billiard tables range from barely playable to first class, with the price reflecting the quality of the table. In any case the price is very reasonable. You can typically rent tables by the hour or in some places there are "challenge" tables, where the winner stays on, and the loser pays for the game.

- **Badminton**.

Most cities offer indoor badminton facilities. Badminton is a popular sport in the Philippines

- **Table Tennis (Ping Pong)**

Not one of the most popular sports but tables can be found for rent in some locations.

- **Cock Fighting**

Cock fighting is one of the national pastimes in the Philippines, and you will never convince Filipinos that it's a cruel sport. Actually, since the losing cock is almost always eaten, I myself don't really see the big deal. What's the difference if one cock kills another, or if you chop off their head at a farm? In the meantime, between fights, the fighting cocks are treated like kings, given the best food and care in the hopes of producing a winning cock. If I was a cock I would rather be a fighting cock than a farm cock.

There are a number of interesting curiosities about cock fighting. One of the most fascinating aspects to me is the way the betting is handled. When you go to a cock fight there are professional bet takers called Kristos. People who want to bet call out the bets verbally or with hand signals and if anybody agrees to the bets the Kristo sets it up. Everything is done verbally or by hand signals. Nothing is written down. The Kristo may handle dozens of bets for a single cock fight. The Kristos seem to have a photographic memory, they never forget a bet and they never seem to make a mistake. If you don't know what you are doing I strongly suggest you don't try betting. You might accidentally agree to a large bet when you think you are making a small bet. You can get yourself In trouble that way. They will insist that you cover your bet. If you do want to go to a cock fight and want to bet, go with an experienced person, and tell him what you want, and let him place the bet.

Of course I am an inexperienced observer, and I'm sure experienced Filipinos would disagree, but to me the fights seem kind of stupid and random. Here is why: The cocks do **not** fight naturally to the death in a test of stamina and ultimate fighting skill. If they were allowed to do that the fights might last many minutes or even an hour or more. This is not what the audience wants. Cock fighting is all about betting and the audience wants many fights. To speed up the fights razor blades are strapped to the feet of the cocks. As a result the first cock to get in a good slash is usually the winner. The fights usually last between 30 seconds and two minutes. They rarely last more than three minutes. To me this would be like strapping deadly razor blades to the fists of boxers. Then instead of boxing being a test of stamina and skill, it would be a test of who could get in the first good punch.

- **Volleyball**

Volleyball is played at many schools and at beaches.

- **Chess**

There are many chess clubs in the Philippines and many good chess players. Eugene Torre is a Filipino Grandmaster residing in Baguio. I once had the privilege of playing tennis with him.

- **Bicycling and Hiking**

Hiking and bicycling clubs are common in the Philippines, if you are fit enough to participate in them. Most Expats are not!

- **Bowling**

Not really that popular in the Philippines, but some bowling alleys exist in the popular high end SM malls.

- **About Soccer (Football)**

I don't know why, but soccer is not at all popular in the Philippines. In fact, in my more than 7 years in the Philippines I have never seen soccer being played. When I recently brought up this point at a party I was told I was wrong, and that soccer is played in the Philippines. Ok, but still I have never seen it!

## Topic iii: *Filipino Mosquitoes are Very Clever!*

I'm not sure why I am bothering to include this topic in my book, it's not like it's going to help you in anyway. But it's true, and I think it's interesting, so I decided to talk about it.

Filipino Mosquitoes are nothing like the mosquitoes in the USA, at least the ones I'm familiar with in the Northeast part of the USA. American mosquitoes are sort of like B17 bombers. They are big and lumbering. They make a buzzing noise that you can hear and they don't maneuver very fast. If you get a clear view of one you can usually kill it.

Filipino Mosquitoes are more like fighter planes. They are small, quick, hard to see and very maneuverable. They are damn hard to kill. And there's more! You could swear they are intelligent! If you see one flying around you coming in for a bite, the mere noticing of it, or looking at it makes it fly away. It's almost as if they catch your gaze and know that they are in danger. I don't know how they do it, but it's not my imagination. So when you come to the Philippines get ready for a whole new type of mosquito!

## Topic iv: *Internet Information, Expat Discussion Forums, Yahoo Groups*

Some people, when deciding whether or not to buy a book like this one, may think to themselves:

"Why do I need to spend good money on a book  about the Philippines when there is so much information available for free on the internet?".

Well it's true, there is a ton of information available on the internet. In fact that's the problem, there is too much information available, some of which is good, much of it useless or misleading.  Weeding through it and integrating the information in your mind is the problem. It can be a very time consuming process.

One of the problems is what I will call the tendency to sugar coat things. This is especially true of an sites sponsored by Philippine organizations like city or regional tourist offices. They will give descriptions that are overly positive without exploring or admitting to the negative aspects.

One way to get more honest and realistic points of view  and information about everyday life and problems for Expats is to visit the various forums and discussion threads that are available.

One easy way to find such forums is to visit www.yahoo.com and then click on GROUPS. Then enter something like "Cebu" or "Expat Philippines" into the search box and click on "search".

You will be presented with a list of groups. For example "Living in Cebu" and "Living in the Philippines" are two groups you might want to explore.

All the groups have discussion forums. A discussion forum is basically the ability for a group member to post an initial question or topic. You can list or search through the initial topics, there might be hundreds or even thousands of them. If you click on a topic or "thread" you then get a list of all the people that wrote in answers to the initial topic. When somebody answers a question, somebody else can respond to the response, and so on.

For example consider the discussion thread below. The level of indentation shows the hierarchy.

**BILL asks**: I currently live in the USA but I will soon be coming to live in the Philippines, and I am a bit of a handy man. Is there any reason I can't bring over my electric power tools to the Philippines?

> **ALEX responds to BILL**: There is no problem. Of course the USA is 110 volts and the Philippines is 220 volts, but this is not really a problem. Simply buy a step down transformer that converts 220 volts to 110 volts, these transformers are readily available in the Philippines.
>
>> **Barry responds to ALEX**: I don't recommend bringing your electric power tools. Yes it's true you can buy a transformer, but my experience is, sooner or later you or somebody else will accidentally plug it into 220, and poof, that's the end of your tool. I personally have had three of my electric power tools ruined this way.
>>
>>> **PAUL responds to Barry**: Yes Barry, what you say is true, but I found a way around it, so that there is no danger. I

replaced all the normal plugs of my 110 volt tools with special three prong air conditioning type plugs which can't fit into normal Philippine electric outlets. I then attached the receptacle for the special plugs to my transformer. Now the only place the tools can be plugged into is my transformer.

**JOHN responds** (directly) **to BILL**: I don't recommend you bring your tools. You might run into customs problems. I had to pay large customs fee's on some of my tools. There are plenty of tools available in the Philippines, why go through the bother of bringing them here.

**BOBBY responds to JOHN:** John, no offense, but what a dumb answer! Why bother? To save money, of course! Who wants to spend good money buying electric tools when you don't need to. I brought over some of my electric tools and had no problem with customs officials. Maybe your tools were new, and that's why they charged you customs fees.

Discussion forums are a good way to learn about the life of Expats as they present real problems and real solutions and unfiltered, non sugar coated discussions. However reading discussion forums is not an efficient way to learn. It's very time consuming. Be prepared to spend many hours reading such forums to glean perhaps just a few golden nuggets of knowledge.

## Topic v: *NO DIVORCE and It's Implications*

As I've mentioned in passing in previous sections there is no divorce in the Philippines. Many laws in the Philippines are influenced by the Catholic church, and this is certainly one of them. The Philippines is one of the very few country that does not allow divorce. So what does the "no divorce" rule mean to Filipinos  and what does it mean to Expats marrying Filipina woman?

### ♦ What are the Implications of No Divorce for Filipino Families?

Believe it or not most Filipino men,  especially men with some wealth  and power (in other words, the ones making the laws), like the fact that there is no divorce in the Philippines. For most this has nothing to do with religious or moral beliefs, rather it has to do with practical reasons. They have lived under this system for many years and have adapted to it and they do not want to change it for reasons I will now describe.

Suppose you are a western man living in a typical western country like the USA. Suppose you are reasonably well off having considerable wealth and power.  Further suppose you are a playboy and like to enjoy women outside your marriage. In a country like the USA this can have dire consequences. If your wife so desires she can file for divorce and if she can prove your infidelity she is likely to get a large share of your assets.

You have no ability to prevent the divorce and no ability (other than hiring a good lawyer which will only help somewhat) to prevent the transfer of much of your assets to your soon to be ex-wife.

The Filipino man does not have to worry about this. Sure he has to worry about the fact that he is living under the same roof with his wife, and that it's not pleasant to have someone angry at you, but that's about it. He does not have to worry about losing his house or property, his assets or custody of his kids. This is a big burden off your shoulders if you choose to have an affair.

Well in fact that's the way it works in the Philippines. In a western country if your marriage does not work out you get a divorce, in the Philippines (if you have the money to do so) you take on a mistress.

Actually, this does not only apply to bad marriages, but it also applies to perfectly good marriages where the couple has been together many years. Consider this example. A couple got married when they were each 20 years old, and they are now 50. They have a house and five kids. The excitement has long ago left the marriage. The man is no longer interested in having sex with his 50 year old wife, but they still get along perfectly well. The woman is comfortable in her house and takes comfort in her family life and being with her five kids, her relatives and all her friends. The man, not yet ready to give up on the excitement of sex has an ongoing affair with a younger woman.

Truth be told it is often the case that the woman does not even care that much. She is likely to look the other way. Why should she make a big deal about it. She has a good life, let her husband have a little fun, as long as he is not serious with that woman.

So in fact the no divorce law encourages affairs because there are no dire consequences and because it also prevents the affair from being too serious because the mistress knows the man is married and can't get divorced. All things considered, in my opinion, all in all, the no divorce law benefits Filipino men far more than it benefits Filipino woman.

### ◆ What are the Implications of No Divorce for Expats Marrying Filipinas?

Well I guess it means you should choose carefully before you Marry.

It means you probably won't get a second chance to marry a second Filipina woman.

It means that if you put property in your wife's name and it does not work out, you will probably be forced to walk away and may not get a penny (I mean centavo).

It could mean, if your wife is a vindictive type and she can prove you have been with other women, she could file a motion to have you deported. I've seen this happen once and although the wife ultimately failed in her attempt to have him deported, he spent a fortune on lawyers fees defending himself and his life was miserable for several months.

So if it does not work out, is it always the end of the world, does something terrible always happen?

Not always. You could make some kind of agreement with your wife to go your separate ways. Usually she will want some compensation. You could just give her some money and then just take off and disappears to another part of the country and hope she does not have the resources or the state of mind to pursue you.

If you make some kind of agreement to go your separate ways, be a little bit careful. If you give her a lump sum of money, unless there is some kind of written agreement legally set up with a lawyer, who is to keep her from requesting or pressuring for more at a later time.

Another possibility is to inform her that you are going your separate way, and there is nothing she can do to stop you, but you will continue to voluntarily send her, say, p10,000 a month. This then puts her in a difficult position. If she fights you she could wind up with nothing, so it is likely she will take the offer and not give you any problems so long as you keep paying her the money every month.

There is also the issue of permanent residence. As I understand it (and I'm not sure I understand it that well) permanent residence is not really permanent and must be renewed after ten years. If you are separated from your wife I don't how this will affect your application renewal.

I guess the bottom line is, if things don't work out with your wife, it's not a good thing. I guess it never is, no matter where you live.

This might be a good reason to avoid marriage all together and go the SRRV route. Unfortunately most Expats don't think about it or are not even aware of it until it is too late.

## Topic vi: *The Scam of Annulment*

I'm not on expert on the Catholic church and it's doctrines, but I'm pretty sure the concept of marriage annulment was as a way to reverse marriages that are scams. Marriages coerced by force or bribery, or perhaps cases where a drunken couple tied the knot in a fit of drunken silliness, or, perhaps to reverse marriages where it clear after a very short time that the initially happy couple is absolutely miserable with each other.

However, in the Philippines, instead of legitimate annulments being used to reverse scam marriages, scam annulments are used to reverse legitimate marriages.

Men with power, money and influence can usually get an annulment if they want. Poor men don't have a chance. Annulment is the Philippine version of divorce available only to the wealthy and influential.

Annulments in the Philippines have nothing to do with the legitimacy of the marriage and have everything to do with the wealth, power, influence and skill of the person requesting the annulment. I talked to one man who had received an annulment from the Catholic church who had been married 20 years and had six kids! To me this is more than a bit weird! After all that you pretend the marriage never happened? Anyways, that's the way it is.

What about annulments for Expats? Actually there are two situations in which an annulment could conceivably benefit an Expat.

The first situation is where you meet a Filipina and fall in love with her but the trouble is, she is already married. Well most Expats would strongly advise you to just find somebody else, as there are plenty of wonderful Filipina fish in the South China Sea. They would certainly be giving you prudent advice. But let's just say hypothetically that you have your heart set on this woman, you feel she is one in a million and you are willing to do whatever it takes to be with her. In this case you might attempt an annulment.

The other situation of course is where you are already married to a Filipina woman and it didn't work out. In this case it would be even harder for you to obtain an annulment because the woman, your wife, would be working against you instead of with you (unless of course your wife also wanted an annulment).

In any case, let's just suppose you have made the decision to attempt it.

The first thing I want to say about this is, that for a foreigner to attempt an annulment is a very dangerous business. I don't mean physically dangerous, I mean monetarily dangerous. You have a very high probability of getting scammed. Even in cases were somebody is basically legitimate in trying to obtain an annulment for you, they will try to suck all the money that they can out of you. If will be very hard for you to tell whether they are working legitimately on your behalf, or whether you are being scammed. You could spend a whole lot of money and never get your annulment and there would be nothing you could do about it. It will always start with them telling you something like they only need p20,000 to initiate the procedure, and then after that they will always be asking you for more and more and more. The more you put in, the more you feel invested, the harder it is to walk away, the more they will want. Imagine a situation where you have already paid the facilitator p300,000 and then he tells you , it's almost done! P50,000 more and the deal is done! So you give him the P50,000, and guess what, a little while later he needs just a little bit more.

So hopefully, by knowing the pitfalls you can improve your chances. If you do attempt this very difficult task, here are two suggestions I can make.

First and foremost make sure you get the right facilitator to help you. Of course you can't petition for an annulment directly, you don't know the system, it's impossible. Somebody who claims to be an expert will have to help you and your most important task is to make sure that person is legitimate. If you can find an Expat who did it, or at least a Filipino who did it, and use the same facilitator that is your best bet.

Second consider your financial arrangement very carefully. You can be sure it's going to cost you a whole lot of money to get an annulment. If somebody claims they can do it for just 20, or 50 or even p100,000, they are just trying to suck you in. So you should have an idea how much an annulment for a foreigner is going to cost and you should figure on a budget and not go over it. Don't have an open ended agreement where you just pay more and more and more. Specifically it might be prudent to make an arrangement something like the following:

Suppose you have decided you are willing to spend p300,000 ($6000) dollars for your annulment. Set up a contract with your facilitator where you give him P100,000 for expenses, and you will put p200,000 into an escrow account to be released to your facilitator upon the successful completion of your annulment. Set a time limit so that if the annulment is not complete by a certain date the money will be released back to you. Make it all legally binding with a real lawyer and all of that. After that make sure you don't get sucked into paying another penny (I mean centavo).

Now if your facilitator is a scam artist he might just take the money, pretend to try for a little while and then tell you sorry, it's not possible. Don't expect to get any of your P100,000 back. Or if he is a real superstar scam artist he might even tell you he needs more for expenses, as the people he needs to pay off need the money in advance. Don't fall for it. Be ready to walk away and lose your initial investment.

If the facilitator is legitimate he is of course going to want to work for that extra p200,000. He should be able to convince the people who need paying off that there is definite money available because the client has already paid p100,000 and there is p200,000 more waiting in a legally binding escrow account.

Ugh! It's a tough road! My best advice is don't try it!

## Topic vii: *Water Situation*

The quality of tap water varies greatly from place to place within the Philippines. In some places the tap water is actually drinkable. In other places it's pretty bad and dangerous to drink. Most Expats try to avoid drinking tap water as much as possible.

The good news is that almost everywhere in the Philippines there are water stations, places where they sell water, typically in 5 gallon containers. These water stations create the water using modern state of the art (or so they tell us) filtering techniques. From personal experience it seems the water from these stations is pretty good. At least it tastes good and I seem to tolerate it well. I have not done any research on the quality of this water or it's long term effects.

If you are really paranoid about the water you can buy name brand water in smaller quantities available in most locations in the Philippines. However this is far more expensive. Whereas a five gallon container of filtered water typically costs between 30 and 50 peso, a 1 gallon (4 liter) bottle of name brand water may cost about 80 peso. So, as an approximation, it would be ten times as expensive to buy name brand water.

In locations where the Filipinos themselves don't hesitate to drink the water, you may have a hard time avoiding tap water completely. They are likely to use it in their cooking, coffee and ice. Unless you avoid restaurants completely you may wind up drinking some of the local tap water. Most likely you will be fine, particularly after you have been here a while and your body has adapted to it.

## Topic viii: *Electricity Situation*

There are two things to know about electricity in the Philippines. The first is that the voltage is 220. If you accidentally plug your 110v appliance into a 220v receptacle there is a good chance it will be destroyed instantly. For more information on this subject see the example forum discussion thread in the section titled

### "Internet information, Expat discussion forums, Yahoo groups"

The second thing to know about electricity in the Philippines is that it is not that dependable. It's nothing like what you are used to in a typical first world country.

In general you can expect an average of about one outage (which they call a brownout – not a blackout) per week, in some places even more often. There is typically no power grid, so if there is a problem, there is no backup system. The brownouts generally last from just a few minutes up to several hours or more. Sometimes they even have scheduled brownouts for maintenance, which are typically on Sunday and may go from 8am to 5pm.

So what can you do when these brownouts occur?

You can just suffer in your house or apartment.

You can escape by going to the beach or a swimming pool. You can escape by going to a restaurant that has its own generator, many do. Some establishments have generators only powerful enough to run the lights and other normal appliances, but not the air conditioner. Other establishments have more powerful generators that can also run the air conditioners.

What if you really don't want to suffer and you don't want to be forced to leave your house.

One choice is a UPS (un-interruptible power supply) with a large battery. Such a UPS may be able to run your computer or TV, a small fan and a light for a few hours. Two hours will cover the majority of brownouts. However you will still have to suffer without air conditioning.

Or, as an alternative to a UPS, you can by a small generator which is equivalent in power to the UPS (no air conditioning) but which can last indefinitely as long as you have gasoline. You can buy a small cheap Chinese generator for as little as p10,000. A small name brand generator will cost double that.

If you want a generator large enough to power your TV, computer, lights, refrigerator and air conditioner you will have to spend p50,000 or more.

The problem with generators are they are noisy, messy, create potentially dangerous fumes (make sure the generator is properly vented) and require the handling of dangerous gasoline. Most Expats do not bother with generators.

## Topic ix: *What Bathrooms are Like*

Bathrooms vary greatly from place to place within the Philippines. In many places, particularly outside of cities, it's hard to find a decent bathroom. Most of the bathrooms are very dirty and lack both toilette seat and toilette paper. Even in the cities, although the bathrooms will typically be cleaner, they often lack toilette seat and toilette paper. If you need to find a toilette with a toilette seat you may have to look for an upscale hotel or restaurant. If you are traveling within the Philippines and you don't trust your ability to hold your poop (technical term), you should be sure and bring some kind of kit with you that includes toilette paper and disposable plastic to put on the dirty seatless toilettes.

# Topic x: *About Philippine Languages*

## ♦ General Discussion

The topic of languages in the Philippines is a fascinating subject. I'm hardly an expert, but nevertheless I will attempt to shed some light on the subject and offer you a few of my insights.

According to Wikipedia (online encyclopedia) there are approximately 166 original native languages of Malayo-Polynesian decent. There are 13 native languages which each have one million or more speakers. One or more of these 13 languages is spoken natively by more than 90% of the population.

Most Filipinos refer to the different languages as different dialects, which confused me, since to me, something like Australian English and American English are different dialects, easily understood by each other but with different accents and phrases.

You know what I mean mate? Now now, don't be a Bullbag, just calm down and she'll be apples. No worries mate.

Since Filipinos speaking different Philippine "Dialects" can't understand each other, this to me seems like different languages. To alleviate my confusion I went to ASK.COM and asked "What is the difference between a language and a dialect?"

The first listed site, called "The Five minute Linguist" had this to say:

*Strange as it may seem, there's no really good way to distinguish between a "language" and a "dialect."*

The article went on to say that the word "Dialect" means different things to different people. So there you have it, for a foreigner you can consider it 165 different native languages, but Filipinos prefer to think of it as 165 different dialects. Perhaps the fact they are all spoken by native Filipinos for them determines that they are different dialects, as opposed to languages like Spanish and English, which originated outside the Philippines.

Although there are so many languages spoken in the Philippines, there are three main languages which really dominate, both in terms of total usage and in cultural significance. These are Tagalog/Filipino, Cebuano/Visayan and of course English.

### ♦ Tagalog / Filipino

Originally Tagalog was the main native language of Luzon, particularly the area around Manila.

A question that visitors often ask is: What is the difference between Tagalog and Filipino?

Well the first answer is, "not too much". They are basically the same language and the terms are often used interchangeably.

That being said, I will now describe the official difference. Tagalog is the language of the ethnic group by the same name. Filipino is the official language of the Philippines. Whereas Tagalog is simply the language of the Tagalog people, the Filipino language is supposed to be based on Tagalog but includes other commonly used words from other native Philippine languages as well as some words borrowed from Spanish and English. For example, the word kumusta (how are you – from Spanish) is considered part of the Filipino language, but certainly not part of the original Tagalog language.

Now once again, as far as the official distinction goes, this is mainly something for politicians and academics to talk about. For the common Filipino they are the same language, and some Filipinos choose to call it Tagalog and some choose to call it Filipino.

## ◆ Cebuano / Visayan

Similar to the relationship between Tagalog and Filipino, the languages **Cebuano** and **Visayan** are almost the same.

Cebuano is the language of the people of Cebu, called Cebuanos. As it so happens the language all over the region known as the Visayas is very similar (but with very small differences) to the language known as Cebuano. Many people use the designations interchangeably, but theoretically Cebuano is the language of the people of Cebu, whereas Visayan is the language of all people living in the Visayan region. The differences in language between different islands in the Visayan region would be analogous to the differences in language between England, Australia and the USA. What I (but not Filipinos) would refer to as different dialects.

Visayan is actually the most widely spoken native language in the Philippines (i.e. spoken as the native tongue as opposed to the people that learned Tagalog as a second language because it's the official language of the Philippines). Among the islands where Visayan is common are Negros, Cebu, Leyte, Bohol and Mindanao.

## ◆ English

English is probably the most widely spoken language in the Philippines, even more universally spoken than Filipino/Tagalog. The difference is, English is nobody's native language and everybody's second language, as opposed to Filipino and Visayan which are spoken natively by millions of Filipinos. Almost everyone in the Philippines knows at least a little bit of English and English is well spoken by the educated all over the Philippines.

In many parts of the Philippines where Filipino/Tagalog is not the native language, Filipinos actually feel more comfortable speaking English than they do Filipino.

English is the language on most road signs, the language of choice for government and business discussions as well as the language used for instruction in all the best schools.

### ◆ History of the "Official Language"

The history of Filipino as the "official" national language is actually quite complex and rich involving numerous controversies, name changes and evolving philosophical thoughts. Here are the basics:

Prior to 1939 Tagalog was only spoken by 25% of the population.

In 1935 the Philippine National Assembly decided the country "shall take steps toward the development and adoption of a common national language based on one of the existing languages".

In 1936 a seven person commission was set up to study the problem and make a recommendation.

In 1937 after ten months of study the commission chose to recommend Tagalog as the official language of the Philippines. Tagalog was the language used in Manila and surrounding areas.

The recommendation was very controversial and fiercely debated, especially among Visayans who correctly noted that Visayan was spoken by far more Filipinos than Tagalog.

In 1939 Tagalog became the official language of the Philippines. The next significant change did not come until 1979, when the government, aware of criticism by some that Tagalog is an ethnic group and thus should not be the name of the national language, changed the name to Pilipino. Interestingly, in seeming conflict with the philosophy of the name change, the government defined the new Pilipino language to be a very pure form of Tagalog, removing Spanish, English and other outside influences. Sort of like the French government trying to change the word EMAIL to "courriel", or the word "air-bag" to "sac goneflable".

This new definition of Pilipino riled many Filipinos who stated that the new Pilipino language was more closely tied to Tagalog than the language it supposedly replaced.

In 1987, in response to these criticisms and also aware that a pure form of Tagalog was no longer working in the modern world with all the new technological terminology being introduced, the government changed directions once more. They changed the name of the language again, to Filipino, and at the same time changed the definition of the language.

Instead of trying to maintain a pure form of Tagalog, Filipino was described as a constantly evolving language embracing outside influences and incorporating words from Spanish and English as well as words from other local dialects.

It is interesting to note that during all this time when the national language was being debated, English was never seriously considered as a possible choice. I don't agree with this, but I understand it. The people involved in this decision wanted to bring the country together with a sense of pride in a common national language. How could they take pride in a language which was not their own?

Even so, it is my personal belief that the adoption of Tagalog as the national language was a big mistake and really hurt the Philippines. Tagalog/Filipino has never really been totally accepted as the national language. As I mentioned before all road signs are in English, the government conducts it's business in English and almost all the major universities and private schools teach in English. It's a very confusing situation!

By choosing Tagalog as the national language the government essentially forced most educated Filipinos (except native Tagalog) to learn at least three languages, their local language, Tagalog and English.

Things would have been a lot simpler if English had been made the official language, but it was not to be!

#### ♦ Should You Learn a Philippine Language?

Many would-be-Expats want to know if they can get by with just English, or even if they can get by, is there any significant advantage to learning Filipino or some other local language?

First of all, you don't need to learn any Philippine language. Most Expats don't. You can certainly, and fairly easily, get by with just English.

Second there is no point in learning a Philippine language unless you are sure where you want to live. Suppose you learn Filipino and then move to Cebu. People in Cebu speak Cebuano, and are probably just as fluent in English as they are in Filipino. Thus your knowledge of Filipino would be more or less useless except for possibly watching Philippine TV or seeing a Philippine produced movie.

It would be even more useless if you learned Cebuano and then moved to Luzon. There most people wouldn't understand you at all if you spoke Cebuano.

Ok, suppose you are sure where you want to live. For example, Cebu is to be your new home. Would it then be worth learning Cebuano? Well sure, if you have the ability and the inclination, why not, it can only help you and there are sure to be many situations where your knowledge of the local language will be to your advantage.

One Expat who learned the local language (Cebuano) told me he got endless satisfaction whenever he went to places where they did not know him. He got to hear what they said about him in Cebuano, thinking he did not understand. Sometimes he would keep his secret, sometimes he would have fun watching their faces when he started to converse with them in the Cebuano.

## Topic xi: *Christmas Eve, New Years Eve and Fireworks in the Philippines*

Christmas and New Years eve are enthusiastically celebrated in the Philippines.

Fireworks are legal in the Philippines and in the two weeks or so prior to Christmas and the New year it is common to see temporary fireworks stores spring up in various locations selling a wide variety of fireworks. For those on a budget simple "Triangles" are available for about one peso each delivering a lot of "BANG for the buck" (I mean peso). For those willing to be extravagant there are fancy multi stage rockets and everything in between. Some of the fireworks are pretty intense. For example the largest firecracker available looks almost like a small stick of dynamite, being about 1.5 cm thick and 8 cm long. Have one of them go off in your hand and you won't be playing the violin any time soon!

Walking around the city or neighborhoods on Xmas or New Years Eve can be both a fun and terrifying experience. On the fun side it is very festive, with people drinking in the streets, being very friendly and offering you food and drink. All around you fireworks are going off all over the place which is very exciting.

On the terrifying side, dangerous fireworks and a lot of drunk people are not a particularly good mix to say the least. Every year hundreds of people are injured and is not unusual to read about a person or two being killed in fireworks accidents.

The first couple of years I was in the Philippines I enjoyed walking around the city and taking in the festivities. Then one year some kid threw a fire cracker into the air and it landed and exploded on my leg. Fortunately it was a small fire cracker and I was wearing jeans. Nevertheless the wound took about a month to heal and I had a scar for more than a year. After that my enthusiasm for walking around on Xmas and New Years eve was dampened a bit.

## Topic xii: *In the Stores*

If you ask for something in a store and the sales lady does not know what you are talking about, or does not know if the item is in the store, she is likely to just say "Out of stock". In Filipino culture they don't like to admit they don't understand you or don't know what you are talking about. When they say this, you sort of have to read the body language to know if it's true or not. If they look confused they probably have no idea. Just go look for it yourself or ask a different sales lady.

If the sales lady does know where something is she is likely just to point and say there, which could mean there 10 feet away or there on the other side of the store. You have to be assertive to have her either show you or give you more specific instructions.

When buying things keep in mind that the laws (if they exist) about proper labeling of name brand items are not enforced. Particularly with electronic equipment such as TVs or DVD players it is common to find cheap Chinese goods labeled with names such as SONY. When I first came to the Philippines I was amazed that I got a great deal on a Sony DVD. When I got it home it broke within a few minutes. When I brought it back to the store to exchange it the conversation went something like this:

Her:   Perhaps you should buy something of better quality

Me:   But it's a SONY

Her:   No, it's Just a SONY label, it's not real SONY

Me:   Well how should I know it was not a real SONY?

Her:   You should have known by the price, you can't get a real SONY for that price!

Me:   (Dumbfounded) Oh.

Years later looking back at the incident I now realize it would be obvious to the experienced Expat, but at the time I applied my western filter to the Filipino experience.

Another thing to keep in mind about shopping in the Philippines is that you can NEVER get your money back. Once the money leaves your hands and the transactions complete, your money is gone. The more reputable stores will allow you to exchange something you bought for something else (within a short period of time) but they will never give you your money back. The concept does not exist in the Philippines.

## Topic xiii: *Negotiating with Street Venders*

There are many street venders in the Philippines. They sell a wide variety of goods such as sun glasses, athletic shoes, towels and clothes, watches, rings, tools, novelty items, etc etc.

As a Westerner it is often difficult to get a truly good deal from these street venders, as from their point of view, you represent a golden opportunity to charge an exorbitant price and make extra money. In other words their goal will be to rip you off!

Still, sometimes you may see something that you like, and you should have some idea how to deal with these people.

First of all, it is best to decide from a distance if you are going to be interested. If you decide not to be interested walk on by without ever letting your eyes make contact. As soon as a street vender detects any interest on your part he will be on you like a hungry wolf on an innocent lamb.

When negotiating for an item it is really important that you have some idea of the value. If you don't, you are very likely to get ripped off. For example, you might see a pretty watch. That watch may be only worth p200. However, if you ask how much, the vender is likely to say something like, "it's an original Armani but I will sell it to you for only p1500". You might then spend five minutes negotiating him down to p800, and feel pretty good when you walk away, not knowing that you really could have got the watch for p200! With street venders you have to negotiate from a position of strength, and strength comes from knowing the value of the item.

If something catches your eye here is a technique you can use. Stop, look at the item, show some interest and ask how much. He will then (almost 100 percent of the time) give you a wildly inflated price. Look incredulous and just walk away. As you walk away he will probably start shouting out new prices at you, lowering the price as you walk away. Don't turn back, but remember the lowest price he shouted out.

Next, see if you can find the item you want in a normal store. Often you can, and often you will be surprised that the price in the store is way lower than what the street vender offered you. If you find the item in a store, buy it there, or use the store price for further negotiation with the vender.

If you can't find it in a store, look for another street vender selling the same item and offer about half the price of what the first vender shouted out as you left, and see what kind of response you get.

If the item you want seems to be unique and is not sold by other stores or street venders, then decide ahead of time how much is the most you are willing to pay for the item. Go back and offer the vender half of your secret maximum and negotiate up. If you can't get it at the price you want, don't hesitate to walk away.

## Topic xiv: *Beggars and Begging*

There are many beggars in the Philippines. As a Westerner one of the things you will have to learn to live with is begging. As a Westerner you are a marked man and all the beggars will seek you out and beg you for some money. On a typical walk through town you are likely to be solicited a half dozen times. You can categorize the beggars into basically two groups, passive beggars and aggressive beggars.

The passive beggars, mainly the old, infirm and blind will sit on the sidewalk, tin can in hand and (assuming they are not blind) try to catch your eye, and beg you for money with a plaintive look upon their face.

The aggressive beggars, usually young, will come right up to you and stick their hand in your face as if it is your obligation to give them some money. Sometimes if you are not looking they will come up to you and tap you on the shoulder and then stick their hand in your face. Among the aggressive beggars there is a further sub category that look for people in captive situations where they can't walk away. This includes when you are getting money from an ATM machine, standing in line at a drug store or even eating at an outside restaurant.

The beggars come in all age ranges from very young to very old. Some of them start as young as five or six years old. These kids are often begging during school hours so you might wonder why these kids are not in school. Well as mentioned in passing before, truancy laws are not enforced in the Philippines. Many young poor children do not go to school. The parents of these kids find it more lucrative to teach their kids to beg then to put them in school.

One common trick among beggars, particularly young mothers and young kids caring for their baby brothers is to carry around a young child with them, anywhere from a few months old up to 3 or four years old (young beggars in training). These very young kids or babies usually have a standard uniform consisting of a tattered dirty tee shirt and naked from the waste down. I mean completely naked. I think the idea is that they are trying to show they are so poor they can't even dress their kids.

As a Westerner living in the Philippines you will have to figure out how you want to deal with beggars. It's a personal decision and different Expats handle it differently. Some make themselves very hardened and never give out money under any circumstances. Others make a point of carrying around loose change and give out a peso or two to every beggar who requests it, with the attitude that it is sort of a Westerner tax. Still others give out a few pesos here and there when their mood and circumstances suit them.

As for myself I fall into this latter category. I have sort of have my own rules that eliminate certain beggars from consideration. I will never give to overly aggressive or "captive strategy" beggars, as I don't want to encourage this kind of begging. I will never give to school age kids during school hours as I feel they should be in school. I won't give to those carrying around naked children as I feel this encourages  child abuse. Among those left it's basically random as to who I give money. Sometimes I just take a moment to reflect on the kind of life they live and it's pretty tragic. It pulls at your heart strings. If I do give them a few pesos I don't fool myself into thinking I've really helped them that much or that I'm any kind of great hero. Sometimes when I pass a beggar that did nothing wrong, without giving any money, I feel guilty, but then, who ever said life was fair.

# Part 5: *Filipino History and Culture*

**Filipinos love festivals, like this one in Cebu**

# Chapter 29: A Very Brief History of the Philippines

I realize that many of you reading this probably don't care that much about the history of the Philippines. You are interested in the moment, what the Philippines are like now, and how it effects you personally.

Nevertheless I would feel remiss if I didn't at least offer a very brief history of the Philippines, as doing so should give you some additional insight into Philippine culture.

Did you ever wonder why the Philippine Islands are the Philippine Islands? I mean the Philippines consist of about two thousand inhabited islands spread out over a longitudinal distance of 1800 km, and a latitudinal distance 2500 km. What do these islands have to do with one another? How are they connected?

Well, if you go back far enough, before the Spanish occupation which started in 1565, the answer is, they had pretty much nothing to do with each other. They were separate islands with separate rulers, separate cultures and separate languages. It was only the Spanish that brought these Islands together by occupying them and naming them the Philippine islands (after King Philip II of Spain, who reigned from 1556 to 1598). It was the Spanish that installed a common language (originally Spanish, later to be morphed into English) and a common religion, namely Christianity. Even so, it was not until the writings of Dr. José Rizal in the late 1800's that the Philippines even began to develop a national identity. This is a point worth noting because as a Westerner you might tend to think of the Philippines as a small country with a homogenous population. Nothing could be further from the truth.

Prior to 1521 the only main interaction between the Philippine Islands and the rest of the world was with the Chinese who visited the Islands often for the purpose of trade. The Chinese never attempted to occupy the Islands.

The first European known to have visited the Philippines was the famous explorer Ferdinand Magellan who discovered the Islands in 1521. Unfortunately for Ferdinand this was his famous last voyage. In attempting to take over the Island of Mactan (near Cebu) he badly misjudged the skill, ferociousness and fighting spirit of the great tribal chief Lapu Lapu. Most of the Spanish, including Ferdinand himself, were massacred. The remaining Spanish hightailed it back to Spain. There is still a city called Lapu Lapu named after the famous chief, and to this day Filipinos hold a warm place in their heart for the famous chief who was the first to standup to foreign imperialism.

Unfortunately for the Philippines the death of Ferdinand did not discourage the Spanish. They continued to send expeditions to the Philippines and started their policy of occupation starting about 1565. The Philippines, basically a bunch of separate islands with no national identity or common ruler, put up little or no resistance to the vastly stronger military capability of the Spanish, the battle of Lapu Lapu not withstanding.

Although the Spanish taught the Filipinos Christianity they denied most other forms of education and common rights and in general kept the Filipino population suppressed and treated the Filipinos more or less like slaves. They were not very nice occupiers. Resistance to the Spanish rule slowly but surely started to build in the 1800s with the advent of secret societies that plotted against the Spanish. Dr. José Rizal was perhaps the first to openly defy the Spanish with the writing of several books, starting in the 1880s, which the Spanish considered subversive. These books were banned and Rizal himself was exiled, later to be executed. Dr. José Rizal was truly a great man and hero and his story is fascinating. I end this book with a small biography of Dr. Rizal.

Although the Spanish executed Rizal, his martyrdom marked the beginning of the end for the Spanish occupation.

Starting in the 1890's, perhaps partly because of Rizal's writings, and spurred on by writings in American Newspapers, the American people and their leaders started to develop a sense of moral outrage towards the Spanish for their abuse of human rights in their occupied territories. Of particular interest were the Spanish held territories of Cuba, Puerto Rico, Guam and the Philippines. The U.S. government issued a series of ultimatums to the Spanish that were of course ignored. This resulted in the Spanish American war which started in 1898. The Spanish were no match for the Americans and the war was quickly over, as was the era of the Spanish empire. The Spanish surrendered the territories of Cuba, Puerto Rico, Guam and the Philippines to the Americans.

The Americans promptly declared themselves as the new rulers of the Philippines, which was a shock, since most of the Filipinos had assumed that with the defeat of the Spanish in the Philippines they had finally gained independence. Thus the American-Philippine war broke out, which was not much of a war at all. The rebelling Filipinos were quickly massacred.

You might think that this start would cause there to be a deep seated hatred towards the Americans. However it turned out the Filipinos did not have that much to worry about. Unlike the Spanish who suppressed the Filipinos, the Americans were content to let the Filipinos pretty much govern themselves. Their main influences were positive, including the implementation of universally available education and the teaching of English.

Every empire builder knows that if you want to keep your occupied inhabitants suppressed, you don't educate them, but this was not the intent of the American occupation. The Americans were content to pretty much let the Filipinos do as they pleased, so long as they did not question the ultimate authority of the U.S. The U.S. was mostly interested in the Philippines for strategic military purposes. Most Filipinos, including it's leaders, were content to let the Philippines be the official territory of the USA, since the Americans offered protection (particularly from the Japanese who the Filipinos feared) and guidance, without medaling too much in their day to day affairs.

Still, many Filipinos longed for total independence, and in fact the U.S. government proclaimed that it was their intention to eventually grant this request – but not right away.

In 1935 the U.S. Government granted the Philippines the status of "commonwealth". A commonwealth is a self-governing nation or state that voluntarily aligns itself with, and gives certain rights to another nation in return for protection, this nation of course being the USA. To this day Guam and Puerto Rico are still commonwealths. The other two countries won during the Spanish American war, Cuba and the Philippines, are now independent nations.

Then of course came world war two, and the Japanese, whom the Filipinos feared, conquered and occupied the Philippines. Turns out the Filipino's fear of the Japanese was justified as thousands of Filipinos were brutally murdered by the Japanese,

When the Americans emerged victorious in world war two they again took over occupation of the Philippines, but quickly granted them their long desired independence in 1946, only insisting that they be able to keep ownership of their military bases.

It would be a nice story if the granting of this independence was the start of a beautiful new era for the Philippines. Unfortunately this was not the case. The Philippines, after centuries of occupation, did not really know how to govern themselves. Fierce power struggles ensued and corruption became entrenched into the system.

Then in 1965 began the disastrous reign of Ferdinand Marcos. In 1972, afraid that he might lose the next election, Marcos dispensed with the silly notion of democracy, declared martial law, and installed himself as dictator. For the next 14 years Marcos ruled like a tyrant rewarding himself and his close followers with untold riches at the expense of the Filipino people, while torturing and/or killing any who opposed him. Marcos embezzled from the Philippine treasury, extorted money from both domestic and international businesses and even foreign governments. The entire country became one giant system of corruption and kickbacks. To this day the country has not recovered as corruption remains rampant in the Philippines, one of, if not the main stumbling block, to a prosperous Philippine nation.

In 1986 Marcos was finally deposed by the famous "people power" revolt. With hatred towards Marcos reaching a critical level, Marcos ordered the military to brutally suppress the revolt. In response thousands if not millions of common Filipinos poured out onto the streets creating (mostly unarmed) human shields around all those that were in danger. The military refused to massacre the human shields and support for Marcos began to quickly dissolve. Marcos, in fear of his life, asked the American government to help him. President Reagan was friends of Marcos and he complied, agreeing to exile him and his famous wife, Imelda, to Hawaii.

Since the time of Marcos the Philippines has been struggling mightily to right themselves, and some progress has been made, but it continues to be a long and difficult road.

# Chapter 30: Core Values

## Topic i: *Religious Attitudes*

I have not found the majority of Filipinos to be overly religious. They almost all claim to be religious, to believe in God and Christ and to follow the teachings of the Church. Most of them go to Church at least occasionally. Most of them pray. But when it comes to living their life they are pragmatic and religion does not usually get in the way. From my point of view this is a positive, not a negative.

For example, most women dating foreign men will not use religion as an excuse for not having sex.

Suppose you are having a sexual relationship with your GF. If somebody were to question her about this telling her it's wrong, the conversation might go something like this:

Questioner:    Do you believe in Christ and follow the teachings of the Catholic church?

GF:            Of course!

Questioner:    Well don't you know the church does not allow sex before marriage?

GF:            I'm sure God understands my situation.

## Topic ii: *Family Values*

Family values are very different in the Philippines than they are in the USA or most western countries.

For example, in the USA it is common for most children to move out of their parents house when they finish school and get their first job. In the Philippines it is common for children to live with their parents indefinitely.

In the USA it is extremely rare for a married couple to live with their parents. In the Philippines this is common.

In the USA, as a boy or girl reaches their upper teen years they do not take kindly to being micro managed by their parents. They don't want to be told who to hang out with, or what time to come home or who they can or can't date. In the Philippines it is common for the parents to be "boss" even when a person is in their 20's or 30s. It's a bit weird to most Westerners when they hear a 30 year old girl saying something like: "I have to get home now, my mother does not like me staying out late".

In the USA when a parent gets very old, if the family has the means, it is common to place the parent in an old age home. In the Philippines the children consider it their obligation to take care of their parents until they die.

In the USA a large family with many kids is considered irresponsible. In the Philippines it is considered insurance against being alone in old age.

In the USA a typical home consists of Parents and children. In the Philippines it may consist of up to four generations, plus an occasional aunt and uncle, plus helpers.

## Topic iii: *Attitude About Abortion*

Abortion in the Philippines is illegal and rare. Most women who get pregnant do not consider it an option. Even a woman who is say 17, in school, and has everything to lose by having a baby, will not typically consider an abortion.

Part of this may be do to the teachings of the Catholic church, but I think this is not the whole story. Filipinos have a very strong sense of family and the idea of ending the life of a potential family member is just not acceptable for them.

For young girls there is usually a period of extreme anger on the part of the parents of the girl, followed by eventual acceptance of the situation, and assimilation of the new baby into the extended family. The good news for young mothers is that because of the extended family they can often lead a semi normal life, able to do activities and go to school while the extended family helps her to take care of the baby.

On the other hand, life is never the same for a young Filipina single mother. For one thing most Filipino men are not interested in single mothers.

If you accidentally get a young woman pregnant, don't expect her to have an abortion, even if you are willing to pay for it. If a girl does agree to an abortion, you will have to obtain the abortion on the black market, complete with all the extra expense and risk (both legal and physical) associated with such an abortion.

# Chapter 31: Driving in the Philippines

**Typical crazed Filipino Traffic**

Philippine driving culture is not one of politeness and courteousness. In fact it's quite the opposite. By western standards Filipino drivers are quite rude, although it's safe to say they don't perceive it that way.

It's very interesting to note that Philippine culture is quite demanding in it's face to face etiquette requiring people to be soft spoken, courteous, polite and non aggressive. Why is it then that the driving culture is quite the opposite? Well, if you are looking for an answer – sorry, I don't have one. It mystifies me.

Driving a car or motorcycle in the Philippines is an "interesting" experience to say the least.

The good news is that unlike Thailand and some other countries driving is (theoretically) on the right side of the road (well not good news if you are from England I guess).

As for the rest of the good news, I will include it in the brackets to follow:

[ ]. In other words, None! Nada!

It's a crazy experience and most foreigners at one time or another become exasperated, but you will get used to it to some extent if you just resign yourself to it.

To get a license you basically just buy one, like you are buying a pair of socks in the local store. There is no driving test to get a license. If you have any trouble, simply go to a facilitator who knows someone in the land transportation office, like your insurance agent, who for a modest fee will make sure you get your license no trouble. There are many people who get licenses who have absolutely no clue about the formal rules of driving, and this is especially true of motorcycle drivers.

Here are some things that will frustrate western drivers:

Most Filipinos don't bother to signal. The only ones that sometimes signal are motorcycle drivers, and they are signaling only because they fear for their lives by not signaling.

Nobody follows any rules about right of way. Oh, sorry, I'm wrong. They do, but it's called MIGHT OF WAY, not right of way. Basically whoever is bigger gets the right of way. Buses and trucks are highest priority, followed by cars, followed by motorcycles, followed by bicycles, followed by pedestrians. If you are a pedestrian don't expect anybody to stop for you and let you cross.

Filipinos have this interesting idea about "wasting". They feel it is a waste to slow down or stop if you don't absolutely have to. I guess there is some logic to this, since you can't dispute that it uses extra gas to slow down and speed up, but the result borders on insanity.

Suppose you are driving on the highway and up ahead you see a potentially dangerous situation developing. You see some kids on the left side of the road, you see a car approaching an intersection on your right and from the opposite direction you see a bus approaching. For me, and most western drivers the natural reaction would be to slow down and let the dangerous situation resolve itself. Not so for most Filipinos. Their reaction is to start honking their horn, and not slow down at all. It's absolutely amazing to me the way drivers will approach such situations at full speed, only using there horn as if to say, hey, I warned you, get out of my way.

Also the way that Filipino drivers approach intersections is totally different than western drivers. Western drivers slow down and often stop when approaching an intersection. Most dangerous intersections in America have stop signs. In the Philippines very few intersections have stop signs and most drivers approach intersections at fairly high speeds with the intent of slowing down as little as possible. I think the psychology as they are approaching an intersection is some kind of prioritized thinking similar to the following:

1. Hope that there is no traffic and they can continue without slowing down.

2. If there is traffic, try to pick out a hole to shoot through so you don't have to slow down.

3. If there is traffic and no holes continue as long as possible at a high speed in the attempt to intimidate someone into slowing down so you can continue without slowing down.

4. If all of the above fails, Jam on your brakes at the last moment.

Motorcycles have an additional strategy. Without slowing down they will take a very hard right turn staying close to the side of the road. The idea is that any traffic flowing in their direction should be able to make the slight adjustment to move a little bit to the left so as not to collide.

Much of the time, when taking turns, the "shortest path" philosophy applies. The smaller the vehicle the more true this is. For example, if you are a car approaching an intersection, and you are properly on the right side of the road, and there is a motorcycle approaching the intersection from your right desiring to take a left turn, the motorcycle will often cut in, passing your car on your right side, on the wrong side of the road. When motorcycles are about to take left turns, they will frequently get to the left side of the road, driving on the wrong side of the road, prior to taking the turn.

One way roads are often ignored, especially by motorcycles, if the distance to go is short. Suppose a driver is parked on a one way road, having just gone into a store. Now the driver wants to get to a road in back of him (opposite the legal flow of traffic). The road is 50 meters away. The choice is go 50 meters illegally, or get to the road by traveling around the block, perhaps half a kilometer. Many drivers just don't want to be so wasteful as to travel half a km when their destination is only 50m away. Motorcycles do this all the time. Cars will also do it if the traffic is not too heavy.

Continuing on the subject of one way roads, here where I live in Dumaguete, they have a number of roads that are one way during the daytime, and two way at night between the hours of 8pm and 6am. I don't know if they do this in other cities, but personally I think it's a bad idea. You get used to a road being one way, and it's easy to forget that all of the sudden it's two way. In addition, drivers start to use the road as two-way starting about 730pm. I guess they feel that's close enough!

Tricycles or pedicabs are another problem. For those not knowing what I am talking about, tricycles or pedicabs – two different words for the same thing – are the Philippine version of taxi's. Only large cities have normal taxi cabs. Some large cities prohibit pedicabs. Many smaller cities only have pedicabs. Some allow both pedicabs and taxicabs.

The word "pedicab" is a bit of a misnomer, it's history being that of a sidecar powered by a human pedaled bicycle. When motorcycles replaced most of the bicycles they continued to call it a pedicab even though is was no longer being pedaled. I think you would have to agree that the word "MotoCycleCab (which I just made up) does not have as nice a ring.

A pedicab is a motorcycle with an attached side car. The motorcycle of course has two wheels, and the side car has only one. Thus the name tricycle. Tricycles or pedicabs are designed as extremely simple vehicles, fabricated out of welded steel at a minimum of cost. In the event of an accident they would essentially offer zero protection to the passengers. Filipinos have the fabrication of pedicab side cars down to a science. Sometimes they look like they couldn't support a bag of feathers, yet somehow they seem to be amazingly strong. It's not unusual to see side cars carrying up to ten people. Sometimes you will see them being used as trucks, carrying twenty 60-pound-bags of cement. Sometimes I am amazed that the things don't break, they just don't seem strong enough for the load they are under, yet I have never seen one snap – although I'm sure it has happened. Another thing about pedicabs is that the side car has no brakes. This means that all the braking is done only with the motorcycle. This means the braking is really off balance since all the braking is on the left side, but the center of balance is more towards the middle, especially when the side car is fully loaded. The result is that a fully loaded pedicab can't stop very fast. For that matter, they can't accelerate very fast either. They are like sloths on the road, doing their own thing and it's up to us to avoid them.

One thing pedicabs are good at doing is turning around in a small space. Because of the way they are built, with the wheel used for steering at the front left, and only a single wheel on the right side, located in the middle of the right side, they can make left U turns in a very small radius. The pedicab drivers use this to their advantage – and our annoyance. Often after letting off a passenger on the right side of the road, the pedicab driver wishes to do a U turn. They seem to have perfected the art of this. They have a technique that most of them seem to use. When they start their turn, they don't look. They just start turning around, quickly, and it appears that they are crazy men making a u turn without even looking. But after the first two feet they look and evaluate, and stop quickly if needed. The technique is genius. Although they probably couldn't put it into words or conscious thought, here is what is happening:

The pedicab drivers know that if they were to look normally and establish eye contact and wait for an opening so they could turn around, it might take them a long time. Filipino drivers do not have a culture of courteousness, and it is unlikely anybody is going to stop and allow them to turn around. They also know, that by only going two feet quickly it is almost always the case (I have never seen an accident from this technique) that if there are any cars behind them they can swerve at least two feet and avoid them. By going the first two feet crazy without looking, they intimidate most drivers behind them into stopping. It certainly works for me – or against me. I see them start to turn without looking and it's just my natural instinct to stop, I almost can't help it. After the first two feet of the turn the pedicab driver looks and evaluates. If necessary they stop quickly, but if they detect even the slightest hesitation they continue the turn. The technique is exasperating, but works to perfection!

The motorcycles powering the pedicabs range from new reasonably powerful four cycle machines, to very old two cycle motorcycles, seemingly on their last legs – or wheels. The two cycle motorcycles spew pollution. For those not familiar with motorcycles they mostly fall into two categories of engines, two cycle and four cycle. Most modern motorcycles are four cycle, meaning they are quiet and their emissions are very low. By contrast two cycle engines are noisy and spew black smoke. This brings up the question: why do two cycle engines exist? Well I really don't know. I guess they are cheaper to produce, and I have been told you get more power per engine size with a two cycle engine. In my opinion they should be outlawed.

Now let's go off on a tangent and talk about emissions testing.

I mentioned above that some cities do not allow pedicabs. These cities typically rely on Taxi's for people who have money, and jeepneys for those that don't. Jeepneys are essentially small busses with bench seats, used for low cost transportation within the city. Most jeepneys use rebuilt diesel engines and like the two cycle pedicabs, they spew pollution, only much worse, because they are much bigger.

The Philippines theoretically has emissions standards. Every year you are supposed to bring your car or motorcycle into an emissions center for testing. So if this is true why are there so many pedicabs, jeepneys and other vehicles spewing toxic emissions? Well the answer is of course, as is often the case – corruption. In this case small scale or petty corruption. If your car or motorcycle fails the test, simply fork out a few hundred extra peso as a bribe, and they will fake the test.

It's hard to blame either the employees or the customers. Imagine you are an employee making p150 a day (about $3). If several times a day you take a bribe for 300 peso, well you can see how this will effect your life style! Maybe you need those bribes to even survive.

Now imagine you are a pedicab or jeepney driver, barely making enough money to survive. Do you think you want to shell out p75,000 for a new motorcycle or p30,000 for a new engine? No, you can't afford that. You can't even afford p10,000 to have your engine rebuilt. No, your best solution is to offer a few hundred peso to have them fake the test.

No, you can't blame the employee or the customer. If you really want to stop this practice, it has to come from a higher level. But now let's imagine the emissions testing was really enforced properly. What would be the result? You would have a lot of poor Filipinos, drivers of pedicabs and jeepneys, unable to pass the test, and unable to afford the money to fix their vehicles or to buy new ones. Fixing an emission problem is not usually a simple fix. It will often involve buying a new engine or rebuilding your current engine, both very costly.

So the result would be to cause a lot of hardship. To cause a lot of poor but hard working and honest Filipinos to be unable to do their job. Is this really what you want? Well it's not what you want, and that's why people look the other way. Nothing is simple.

Anyway, getting back to the subject of driving,

In addition to the pedicabs you also have a significant number of bicyclists and bicycles with side cars. Bicycles with side cars are similar to pedicabs, but smaller and powered by bicycle, and of course even slower and even more sloth like than the pedicabs. Bicycle side cars are sometimes used to transport people, but more often used by small businesses, or as traveling food stations, offering drinks or certain kinds of foods for sale.

Real highways, as we know them in the USA – multi lane and divided with limited access and exit, only exist in a few areas, most notably Metro Manila. What most Filipinos call highways are simply normal long roads that go on for many kilometers. National highways they are called. They are nothing like modern western highways. They have the following characteristics:

- Very traffic (That's Filipino English!)

- One lane on each side

- No divider

- There are many commercial establishments along the side.

All types of vehicles share the road, buses, trucks, cars, pedicabs, motorcycles, bicycles and bicycle side cars. Plus cows, goats dogs and chickens.

Typically these national highways are very slow and crowded in or near cities, and speed up quite a bit between cities. However, even between cities all the above mentioned vehicles share the road.

Well as you can imagine, it can be a bit frustrating driving on one of these highways if you have a distance to go and you are always being slowed down by pedicabs and bicycles side cars as well as other slow moving vehicles.

Many drivers are patient. Many are not. The level of impatience ranges from mild to extreme, as does the resulting behavior. Some drivers seem to take extreme chances in overtaking vehicles, yet it seems, that at least most of the time, they get away with it. It never ceases to amaze me.

The philosophy of passing is different than what most foreigners are used to. In the USA you basically wait for a free space before passing. The idea is that you want to have time to completely pass the slower vehicle and get back into the proper lane before any oncoming traffic reaches you. This is not the philosophy in the Philippines. It goes back to the MIGHT IS RIGHT rule. If, for example, a car wants to pass and the oncoming traffic consists of motorcycles and side cars, it will go ahead and pass and expect the oncoming traffic to get out of the way.

Whereas in the USA, you would want to have time to pass and merge back in before oncoming traffic reaches you, in the Philippines the rules go something like this:

- Is the oncoming traffic of a lower stature than you?

- Is there time for the oncoming traffic to get out of the way.

- Is there a place for the oncoming traffic to get out of the way (such as a dirt shoulder).

- If the answer to all three of these questions is yes, go ahead and pass.

Since large trucks and busses are of a higher stature than cars, they will pass even when the oncoming traffic is cars. If you are driving a car, you had better get out of the way.

Buses are particularly notorious for this practice since they have a schedule to keep. Here where I live in the Negros/Cebu area we have Ceres liner busses which are infamous for their extreme driving behavior. They travel along at very high speeds even when approaching crowded situations. Their main means of accident avoidance is to honk their horn. They pass at will expecting oncoming traffic to get out of the way. If you don't get out of their way, there is not time for them to stop. You will die. Fortunately most people are aware of this and get out of the way. Does an elephant slow down for a rabbit? No, it's up to the rabbit to get out of the way, and the rabbit accepts this.

I have heard from a number of people – and I can't confirm it, but I believe it, that when a Ceres bus does kill someone their standard practice is to offer the family p100,000 (about $2000) compensation and if the family does not accept this, fight the family to the death in court. As I understand it, almost all the time, the families accept the compensation.

Unlike in the USA where criminal charges can be filed against the driver by the state regardless of any compensation offered, in the Philippines, if the family agrees to compensation, all charges are dropped.

In regards to passing and crazy driving, since motorcycles are of the lowest cast, they can't rely on intimidation to make other vehicles get out of their way. Instead, a certain percentage of motorcycle drivers, most often young teenage boys, drive absolutely crazy, weaving in and out of traffic at high speeds leaving no room for error or unexpected circumstances. Well they seem to get away with it most of the time. A policeman friend of mine told me there are about 70 motorcycle fatalities a year in the city of Dumaguete, the great majority of them involving teenage boys. In a way this is good news. It means if you drive your motorcycle conservatively your odds of getting killed are pretty small.

Another interesting thing about motorcycle driving, at least here in Dumageute, is that at night a lot of them don't use their lights. Perhaps one in ten motorcycles drive at night without lights. Believe it or not, after three years here in Dumaguete, I still can't figure out the reason.

When I ask my educated Filipino friends I get different answers such as:

- The lights are broken and they can't afford to fix.

- They think it wastes gas or the life time of the lights.

- They don't have licenses, so they don't want the police to be able to see them or the plates.

- Why do they need lights? They can see where they are going.

The first reason is definitely true some of the time, but definitely not true all of the time, as I often see these drivers switch on their lights for a few seconds and then turn them off again. As for the other reasons, I have no idea. Most of the drivers driving without lights are young uneducated drivers. When on several occasions I have had the opportunity to ask them why, they just look at me like I'm crazy and don't answer. I don't know if they don't understand me, or if they just don't want to answer.

The philosophy about drunk driving is also highly different than in western countries. Whereas in the USA drunk driving is a serious crime, in the Philippines it can be best summed up like this:

"It's ok to drive drunk as long as you are careful and don't get into an accident".

You can pretty much drive drunk with impunity so long as you don't get in an accident. The police department doesn't even have breathalyzers. If a policeman sees a drunk driver they might ignore it, they might tell the driver to be careful or in extreme cases they might tell the driver to stop driving. They very rarely arrest somebody for drunk driving if there is no accident involved. Is this good or bad? Well that's up to you. I will not impart my moral judgment.

While on the subject of police, don't the police enforce the traffic laws? Well different cities and provinces have different philosophies so far as their police go. Here in Dumaguete the police are very laid back, they are not looking to cause trouble or hassle people about petty things. If they see a minor infraction most of the time they will look the other way. The police reserve their energy and time for serious matters. Is this good? Well I think so, but again, this is a matter of opinion. It has it's up and down sides.

In my three years in Dumaguete, on a few occasions I have been told by traffic enforcers (a lower level of police without guns) that I am doing something wrong. On all occasions except once, after saying I was sorry, they let me continue driving without a ticket.

The one occasion I did get a ticket involved a very nasty woman traffic enforcer. I was accidentally going the wrong way on a one way street. I was stopped by this woman enforcer and told that it was a one way street. I said it was a mistake and I was sorry. If she had then said, "well it doesn't matter that it was a mistake, I still have to give you a ticket". if she had done that, I would have been fine with it.

Instead she started saying things like this: "That's bull shit. Can't you read? You can't read signs? You Americans think you can do anything you want. Well you can't, this is the Philippines, and you had better obey our rules".

I can't tell you how much I hate that kind of talk, since I try hard to be a good and law abiding resident. Unfortunately there are a small percentage of Filipinos who hate foreigners. They are in the minority, but they do exist.

Incidentally, she did give me a ticket, and I went to the traffic office the next day and paid it. It cost me 50 pesos. I almost laughed when the clerk told me the fine. In the USA, if you got a ticket for going the wrong way on a one way street it would cost you plenty. The ticket itself would be two or three hundred dollars and it would effect your merit rating which would cost you more in insurance.

Concerning police and traffic violations there is one common scam that police officers sometimes play, particularly when you are from out of town. They will ask to see your license. When you give it to them they will inform you that they are going to give you a ticket and that you can get your license back after you pay the ticket. I have talked to a number of Filipinos about this practice including police, lawyers and insurance agents. The police are not supposed to take your license for a simple traffic violation. When the police tell you they are going to take your license, they are looking for a bribe. Don't be arrogant and say something like "hey I know the law, and you are not supposed to get my license", such talk will only anger them. The best thing to do is to pay the bribe. Two or three hundred peso is usually plenty.

Also, when handling this situation don't say something like "ok, I know you want a bribe, how much do you want?". That is definitely bad as it puts the policeman in the awkward situation of admitting he is looking for a bribe. Here is the proper way to handle such a situation:

Stay calm and submissive. Start by telling how difficult it will be for you if you don't have your license. How you have plans to travel somewhere else and you can't afford to wait. Then say something like, "how about if I pay you the money and you be the one to pay the ticket?". Of course you know and he knows it's a bribe, but at least neither of you have admitted it directly.

Well in conclusion, I have one observation, and one suggestion.

My observation is this, despite all this craziness there does not seem to be any more accidents here than in the USA, maybe less so. In my seven years in the Philippines I have never witnessed a serious accident and only a few times witnessed minor accidents. I don't understand this. Perhaps all this craziness causes the drivers to be more alert and attain a higher level of skill, I don't know.

My suggestion is this: The best way to cope is to accept it. Just relax and let the crazies do their thing. Keep on repeating to yourself, "I can't control them - I can't control them". Drive defensively and most importantly drive predictably. If you drive predictably most likely the crazies will avoid you.

# Chapter 32: Lying is Common in Filipino Culture

Example internet conversation with a Filipina woman:

| | |
|---|---|
| Filipina: | Do you have web cam? Can I see you? |
| You: | Yes, I have camera, do you also have cam? |
| Filipina: | Yes, but you first. |
| You: | Ok, but if I go first you promise to also start your cam? |
| Filipina | Ok. |
| You: | Ok, (as you start up your web cam). Do you see me? |
| Filipina: | Yes, I see you now. |
| You: | So your cam now? |
| Filipina | I'm sorry but I don't have cam right now, it's broken. |
| You: | So you are a liar. You promised cam, but you don't have. |
| Filipina: | I am not a liar. |

This little conversation – which is so very typical – illustrates a number of points. Many (not all, but many) Filipina think nothing about lying to get what they want. They lie easily and naturally and don't give it a second thought.

Now at the end of this conversation, when the Filipina was confronted with her dishonesty and told she was a liar, her reaction was, "I am not a liar". Well shocking news, a person that lies is a liar. But she lies so easily and naturally that she doesn't even realizes it's bad, doesn't even realize that she's doing it, and that in doing so makes her a liar!

Try this little experiment next time you catch a Filipina red handed in a lie. Say, "you lied,  that makes you a liar", their reaction will almost always be, "I am not a liar"

So it is very common for Filipinos to lie in situations where Westerners would consider it unacceptable, and you have to get used to this and read the body language and signals.

For example suppose you are having a party and you invite someone to come. If they say "ok, I'll be there", in many cases they are just trying not to hurt your feelings. Sometimes a more educated Filipino might instead say, "I'll try to be there". If you hear the expression, "I'll try", it almost always means "I won't try at all".

Now of course there are exceptions. You will find some Filipinos to be very reliable and honest, so I don't want to paint a picture that all Filipinos are this way, but unfortunately, many are this way.

When it comes to money the lying is particularly common. For example a Filipino might say, "can I borrow a few thousand peso?, I'm getting a check Monday and I will pay you back then. So you loan them the money and Monday comes, and guess what, they can't pay you back. They will always have an excuse, and the excuse is more lies.

Don't be dumb enough to send a Filipina that you don't know well any significant amount of money to be used for a particular purpose. Here is an example: Suppose you are in Baguio and you are corresponding via the internet with a girl from Manila. She wants to meet you. You also want to meet her, but you really don't feel like taking the seven hour bus ride to Manila. So you ask her to visit you in Baguio. You tell her after she gets here you will pay her back for her expenses. The answer will ALWAYS be the same. She will say, "I'm sorry, but I don't have any money". You might say, just borrow the money, I promise to pay you back. But it will never happen. She will say she can't. In some cases it might be true, in some not.

Now suppose you then say, ok, I'll send you the money if you promise to come. She will say "ok". Suppose you then say, "well, I'm worried, I have heard that many women will accept the money but then not keep their promise". Her response will typically be: "Don't compare me to them, I'm not like that".

So, you send her the money, and guess what, she is like that and she doesn't come. Maybe she never talks to you again. Or maybe she says, sorry I couldn't come, my mother got sick. So you say, ok, come tomorrow or next week, but again it never happens and you never get your money back. And on and on and on. If you are gullible you will fall for many lies.

# Chapter 33: **Filipino English**

Concerning English, the Philippines has it's own unique expressions and vernacular. I would say in general that English as spoken in the Philippines is more restrictive and less expressive than American English. The Filipinos have simplified the language a bit. This makes sense of course, since English is not the native language of the Philippines.

For example, in American English people might use words such as huge, gigantic, humongous, enormous and gargantuan. In the Philippines they are likely to just say "Very Big".

Also there are expressions people are used to, certain ways of saying things, and if you don't say it that exact way, they won't understand you.

For example go to a McDonalds and request your order "to go", and they might not understand you. They want to hear the particular expression "Take out".

Request that you want to borrow a pen, and they won't understand you. You must say "Ball Pen".

Ask where the rest room or bathroom is, they are likely to be confused. They want to hear the word CR (comfort room).

Here are a few more example words and expressions along with some of my comments. This list is by no means complete.

**American**
When most Filipinos talk about somebody being an American what they really mean is the generic concept of Westerner. They are not referring to someone specifically from the USA.

**Aircon or just Air**
They don't use the abbreviation AC.

### American Time

Come at six o'clock American time. Means come at exactly six o'clock, referring to the American habit of being on time, as opposed to the Filipino habit of being late.

### Allergic

Referring to somebody that is obsessed about or always thinking about or very sensitive about a particular subject. Example:

Man:        Wow! That girl has great looking breasts
Woman:      You are so allergic about breasts!

### Avail

To my surprise I found that AVAIL is a real word, but it is not used very much in American English. Filipinos love the word AVAIL and use it all the time. Would you like to "avail" of our special offer? As sort of an inside joke to myself I have used the word AVAIL throughout this book. Did you notice?

### Brownout

Brownout means Blackout. They don't use the word Blackout.

### Cotton Buds

They won't understand the word Q-tips

### For a while

Means please wait, or hold on, or hold on for a while. But "for a while" is the way it's said in the Philippines.

### High Society

Usually used as an insult when talking about somebody that is overly concerned with their status or how they are perceived. "I don't want to invite her to the party, she is very high society."

### Ref

Means refrigerator. They don't use the word "fridge".

**Rubber Shoes**
Means sneakers or athletic shoes. They don't use the word sneaker.

**Sala**
Means living room. They don't use the expression "living room".

**Simple**
In American English if you call somebody simple it is an insult. It implies they are dull or stupid or not very interesting. In Filipino English it is a complement. It implies a person who is modest, does not need a lot of money or fancy jewelry and someone who just wants to live a simple good life. Example: "I am just a simple women". Simple in this usage is the opposite of "high society".

**Tomboy**
In American English tomboy refers to a normal healthy girl who likes doing traditionally boy activities. In Filipino English a tomboy is a lesbian

**Very Deep English**
Refers to a an English speaker that uses big words such as "vernacular", "enormous" or "perplexing". Your English is very deep.

**Very Slang**
Refers to somebody that is hard to understand for any number of reasons, such as he speaks too fast, his accent is strong, or his English is "very deep". "I can't understand you because you are very slang".

**Very traffic**
Don't go that way, it's "very traffic". Simple and clean. Much better than correct English which might state "Don't go that way because the traffic is very bad"

# Chapter 34: **Potpourri of Cultural Observations**

## Topic i: *About White Skin*

It's a funny thing about skin color. It seems if you are black or brown you want to be more white, and if you are white you want to be more brown. In western culture it is common for caucasian people to strive to have that brown tanned look. If you are too white it is thought that you look pale and sickly. People will even go to tanning salons to achieve the nice brown look.

In the Philippines most Filipina have a thing about white skin. They feel that if a Filipino's skin is too brown it indicates they are from a lower class or somehow not educated. Never mind that in a western country it would be politically incorrect to admit you like whiter people, in the Philippines they are quite open about this. There are many skin whitening products on the market and many if not most women will buy one or more of these products in an attempt to whiten their skin. They will also avoid the sun like the plague even going so far as to sometimes use umbrellas to protect themselves from the sun.

If you are with your Filipina girl friend or wife who happens to have fairly white skin and you see another Westerner with a beautiful brown skinned Filipina by his side, you might remark how beautiful she is. Your Filipina girl friend or Wife is likely to respond: "Yuck, she is so ugly, look how brown her skin is".

You might explain that there is nothing wrong with brown skin, and in fact many Westerners find Filipina brown skinned women to be very beautiful. It will not change her opinion that brown skin is ugly.

This aversion to dark skin does not apply to caucasian men that are well tanned but it does apply to black Westerners. There are many Filipinos that are prejudiced against black Westerners, not in an overt hateful way, but just in what they think. If you are a black Westerner you can still have success in the Philippines but it will be more difficult for you than for a white man. Many (but certainly not all) Filipina women will reject you because of the color of your skin.

## Topic ii: *Filipinos Don't Like Being Alone*

Most Filipinos grow up in large house holds and are always around other people. They get used to it. They are always with somebody and they don't like to be alone. Whereas a Westerner often craves some time to be alone where he can have time to think and reflect in privacy the Filipino, and Filipina in particular will always try to avoid being alone. The idea of spending a night in a house all by themselves without even a helper around is terrifying to most Filipina.

## Topic iii: *About Personal Privacy*

As described above Filipino's are rarely alone and grow up in large house holds often sharing a bedroom with many siblings. Because of this they don't have the same views about privacy that most Westerners have. If you want to keep something private from your Filipina girl friend or wife, it is up to you to take the necessary steps, don't expect her to respect your personal space. For example, if you don't want her to look through your cell phone messages and contacts, you had better lock your cell phone. If she finds it unlocked she is almost sure to check it out. She is likely to look through your luggage or draws or even your wallet.   This may make you angry but this is an example of culture gap, she will not understand why you think this is so bad. So again, if there is something you don't want her to see, put it where she can't get it. Don't rely on her respecting your Westerner rules of privacy.

## Topic iv: *About Jealousy*

In general most Filipina women are very jealous. When they feel they finally "have you" they will not want to let any other women take you away. Combine this with their attitude towards personal privacy and you often have an unpleasant situation where you feel they are always checking up on you. Checking your phone, smelling your clothes, asking where you have been, etc etc. Of course if you really are looking around at other women you are likely to be caught. If you are not, and you are being true to your woman, this lack of trust can be a bit upsetting but it is probably something you will have to learn to live with.

## Topic v: *Attitudes Towards Dogs and Cats*

There are lots of dogs and cats in the Philippines and most of them are scrawny, parasite infested and in poor health. Of course there are exceptions. There are wealthier Filipinos with purebred dogs that really care about their pets but this is the exception rather than the rule. Most dog and cat owners never let their pet in the house. The pets are fed bones and other left over scraps including old rice. Try feeding old rice to a dog or cat in the USA! But in the Philippines they eat rice. If the dog or cat gets sick either they get better by themselves or they die. They are not typically brought to the vet. This may seem a bit cruel but you have to understand the situation. Most Philippine families don't have enough money to properly take care of their own kids. Pets are a low priority. You don't take a pet to the vet when you are struggling to put food on the table.

There are also a lot of ownerless dogs and cats running around. They are street smart and mostly scrounge on garbage. For the most part they are well behaved and not aggressive. This is probably because the aggressive ones are quickly killed off. These animals are also smart about traffic. Again the ones that are not are quickly killed. For the most part the attitude of Filipino drivers is not to slow down for animals on the road.

## Topic vi: *Rude Use of Cell Phones*

Well, when I say the way they use cell phones is rude, I really mean rude from a western point of view. In Philippine culture it seems to be ok to use a cell phone any time or any place. For example, you might be on a date with a Filipina woman and all of the sudden she just starts using her cell phone and ignoring you, texting back and forth to her friends. At a party there will always be some people removed from the normal flow, off in some corner texting away. Even sitting around a table enjoying dinner at a restaurant there is likely to be one or two people busy with their cell phones and ignoring the conversation. Women are much worse offenders than men in this regard, but even some men are guilty of this. It really seems that the cell phone takes priority over people and normal conversations. Filipinos are used to this and seem to accept it. It drives most westerners crazy. Depending on the situation you may or may not have some control. If you are just a person in a random situation you have no right to say anything. If however a woman is your date or you are at dinner in a restaurant and you are the one paying for the dinner, you have some right to say something. At least that's my opinion. I certainly do. I might say something like: "Since I'm treating you to dinner, would you mind turning off your cell phone? You know, in western culture it's not considered polite to use your phone at dinner unless it's an emergency". Something like that. Usually they will comply, but sometimes they are visibly uncomfortable, and will continue to hold the phone in their hand and fidget with it. It's apparent in these situations that it's practically physically painful for them to not be in constant contact with their social network.

## Topic vii: *Employment Discrimination*

**Typical employment ad for sales lady**: *Wanted: Sales lady, must be female, friendly, attractive and fluent in English with at least a high school education. Must be at least 5' 3" tall and between the ages of 18 and 22.*

This is no joke. This really is a typical ad! In the USA, besides being extremely politically incorrect, this type of ad is also highly illegal. There are no such qualms or laws in the Philippines. The feeling here is that it is your business and you have the right to hire who you want.

Well since there are a lot more Filipina seeking employment then there are job openings this presents a difficult situation for women that are not young and pretty. By the time a woman reaches 30, or even 25, it becomes very difficult to get a job like waitress or sales lady or any other type of basically unskilled job. This attitude presents a terrible problem for women who reach 30 years old and find themselves neither married nor employed. Neither employer nor Filipino man wants them because they are already too old.

In life and family relationships Filipinos have great respect for older people but in the work force, and for men looking for a wife, youth rules.

## Topic viii: *Filipinos are Terrible at Giving Directions*

I don't know why, but most Filipinos have a very hard time giving directions. If you ask where something is, they will typically just point. Or they will point and say "go that way, then here, then there" pointing with their fingers in all different directions. They hardly ever give distances or landmarks or anything like that. At first I thought it was a language barrier thing, but it isn't. Even when my wife is with me they can't communicate directions to her. This difficulty in giving directions applies even in stores when you are shopping. Ask where something is, and most of the time they just point. You have no idea if they are pointing ten feet away, or to the other side of the store. You will rarely if ever hear something like "Yes, the razor knives are three isles down, on your right, just to the left of the paint section".

## Topic ix: *Apologizing in the Philippines Does Not Work*

Most Filipinos are not that quick to anger. Most are easy going and will give you the benefit of the doubt. However if they do get angry they sometimes have a hard time letting go. If you are in this situation, don't apologize. Apologizing does not seem to be part of their culture and does not seem to work. If you apologize it's almost like it makes them more angry, and they say to themselves, see, he was wrong, he even admits it. In western cultures the attitude is, if someone apologizes (unless the offense was so bad it simply is not forgivable) you give somebody credit for having the courage to admit they were wrong, and in general you forgive them. Not so in Filipino culture.

Does that mean if something happens to create bad feelings you can never be friends again? No, you can be friends again, but the proper way to go about it is to just wait some time for the feelings to cool. Then if you see them again, you might just say, hey, let's forget about it. Or, it was just a misunderstanding, let's forget about it, or "It's not important". Then offer them a beer.

## Topic x: *The Cultural Habit of Just Not Answering*

In Filipino culture it's ok to just not answer a question. The response of silence is acceptable. This is a little weird to most Westerners and takes some getting used to. If you ask a Filipino a question, and he just looks at you, and it's clear that he understands you, then this means he or she does not want to answer the question. You should not push on or repeat the question as he or she might find this annoying.

For example, suppose you see somebody that is normally always with their wife, but today he is alone. So you ask, "why are you not with your wife?"

In western culture you are required to say something, even if it's something very generic like, "she couldn't make it today", whereas a Filipino might answer with silence if he did not want to answer the question.

Actually this is a cultural habit I have become used to and now sometimes employ myself. Sometimes it's nice to just not say anything if you don't feel like talking about it.

### Topic xi: *Filipinos are Sound Sleepers*

Indelibly burned into my brain is an incident that took place many years ago in the USA. A friend of mine who owned a vacation home on a lake invited me and a number of other friends to his vacation home for a weekend of swimming, barbequing and partying. The first night everybody, including myself, went to bed around 2am.

The next morning I awoke at 6am and didn't feel tired. I started to do my normal morning routine of washing up and shaving with my electric shaver. I had been shaving no more than about 15 seconds when my friend stormed out of his room yelling "what the hell is that?", referring to the buzz of my electric razor, which was no louder than any typical electric razor.

When he realized what the sound was he chastised me. "Don't you realize everybody is sleeping? What the hell were you thinking?". For the next two years whenever we were together he would repeat this story to every new person who had not yet heard the story, as if to say, look what a doofus this guy is!

Whether my friend had a point, or whether he was making much ado about nothing is up to you to decide. The point I want to make is this would never have happened in the first place with Filipinos. Filipinos tend to be very sound sleepers. This makes sense because most Filipinos grew up in a house with five brothers and sisters, Parents, Grand Parents, Helpers and perhaps a uncle or Aunt or two as well as two dogs and a cat. Every morning there are dogs barking and roosters crowing. They had to learn to be sound sleepers or they would have never gotten any sleep.

I find with my wife I can watch TV, turn on the lights, listen to music, or set off nuclear devices. Nothing wakes her up before she is ready to wake up on her own.

## Topic xii: *Interesting Medical Beliefs*

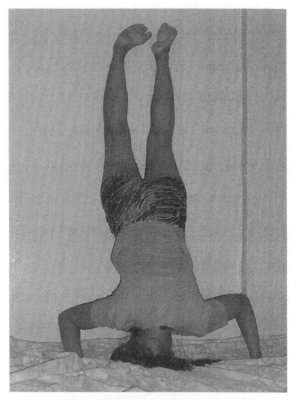

**Hope it works!**

I was going to label this topic "Medical Misconceptions", but then I decided, who am I to decide they are misconceptions, that's only my "Westerner" viewpoint.

Well, maybe the girl I mentioned before, that believed if she stood on her head after sex she wouldn't get pregnant, and now has two kids, maybe I'm ok in labeling that a misconception! Interestingly, I have since heard from other Filipina women that standing on your head after sex is the way to ensure that you **do** get pregnant, not to prevent pregnancy (which actually makes a bit more sense!). Maybe the first women tragically got her belief all opposite (or perhaps you could say she got her belief upside down ha ha ha).

Another "interesting belief" that many Filipinos share is the concept of Pasma. Pasma is something you get if you change environments too quickly. If you go from being very hot outside to a very cool aircon room, you might get Pasma. If you engage in strenuous physical activity you had better wait a while before taking a shower, or you might get Pasma. If your helper is ironing clothes, she must wait a good while before washing the dishes or she might get Pasma.

Now ask them to tell you exactly what the symptoms of pasma are and they might be a bit hard pressed to answer. "You know, like you don't feel well, or your body is shaking, or you get varicose veins, like that".

Don't try and tell them there is no such thing, or that all your life you have been taking showers after exercise and you never got Pasma, such talk will go in one ear and out the other.

If you come across "pasma" or other "interesting medical beliefs" your best approach is usually to just go along with it and let them do what they want.

Many Filipinos also believe in faith healers. Some Filipinos would rather go to a faith healer than a real doctor. Faith healers are often older Filipinos who are reputed to have special healing powers. In some cases there may be some science behind the myth. For example faith healers often resort to a massage to relieve pain in some area of the body. Main stream medicine now recognizes that massage can be very helpful in some cases for stimulating the body to heal itself. Faith healers may also resort to certain herbs or home remedies. Again, main stream medicine now admits that sometimes (but certainly not always) these herbs and home remedies really do work.

In other cases faith healers may resort to techniques that seem dubious at best, such as touching the affected area and reciting some prayer or incantation.

There is a tendency by Westerners and even some educated Filipinos to put down the concept of faith healer. However, in many cases I think they can be helpful for your Filipina wife or GF if she believes in them. In some cases, as discussed above, the actions the faith healers may actually do some good. Even when the actions of the faith healer do not seem to be based on any medical reality they may help her simply because of the "placebo effect". For those not familiar with this concept, the placebo effect is the well proven medical reality that often, if a patient thinks something will help them, it does help them.

The problem with faith healers is that sometimes Filipinos want to forgo traditional medical treatment in preference to faith healers. In some cases the results of this can be disastrous.

## Topic xiii: *Alcohol and Alcoholism*

Alcohol and alcoholism is a definite problem in the Philippines. Many Filipinos, especially men, drink to excess. Drunk driving laws are not enforced unless there is an accident.

Part of the problem may be the cheap cost of locally produced alcohol. For example, for only p60 you can buy a 750ml (25 fl. ounce) bottle of 80 proof Tanduay Rum. That's a whole lot of alcohol for your peso!

If you are an alcoholic the Philippines is a wonderful place to be!

## Topic xiv: *Pee Any Time Any Place*

I'll never forget an incident that happened to me many years ago when I was in my early 20's. Some friends and I traveled to Time Square NY to celebrate the new year. At one point I had to urinate and I couldn't find a place to do so. All restaurants had a policy of making you sit down and order before you could use the bathroom. Finally I found a public bathroom and waited at the end of a long line for my turn to pee. When I finally got to the front of the line I was in pain, ready to burst! However when I tried to pee I couldn't! The long line of people waiting and watching was making me nervous. So I just stood there like an idiot for what seemed like eternity with my dick hanging out and nothing happening!

Thank god I was finally able to pee. But the point of this little story is that something like this would never happen in the Philippines. At least as far as males are concerned. In the Philippines if you have to pee and there is no CR (bathroom) near by, simply pee into the nearest wall, bush, fence or tree. No need to make sure people are not watching. No need to find an isolated spot. Simply get yourself close enough to the wall/fence/bush/tree so that nobody can see your private parts and let loose. Seeing people urinate in public is a common occurrence.

Is this good? Well as with many aspects of Philippine society and culture, it's a mixed bag. On the positive side it's a good thing if you have to go bad and there is no CR near by. On the negative side the smell of urine is a common smell.

## Topic xv: *Sense of Helplessness*

Sometimes Filipinos have a sense of helplessness, a feeling that they are powerless to change anything. They will accept situations or circumstances that a Westerner will not accept.

For example, if a Filipino moves into an apartment and something does not work properly the Filipino will be much more likely to live with the problem, whereas the Westerner will be more likely to bring the problem to the landlords attention.

Here is another example concerning one of my neighbors. She has cable service for her TV. However the problem is that she has a Japanese TV, with all instructions being in Japanese. Nobody can figure out how to put the TV into Cable mode. It's stuck in Antenna mode. As a result she only gets channels two through thirteen.

When I saw the problem I suggested to her that she call the cable company and they could probably help her solve the problem, perhaps by installing a cable box.

She thanked me for the suggestion and the proceeded to ignore my advice. For over a year now she has only been watching channels two through thirteen, not being able to watch many of the most interesting stations. When a special program is on cable, such as a Manny Pacquiao boxing fight, members of her household come over to our house to watch! This kind of example is very common in Filipino society.

## Topic xvi: *Filipino Ingenuity (Or How to Open a Bottle of Beer)*

**Typical Filipino Bottle Opener**

Filipinos are ingenious at making do with what they have. If there are two ways to solve a problem and one costs money but the other takes ten times as long, guess which one they will pick!

Economically of course this makes perfect sense. In the Philippines labor is extremely cheap while material goods are relatively very expensive. Consider the following real life example (which I have witnessed several times) of installing a lock in a door. Installing a lock requires creating a hole about 6 cm in diameter through a 4 cm thick door. A carpenter doing this task in the USA would take out their powerful electric drill and attach a saw hole device and create the hole in about one minute. Most Filipino carpenters don't even own an electric drill.

The way they solve the problem is by chipping out the hole using a screw driver and hammer. The task takes them about an hour.

Does this make sense? Not in the USA where labor costs are so expensive. But in the Philippines it makes perfect sense. The extra hour the carpenter spent chipping out the hole represents about p30 pesos of labor. The cost of a good drill and saw hole set might be about p5000 pesos, so they would have to install 166 locks to break even!

Another example is in fixing their cars. Typically in the USA if a part is defective you replace it, end of story. Not so in the Philippines. If there is any way to fix it, any way to wire it, glue it, weld it, bend it or strengthen it, they will do that before buying the new part.

This concept of labor before material is very ingrained into Filipino culture even around the house. The perfect example of this is the way Filipinos open a bottle of beer.

Perhaps you saw the movie "My Cousin Vinny" where the lawyer (Joe Pesci) asks the witness: "Did you cook instant grits?" To which the witness replies, "No self respecting southerner would cook Instant grits" (the witness thereby shooting himself in the foot).

Well it's sort of the same thing with opening a bottle of beer. No self respecting Filipino uses a bottle opener to open a bottle of beer! Nope, they have many other ways to open a bottle of beer. In fact they take great pride and amusement in showing the Westerner all the different ways a bottle of beer can be opened! They will use one bottle to open another, a table edge, their teeth, a nail in the wall, a spoon or any number of other techniques!

## Topic xvii: *Trash and Littering*

The situation concerning trash, garbage and littering varies greatly from city to city and even from area to area within a city.

Some locations are very clean. Some are disgusting with trash and garbage all over the place.

As far as Filipinos themselves go, for some reason, the idea that littering is bad as never been instilled into the national psyche. Maybe they need an anti littering campaign similar to what they had in the USA in the 60s and 70s.

It is very common to see Filipinos (particularly the less educated) toss trash onto the street.

Finish a pack of cigarettes, toss the empty pack onto the street. Finish your McDonalds hamburger, toss the empty bag onto the street.

Many times the thought has occurred to me to go up to one of these people and say something like:

*"What's wrong with you? Don't you know littering is wrong? Don't you even have any pride in your own country?"*

Alas, it is only a thought. If you said something like that you would only be looking for trouble. Like many other aspects of Philippine society that you may not agree with, the appropriate response is to mumble to yourself and go on your way.

# Chapter 35: Dr. José Rizal

I am going to end my book with a short biography of Dr. José Rizal, followed by his incredibly sorrowful poem written on the eve of his death.

This biography, short as it is, does not do justice to the greatness of the man, and if you find the subject interesting I suggest you do further reading on your own.

### Topic i: *Very Short Biography of Dr. José Rizal*

Although there are other great men in Philippine history, he is perhaps the only one who is so universally proclaimed as a true national hero, a selfless and brilliant man, a true patriot and revered martyr.

Rizal was born in the Philippines on June 19, 1861. Rizal's well off family valued education, and José, a precocious child, grew up to be a brilliant scholar.

Rizal became disenchanted by the heavy handed Spanish occupation and wrote two books on the subject which stirred up the wrath of the Spanish and were quickly banned.

Rizal himself was arrested and exiled to Dapitan in Zamboanga. During his four year stay in Dapitan Rizal did many great things such as set up schools and hospitals, hygienic drainage systems, introduced new fishing methods, write poems and carve sculptures.

Finally the Spanish granted Rizal permission to leave Dapitan but just as he was leaving he was contacted by a secret organization called Katipunan that asked for his help in planning an uprising against the Spanish.

Rizal refused saying they did not have the means, weapons or know-how to successfully revolt against the Spanish. Shortly thereafter the Katipunan plot was uncovered and many arrests were made. Rizal, although on a ship to Cuba, was implicated, and the ship returned to Manila where Rizal was tried, convicted and sentenced to die. Rizal was publicly executed on December 30, 1896 at the tender age of 35. On the eve of his death Rizal wrote a poem which he concealed inside a lamp and gave to his sister. I am no literary scholar – far from it - but in my humble opinion this poem has to be one of the greatest poems ever written. I get tears in my eyes every time I read it. I end my book with this astonishingly profound poem by Dr. José Rizal.

**Dr. José Rizal**

## Topic ii: *Rizal's Farewell Poem*

# My Final Farewell    by Dr. José Rizal

*Farewell, dear Fatherland, clime of the sun caress'd*
*Pearl of the Orient seas, our Eden lost!,*
*Gladly now I go to give thee this faded life's best,*
*And were it brighter, fresher, or more blest*
*Still would I give it thee, nor count the cost.*

*On the field of battle, 'mid the frenzy of fight,*
*Others have given their lives, without doubt or heed;*
*The place matters not-cypress or laurel or lily white,*
*Scaffold or open plain, combat or martyrdom's plight,*
*T is ever the same, to serve our home and country's need.*

*I die just when I see the dawn break,*
*Through the gloom of night, to herald the day;*
*And if color is lacking my blood thou shalt take,*
*Pour'd out at need for thy dear sake*
*To dye with its crimson the waking ray.*

*My dreams, when life first opened to me,*
*My dreams, when the hopes of youth beat high,*
*Were to see thy lov'd face, O gem of the Orient sea*
*From gloom and grief, from care and sorrow free;*
*No blush on thy brow, no tear in thine eye.*

*Dream of my life, my living and burning desire,*
*All hail ! cries the soul that is now to take flight;*
*All hail ! And sweet it is for thee to expire ;*
*To die for thy sake, that thou mayst aspire;*
*And sleep in thy bosom eternity's long night.*

*If over my grave some day thou seest grow,*
*In the grassy sod, a humble flower,*
*Draw it to thy lips and kiss my soul so,*
*While I may feel on my brow in the cold tomb below*
*The touch of thy tenderness, thy breath's warm power.*

*Let the moon beam over me soft and serene,*
*Let the dawn shed over me its radiant flashes,*
*Let the wind with sad lament over me keen ;*
*And if on my cross a bird should be seen,*
*Let it trill there its hymn of peace to my ashes.*
*Let the sun draw the vapors up to the sky,*
*And heavenward in purity bear my tardy protest*
*Let some kind soul o 'er my untimely fate sigh,*
*And in the still evening a prayer be lifted on high*
*From thee, 0 my country, that in God I may rest.*

*Pray for all those that hapless have died,*
*For all who have suffered the unmeasur'd pain;*
*For our mothers that bitterly their woes have cried,*
*For widows and orphans, for captives by torture tried*
*And then for thyself that redemption thou mayst gain.*

*And when the dark night wraps the graveyard around*
*With only the dead in their vigil to see*
*Break not my repose or the mystery profound*
*And perchance thou mayst hear a sad hymn resound*
*'T is I, O my country, raising a song unto thee.*

*And even my grave is remembered no more*
*Unmark'd by never a cross nor a stone*
*Let the plow sweep through it, the spade turn it o'er*
*That my ashes may carpet earthly floor,*
*Before into nothingness at last they are blown.*

*Then will oblivion bring to me no care*
*As over thy vales and plains I sweep;*
*Throbbing and cleansed in thy space and air*
*With color and light, with song and lament I fare,*
*Ever repeating the faith that I keep.*

*My Fatherland ador'd, that sadness to my sorrow lends*
*Beloved Filipinas, hear now my last good-by!*
*I give thee all: parents and kindred and friends*
*For I go where no slave before the oppressor bends,*
*Where faith can never kill, and God reigns e'er on high!*

*Farewell to you all, from my soul torn away,*
*Friends of my childhood in the home dispossessed !*
*Give thanks that I rest from the wearisome day !*
*Farewell to thee, too, sweet friend that lightened my way;*
*Beloved creatures all, farewell! In death there is rest!*

Printed in Great Britain
by Amazon

84185938R00199